THE EVERYTHING

WILD GAME COOKBOOK

From fowl and fish to rabbit and venison—
300 recipes for home-cooked meals

Karen Eagle

Adams Media
Avon, Massachusetts

*This book could not have been possible without
the hunter in my life, my husband, Dick.*

Copyright ©2006, F+W Media, Inc.
All rights reserved. This book, or parts thereof, may not be reproduced in any form without permission
from the publisher; exceptions are made for brief excerpts used in published reviews.

An Everything® Series Book.
Everything® and everything.com® are registered trademarks of F+W Media, Inc.

Published by Adams Media, a division of F+W Media, Inc.
57 Littlefield Street, Avon, MA 02322 U.S.A.
www.adamsmedia.com

ISBN 10: 1-59337-545-X
ISBN 13: 978-1-59337-545-4
Printed in the United States of America.

10 9 8 7 6 5 4 3

Library of Congress Cataloging-in-Publication Data
Eagle, Karen.
The everything wild game cookbook / Karen Eagle.
    p.   cm. -- (The Everything series)
ISBN 1-59337-545-X
1. Cookery (Game) I. Title. II. Series.

TX751.E25 2006
641.6'91--dc22
               2006013595

*This book is available at quantity discounts for bulk purchases.
For information, please call 1-800-289-0963.*

Contents

Acknowledgments

There are many hunters and wild game cooks in our circle of friends, who have shared cooking techniques and offered oral or written recipes while visiting on the phone, in person, in the field, or on a river or stream: Judith Fertig, Jimmy Donnici, Brian Young, Don and Janet Coffey, Bob and Nancy Hatch, LueAnn and Alvin Roepke, Anne and Al Saroni, and Dane and Susie Herbal. For my first meal of smothered quail, I thank my mother, Denise (the cook), and my late father, Bob Conde (the hunter). And for our freezer full of game at home, I thank my husband Dick, the ultimate outdoorsman.

Introduction

Hunters and game cookers everywhere, welcome to *The Everything*®
Wild Game Cookbook. Just like the title says, the recipes within these
pages are designed for wild game. It's the leaner and richer-flavored
version of the domesticated poultry, beef, pork, and fish you can purchase from the grocery store. Also included are recipes for sauces, side
dishes, and desserts that go with wild game. Some of the sides and desserts have ingredients that may be gathered from the wild: nuts, berries,
fruits, and mushrooms, for example.

To begin with, wild game must be properly field dressed and trans-
ported to the meat processor in a timely manner. Some hunters butcher
their own meat. Most send it out for butchering. Soaking game meat in
brine (a mixture of water and salt), milk, or even vinegar can reduce the
gaminess, if desired.

Since most game is leaner (there is less fat throughout the meat)
than its domesticated counterpart, when this meat is overcooked, it
tends to be dry and tough. We recommend cooking good-quality lean
wild game to medium-rare for optimum tenderness and juiciness. Cooking to medium doneness is acceptable, too. Medium-well and well done
are best saved for braising wild game, when it's immersed in a liquid
that helps to keep it moist while cooking.

Game can be grilled, braised, broiled, baked, smoked, roasted, spit-
cooked, pan sautéed, and fried. Tender boneless and skinless breasts of
duck, turkey, goose, grouse, and other birds are delicious when licked
with a hot flame. They may be wrapped with a slice of bacon or prosciutto or basted with butter or olive oil while on the grill. Sear them hot
and fast and use a thermometer to test their doneness (135°F to 140°F
for medium-rare).

Big-game steaks are also very lean. Most of the gaminess in big game comes from the fat, so any excess fat around the edges of a steak are trimmed off. Quick searing over high heat is the ticket here, too. Marinating in or brushing with olive oil and sprinkling seasonings on the steaks yield wonderful results. A half-inch steak will cook in about 4 to 5 minutes over high heat, turning only once.

Braising, roasting, and smoking are preferred methods for tough game meat, which may come in the form of big roasts, a shoulder, or a leg. It may also come from an older animal. Oftentimes, an older animal is best processed into ground meat. There are ample recipes for ground meat throughout this book. But a good roast that is brined and slowly braised like a stew might be absolutely delicious. For other tough meat, try the delicious soups and stews throughout the chapters. Make them a holiday tradition, and serve them for casual get-togethers throughout the winter.

There are ample short recipes for those who get dizzy looking at a long list of ingredients. But there are plenty of luscious gourmet-style recipes, too, which may require just a bit of effort, but the results are worth every minute of your time.

Chapter 1

Wild Game Basics

Hunting and fishing in the wild is a passionate sport and pastime. The multitude of organizations that contribute to the management and conservation of wildlife and its land is a testament to this passion. Preservation, so that future generations may enjoy not only the bounty of the feast but also the bounty of nature, is paramount in the licensing, rules, and regulations for fishing and hunting. When all of these rules are followed, the legal quarry may be brought home to the table.

In the Field

To take proper care of fish and game in the field, you must package and freeze the meats correctly to ensure top-quality flavor and freshness. You must also use the correct cooking techniques so that a big-game rump roast is slow-cooked or braised for tenderness and a delicate fish fillet or steak is cooked quickly so that it stays juicy and flavorful. The following information is an overview to the recipe chapters that will entice you with flavorful dishes and different cooking techniques. Recipes like Poached Halibut with Red Pepper Aioli (page 68), Rotisserie Goose with Buttered Brandy Sauce (page 216), Braised Venison Roast with Mushrooms and Root Vegetables (page 99), Golden-Fried Squirrel or Rabbit (page 133), Grilled Duck Breast with Blackberry Sauce (page 199), Dutch Oven Fall-off-the-Bone Pheasant Legs (page 151), and more than 100 varieties of wild game and fish compose this comprehensive recipe collection.

QUESTION?

Does game taste better when it is fresh?
Absolutely! A quail, duck, squirrel, turkey, salmon, or other wild game is optimum when freshly caught and cooked immediately. The transportation and shelf life of organ meat is short, so elk and deer hunters out in the wild often celebrate campfire-side with a pan-sautéed dinner of fresh liver or heart. Streamside or shore lunches or dinners are popular for anglers in the wild, too.

Hunting Knives and Scissors

Good knives and scissors are essential to field dressing big and small game. A knife needs to have a sturdy handle, and the blade needs to be stainless steel and hard enough to hold an edge, but soft enough to be sharpened. Different knives for different jobs include an all-purpose blade that ranges from 3½ to 4½ inches long for most jobs. For filleting fish, a fillet knife with a long, tapered blade is preferable. Electric carving knives save lots of time when filleting a mess of bluegill or crappie, but they require electricity. Good-quality heavy-duty scissors are great for field dressing birds. Just don't use the scissors for anything else that will dull the blade.

Field Dressing

All game and fish should be field dressed immediately. Invest in a book with either drawings or photographs to show how to correctly do this. Or see if the state conservation department or licensing bureau has this information. Another option is to hunt or fish with guides who will do this for you. Leaving the hide on big game can protect the meat from dirt and insects. Peppering the meat and enclosing it in net or nylon bags is also a good choice for protection. The next step is to butcher the game.

Most birds, because they are much smaller than game mammals, can be gutted and either plucked or skinned. Put the field-dressed birds in plastic bags, and place the bags in coolers, covered with ice.

Fish can be gutted and scaled or filleted. Put portions in plastic bags and place bags in coolers covered with ice. The plastic bags will keep the cooler and ice cleaner than just placing the meat or fish directly into the cooler.

For big-game, wear rubber gloves for protection from parasites and blood-borne diseases. The rubber gloves will also make cleanup easier.

Processing and Butchering

For many hunters, finding a good meat processor is essential. The meat processor is an expert butcher with the equipment for cutting, grinding, and refrigerating or freezing the game under the best possible sanitary conditions. If processing and butchering your own game, make sure that your butchering area is clean, cool, and sanitary.

Freezing and Thawing

Prior to freezing, fine-clean the game or fish. Rinse and remove any grass, dirt, fur, feathers, or shot. Clean any bloody areas. Cut away most of the fat from any big game. Let game soak in salted ice water for 30 to 60 minutes. Rinse until water is clear. Do any final cutting of game into cooking pieces. For instance, pheasant legs are tough and require longer cooking time than the tender breast meat does. It may be preferable to freeze several pheasant legs together for a meal and freeze the pheasant breast meat separately.

Freezing and Labeling Game

Proper freezing and labeling of wild game and fish are essential. Cuts of meat or fish can be frozen in water, wrapped in freezer paper and placed in resealable freezer bags, or vacuum sealed. Double-wrap game so that moisture does not evaporate in the freezer. Label the packages with a waterproof marker. Include the kind of game, cut of meat, quantity, and date. Also, noting the age of the game can be helpful in deciding on cooking method; for example, choosing to slow-braise an old cock pheasant or roast a young plump hen.

FACT

Fish is tender and has very little connective tissue. Marinate fish or shellfish for only 30 minutes. Overmarinating causes the flesh to become mushy. Cook fish for 10 minutes per inch of thickness. Shellfish and fish like shark and swordfish cook even quicker (about 6 minutes over high heat). Another exception is ahi tuna, which many cooks prefer to sear on the outside and serve rare in the middle.

Thawing Game

Place packages of frozen game in the refrigerator and let thaw for 24 hours prior to cooking. The slow thaw in the refrigerator keeps bacteria at bay. Smaller game can be thawed in a bowl of cold water in the kitchen sink. Change the water several times during the thaw.

Cooking Game Quickly

Tender pieces of meat like tenderloin and steaks, fish, young small game, and breast meat are perfect for cooking hot and fast.

Hot Oven Roasting or Baking

Usually a hot oven is 400°F to 500°F. Tender roasts are the best candidates for dry-heat cooking. The internal temperature of these cuts of thick meat should be from 130°F degrees for rare to 145°F for medium. Well done tends to be too dry with high dry heat. Whole turkey, pheasant, duck, goose, large grouse, and other such birds with the skin on or skinless and larded with fat or bacon strips should be cooked over high heat to begin with and then dropped to a lower temperature to finish cooking.

Pan Sautéing

A pan-sautéed game bird breast, big-game steak, or fillet of fish is undeniably delicious. The trick to sautéing is getting the pan and the oil nice and hot. The meat is then placed into the skillet and cooked for 2 or 3 minutes (depending on thickness) until nicely browned, then turned once to finish cooking. Very thin pieces of meat or fish will sauté in a couple of minutes. Game meat is very lean, so avoid overcooking, which dries it out.

Broiling

Let the broiler get nice and hot. Gas broilers are akin to grilling because the gas broiler is a hot flame that licks from the top of the oven. Electric broilers need to be red hot before cooking food, which is placed on the upper rack. Splay small game birds flat and always broil the bone side first. Steaks, chops, and tenderloins need to be turned to brown and sear on each side. Broil fish fillets on the flesh side only. Fish steaks may be turned once.

FACT

A bouquet garni is often added to poaching liquid to enhance the flavor of the food that is being poached. It is a bundle of herbs and seasonings such as bay leaves, whole peppercorns, cloves, star anise, and garlic placed atop a piece of cheesecloth and tied with twine to enclose. It is immersed in the poaching liquid and cooked for several minutes to release the flavor prior to adding the food.

Poaching

Probably the most commonly poached foods are chicken breasts for chicken salad and fish and shrimp. Poaching is cooking food in hot liquid that is heated just below the boiling point, simmering until the food is cooked through. The liquid can be water, wine, milk, juice, broth, or a combination of these, enhanced by adding vegetables, fruits, herbs, or seasonings.

Cooking Game Slowly

Slow cooking is preferable for tough cuts of game meat and older game and birds. The addition of moisture, whether as a liquid in the bottom of the pan or as a baste, can turn out tender, fall-off-the-bone food.

Slow Oven Roasting

Roasting or baking in a slow oven can range from a low temperature of 225°F up to about 350°F. Game meats can be cooked in roasters, on baking sheets, or in Dutch ovens, covered or uncovered. Roasting bags also fall into this category. Tender birds and cuts of meat can also be slow roasted, basting frequently to keep these lean cuts moist.

Braising

Slow cooking in a liquid is braising. Braising can be done either on the stovetop or in the oven. It is similar to poaching. Tough cuts of meat like shoulder roasts and bottom round are good to braise. An old pheasant or goose can be braised, and the liquid may be used as a stock for sauce, soup, or stew.

Crock-Pot

Crock-Pot cooking became especially popular with busy mothers and working women. Recipes called for assembling the dinner ingredients in a Crock-Pot before leaving the house in the morning. The appliance was turned on to a low setting so the food would slow cook all day (or for about 8 to 10 hours). When the family arrived home from a day of work or activities, dinner was ready. Thus, these homey recipes that produce fall-off-the-bone meat work well with game.

Cooking Game Outdoors

The popularity of cooking outdoors is on the rise. Of course, hunters and anglers have been cooking outdoors over campfires way before the popularity of cooking on an outdoor grill or smoker came onto the scene in the mid–twentieth century. For many, the move from campfire to grill is an easy one.

Grilling

Grilling is cooking fast over medium-high to high heat. Tender food is best. Choose prime steaks, chops, tenderloins, fish, tender small game and game birds, and ground meat for the grill. Cooking times will vary depending on the amount of heat and the distance from the heat, whether grilling over gas, charcoal, or hardwood lump charcoal.

Flame-retardant mats are a great product to place underneath an outdoor deep fryer or grill, especially if cooking on a wooden deck. They come in 36- to 48-inch circles or rectangles. They catch the oil or juices from deep-frying or grilling instead of having splatters go directly onto the wooden deck or patio, too.

The indirect side of the grill is the side where there is no fire or heat. On a charcoal grill, bank the coals on each side of the grill. Place a disposable pan filled with water in the center, in between the banks of coals. The center of the grill is indirect heat. On a gas grill with two or more burners, one side has the burner turned on and the other side, with the burner off, is indirect heat. A whole game bird or thick chop or steak can be direct grilled to char the outside, then placed on the indirect side of the grill, with the lid closed, to cook slowly until done.

Smoking

Usually, smoking is slow versus fast cooking, with wood as a flavor. The fire is low, from about 225°F to not more than 300°F. The lower heat is so the food has more time to cook slowly with the wood flavor enveloping it. A water pan is essential for game smoking, because the meat has little fat. Whole birds, whole fish, large roasts, ribs, and tough meats do well smoked slowly. Slow-smoked food is cooked well done. Allow ample time for slow smoking.

Rotisserie

Tenderloins and roasts, game birds, hams, and even whole fish can be rotisserie (or spit) cooked. Most rotisserie units are motorized. Follow the manufacturer's directions for setting up the rotisserie. Ideally, it is nice to set a disposable pan of water directly under the spit to catch the drippings. This keeps flare-ups at bay and also keeps a gas grill and its gas jets cleaner. Allow plenty of time for rotisserie cooking. Foods can be basted while on the rotisserie.

Deep Frying

The fried smell and mess that hot oil makes indoors isn't necessary with an outdoor deep fryer. Make sure you have a sturdy unit with reinforced tripod legs. Four-legged fryers are even more stable. Solid base fryers, sturdier yet, sit on the floor or on a table. Read manufacturer's directions prior to using. Investing in fryer forks for immersing and lifting foods helps to prevent hot oil spills. Long heat-resistant mitts protect arms from hot oil, too.

Specialty Cooking Techniques

Specialty cooking methods often require the purchase of extra equipment or accessories. Decide if the purchase is worth it and if it is a style of cooking that you will employ and enjoy.

Stir-Frying or Stir-Grilling

Stir-frying is best done in a wok. Similarly, stir-grilling is accomplished by grilling in a perforated grill basket over a hot charcoal or gas fire. Either is a delicious way to prepare tender pieces of meat quickly. By adding a variety of vegetables to the mixture and serving the finished food over rice or noodles, it is a great way to stretch a meal, too.

Packet Cooking in Parchment or Foil

Parchment paper and foil packets allow you to cook meat with vegetables and sauce in one neat package. Foil is a bit more versatile, since it won't burn up if placed by flame. So foil packets can cook over campfires, grills, and in hot ovens.

Planking

Modern-day planking can be done in the oven or on the grill. The most popular woods for planking are cedar, alder, oak, or other nonresinous woods. Some cooks prefer to char or bake the plank prior to placing tender foods atop it for baking. Others prefer to arrange the food on top of the water-soaked plank and place it in an oven or on the indirect side of a grill, closing the door and cooking for 20 to 30 minutes or until food is the desired doneness.

FACT

Baking planks are 2- to 3-inch-thick rectangular planks of wood with two steel rods inserted through the planks on each end. If the planks begin to split apart with repeated use, the steel rod can be tightened with screws. Baking planks cost more than grilling planks, but they last much longer. To clean planks, simply wash with warm sudsy water, rinse, and let dry until the next use.

Stovetop Smoking

This indoor smoker has been around for many years. It smokes finely shredded dry wood over medium-high temperatures. Items like shrimp cook in about 6 to 8 minutes. The shrimp gets a pretty burnished color and a hint of wood aroma in the taste. Smaller pieces of tender meat and vegetables fit better than large pieces in the stovetop smoker, which is smaller than an outdoor smoker.

Cold Smoking

Cold smoking is a process that adds smoke flavor to foods but does not usually cook the food (exceptions include cold smoking fish). Items like sausage or jerky can be cold smoked at less than 120°F. It is best to use curing products when cold smoking to avoid the growth of bacteria that causes food poisoning. After cold smoking, foods need to be stored in the refrigerator for several days or packaged for the freezer. When ready to eat, the cold-smoked items need to be cooked: hot smoked, grilled, baked, pan sautéed, or braised.

Chapter 2

Sauces, Relishes, Rubs, Brines, Marinades, & Pastes

Yields 3 cups

1 red bell pepper, finely
    chopped
1 red onion, finely chopped
1½ cups chili sauce
¼ cup olive oil
¼ cup lemon juice
¼ cup Worcestershire sauce
¼ cup freshly snipped Italian
    parsley
¼ cup packed dark brown
    sugar
4 cloves garlic, minced
1 tablespoon chili powder
1 tablespoon dry mustard
1 teaspoon seasoned black
    pepper
1 teaspoon kosher salt
½ teaspoon red pepper flakes

Game Bird Serving Sauce and Baste

This is a delicious sauce to baste on pheasant, quail, duck, or turkey that is roasting in the oven or cooking on the outdoor grill. Reserve a portion of the sauce to serve on the side, too.

1. In a large saucepan, combine all of the ingredients and simmer for 1½ hours over low heat. Stir occasionally. If the sauce is too thick, add 2 tablespoons of water at a time to thin to desired consistency.

2. Keeps in an airtight container in the refrigerator for up to one week.

Substitutes for Italian Parsley
Substituting herbs is acceptable, especially in a sauce that has many flavors. If you have an herb garden, then you'll have some herbs that are extremely plentiful, like chives, mint, or lemon balm. They can be interchanged in a sauce or marinade recipe that calls for small amounts.

Cognac Cream Sauce

This sauce is especially good served with red meat like venison and bear. It complements pan-seared and grilled partridge, turkey, pheasant, and quail, too.

~

Yields 1 cup

1 bunch scallions
½ stick butter
½ cup cognac
1 cup whipping cream
2 tablespoons horseradish
2 tablespoons chives, freshly
   snipped
½ teaspoon kosher salt
½ teaspoon white pepper

1. Finely mince the white part of the scallions, reserving the green parts for later.

2. Melt the butter in a skillet and sauté the white part of the scallions until they are soft. Add the cognac and cook over medium heat until reduced by half.

3. Add the cream and horseradish and heat until the mixture coats a spoon.

4. Add the chives, salt, pepper, and green part of the onions. Serve immediately.

Cooking with Cognac

An inexpensive cognac will do just as good a job in this recipe as an expensive one. If you like to cook with liquor or liqueurs, keep the inexpensive bottles for cooking in a kitchen cupboard. Keep the "good" stuff in the liquor cabinet. If you rarely use cognac, try substituting whiskey instead.

Yields 2 cups

1 cup of au jus or brown
 gravy
⅓ cup red wine
¼ cup gingersnaps, finely
 crushed
¼ cup currants
¼ cup almonds, sliced and
 toasted
1 tablespoon dark brown
 sugar

Gingersnap Sauce

*Use hard, crisp gingersnap cookies for this German-style sauce.
It is distinctive and best served with red-meat game.*

1. Combine all of the ingredients in a saucepan. Simmer over medium heat for about 7 to 10 minutes, stirring occasionally.

2. Ladle over cooked meat.

Yields 1 cup

1 cup yogurt
2 teaspoons toasted sesame
 oil
3 tablespoons lime juice
2 cloves garlic, minced
½ teaspoon hot sauce
1 teaspoon sesame seeds,
 toasted

Yogurt-Sesame Sauce

*No-cook sauces assemble quickly and save time and cleanup because
there is only one bowl used. Vary this recipe to your liking by using lemon
or orange instead of the lime. Try substituting sour cream for the yogurt
for a subtle difference, too. Serve this with fish or seafood.*

Combine all of the ingredients in a bowl and stir to blend. Keeps refrigerated for a few days.

Béarnaise Sauce

Béarnaise is heavenly served with a meaty steak, tenderloin, or even wild salmon. It can be made an hour ahead but needs to be reheated gently so that it doesn't separate.

Yields 1½ cups

1 stick unsalted butter
2 tablespoons shallots, finely chopped
2 tablespoons hot water
3 egg yolks
¼ cup tarragon vinegar
¼ cup dry white wine
1 tablespoon fresh tarragon, chopped
½ tablespoon fresh Italian parsley, chopped
¼ teaspoon kosher salt
¼ teaspoon hot sauce

1. In a double boiler, melt butter slowly over medium heat. Add shallots and simmer for about 3 to 4 minutes. Whisk in hot water and remove top of double boiler from the heat to cool.

2. Place top of double boiler back on pot. Whisk in egg yolks and then the rest of the ingredients.

3. Over low heat, stir constantly until it thickens.

Béarnaise Butter

A quick version of this sauce is easy to assemble. In a bowl, combine 1 stick softened butter, 2 tablespoons shallots, 1 tablespoon tarragon vinegar, 1 tablespoon chopped fresh tarragon, ½ tablespoon chopped fresh Italian parsley, ¼ teaspoon kosher salt, and ¼ teaspoon hot sauce. Stir to blend. Place in a ramekin. Serve with crusty bread as a spread or dollop on the meat or fish of your choice.

Yields about 2½ cups

6 strips bacon
8 ounces mushrooms, sliced
1 clove garlic, minced
1½ cups sour cream, light or
    regular
1 tablespoon horseradish
1 tablespoon chives, snipped
1 tablespoon Italian parsley,
    finely chopped

Sour Cream Mushroom Sauce

*In a word—fabulous! Serve this decadent mushroom sauce with
dark-red-meat game like venison, elk, moose, and bear. It goes well with
pan-sautéed breast of duck, goose, partridge, and pheasant, too.*

1. Fry bacon in a skillet over high heat until crisp. Remove the bacon and drain on paper towels. When cool, crumble and set aside.

2. Pour off all but 2 tablespoons of the bacon grease. Sauté the mushrooms over medium-high heat for about 3 to 5 minutes. Transfer to a bowl and let cool.

3. Add crumbled bacon, garlic, sour cream, horseradish, chives, and parsley. Stir to blend. Serve warm or chilled. Keeps for 2 days refrigerated.

Peppercorn Gravy

Here's a winning tip for a delicious sauce that comes from a package. Knorr's Peppercorn Sauce is divine when made with half water and half wine, red or white. If you want extra depth and flavor, skip the water and use chicken or beef broth paired with the wine. It's a great convenience to sprinkle a tablespoon of the powder into a pan that you are deglazing with wine, too.

Mandarin Orange Relish

*This is a very pretty relish, with its orange, white, and green colors.
It's flavorful and refreshing, too. Pair it with the game of your choice.*

⌒

1. Combine the oranges, scallions, and celery in a bowl. Add the soy sauce, sesame oil, vinegar, toasted sesame seeds, and honey. Toss well to combine.

2. Refrigerate until completely chilled before serving. Best served the day that it is made.

Toasting Sesame Seeds and Nuts

Why bother toasting sesame seeds and nuts? Because the richness and depth of flavor attained by toasting is worth it. Think of the difference between having a piece of toasted bread for breakfast versus plain untoasted bread. The crispness and char add a whole different texture and taste. To toast the sesame seeds or nuts, place a single layer on a heavy-duty baking tray. Toast in the oven at 350°F for about 5 to 10 minutes, stirring a couple of times while toasting. Nuts will take longer than the sesame seeds.

Yields about 3 cups

1 (11-ounce) can mandarin oranges, drained and rinsed
2 cups scallions, thinly sliced
1 cup celery, thinly sliced
3 tablespoons soy sauce
2 tablespoons toasted sesame oil
3 tablespoons rice vinegar
2 tablespoons sesame seeds, toasted
1 tablespoon dark honey

Yields 3 cups

2 oranges
¾ cup sugar
1 (12-ounce) bag cranberries,
    picked through

Fresh Cranberry-Orange Relish

*This relish is good for you. It is simple, fresh, and made in the food processor.
All wild birds and small- and big-game meat pair perfectly with it.*

1. Peel the zest of the oranges, orange part only, and place in a food processor. Pulse to chop. Add the sugar and process at high speed for 1 to 2 minutes until the zest is very fine and has formed a paste.

2. Add cranberries and pulse to finely chop. Place in a container.

3. Peel the white membrane from the oranges and separate the segments; add to the cranberry mixture. Stir and chill. Keeps several weeks in a covered container in the refrigerator.

Yields 2 cups

1½ cups apricot preserves
½ teaspoon fresh ginger,
    grated
⅓ cup golden raisins
¼ cup dried apples, snipped
1 clove garlic, minced
2 tablespoons cider vinegar
1 teaspoon cinnamon
½ teaspoon white pepper

Quick Apricot Chutney

*Unlike most chutneys, this one does not require cooking. Offer it as a
condiment for game fowl like turkey, pheasant, partridge, and duck.*

Combine all ingredients and mix well. Set aside for at least 1 hour before serving so flavors will blend. Refrigerate unused portions in a tightly covered container.

Cranberry and Golden Raisin Relish

*Wild game and cranberry concoctions just seem to go together.
This relish is a favorite and can be made a number of different ways.
Try substituting pear for the apple or add ½ cup of toasted sliced almonds
to it for another variation. The Grand Marnier is pricey, so try apricot
brandy or orange liqueur as a less expensive alternative.*

1. Combine all of the ingredients except the Grand Marnier in a saucepan. Bring to a boil, stirring, then turn down the heat to medium.

2. Simmer, uncovered, for about 30 minutes. Continue stirring until cranberries pop and mixture thickens.

3. Remove from heat and add the liqueur.

4. Let cool. May be served at room temperature.

Yields 4 cups

2 (12-ounce) bags fresh
    cranberries
2 apples, cored and chopped
2 cups golden raisins
1 cup sugar
1 cup orange juice
1 tablespoon ginger, freshly
    grated
1 tablespoon ground
    cinnamon
1 tablespoon ground cloves
½ cup Grand Marnier

½ cup green Italian olives,
   pitted
½ cup Kalamata olives, pitted
½ cup Nicoise olives, pitted
½ cup Italian parsley,
   chopped
2 tablespoons capers
1 tablespoon anchovy paste
2 tablespoons extra-virgin
   olive oil
1 tablespoon balsamic
   vinegar
1 teaspoon sugar
Freshly ground pepper to
   taste

Salad Bar Olive Relish

*Many grocery stores have fancy olive bars. This recipe is
perfect for making use of the wonderful variety they offer. The French
term for olive relish is tapenade. It is often made with only one kind of cured
olive, the Nicoise. Olive relish is delicious served with grilled, broiled, or
baked fish and poultry. Try it as a spread for sandwiches like grilled
game burgers or grilled Portobello mushrooms.*

1. Add olives and parsley to a food processor and pulse to a coarse texture.

2. Place mixture in a bowl and stir in the rest of the ingredients.

3. This mixture is best if the flavors are allowed to blend at room temperature for an hour. Or it may be refrigerated in a covered container for several hours. Keeps for several days.

Olives
*Make your own olive salads by simply spooning several kinds together
from the salad or olive bar in a grocery store. Legumes like garbanzo
beans, cannellini beans, or red kidney beans are good additions.
Pickled garlic and cocktail onions are nice complements, too. Serve this
as a small salad or a condiment with wild-game dinners.*

Coarse Kosher Salt and Freshly Cracked Pepper Rub

The most simple of rubs is one most cooks use everyday—salt and pepper. If this is your rub of choice, try this one using coarse kosher salt. The irregular shape of the salt crystals and cracked pepper adhere to the meat more readily. Freshly cracked pepper comes from a coarse pepper grinder. If you do not have one, then substitute freshly ground pepper. Lightly coat your meat with olive oil, then sprinkle on the rub. Pan sear, roast, or grill the game of your choice.

Combine the salt and peppers in a glass jar with a tight-fitting lid. Shake to blend. Will keep for several months.

Yields ½ cup

¼ cup coarse kosher salt
2 tablespoons freshly cracked black peppercorns
2 tablespoons freshly cracked green peppercorns

Tandoori Rub

The fragrance of Indian cuisine will permeate your home when you use this rub for game birds or steak.

Combine the ingredients in a glass jar with a tight-fitting lid. Shake to blend. Will keep for several months.

Yields about 1 cup

2 tablespoons cumin
2 tablespoons coriander
2 tablespoons paprika
1 tablespoon dried ginger
1 tablespoon turmeric
1 tablespoon red pepper flakes
½ tablespoon kosher salt

2 tablespoons paprika
2 tablespoons lemon pepper
2 tablespoons white pepper
2 tablespoons black pepper
2 tablespoons garlic salt
2 tablespoons dark brown
    sugar
1 tablespoon dried thyme
1 tablespoon dried savory
1 tablespoon dried marjoram
1 tablespoon dried rosemary
1 bay leaf

Herb Rub for Birds

*This makes enough rub to season four whole ducks
for the oven, rotisserie, or smoker.*

Combine ingredients, leaving the bay leaf whole. Make the blend
ahead of time for the bay leaf to infuse the mixture. Discard the
bay leaf when using the blend. Store in a dark cupboard in a jar
with a tight-fitting lid for up to 3 months.

Rules of Dry Rubs

*Dry rubs are just that, a mixture of dry spices, herbs, or a combi-
nation of both. Because there are no fresh ingredients in a dry rub,
they have a significant shelf life. Rubs may be stored in tightly
covered glass jars for up to 3 months. After 3 months, they tend to
lose some of their pungency, so make only the amount that you'll
use up in that time period. Take care to portion out the amount of
rub to be used for each recipe so that you do not cross contami-
nate while handling raw meat. Sprinkle dry rubs in soups, stews,
and sauces, too.*

Spicy Chipotle Rub

Try this fragrant mixture on a whole turkey or duck or big-game steaks or tenderloin. Sauté sliced potatoes dusted lightly with the same rub.

～

Combine all of the ingredients in a glass jar and cover with a tight-fitting lid. Keeps for up to 3 months.

Giftable Spice Mixtures

Dry spice mixtures make wonderful gifts from the kitchen. They can be made up a few weeks ahead of time. Portion them out in pretty jars. Then affix a nice tag with the name of the rub and how to use it. Don't forget your name on the tag. Your friends will think of you each time they use the rub.

Yields 1 cup

¼ cup garlic powder
2 tablespoons dried ground chipotle
2 tablespoons allspice
2 tablespoons dark brown sugar
1 tablespoon dried cloves
1 tablespoon dried orange zest
1 tablespoon thyme
1 tablespoon dried cilantro
2 teaspoons onion salt
1 teaspoon red pepper flakes

Citrus Rub

A delightful, zesty rub that is perfect for birds and fish. It's lovely sprinkled on pan-sautéed, roasted, or grilled vegetables, too.

～

Combine all of the ingredients in a glass jar and cover with a tight-fitting lid. Store in a dark cupboard away from heat. Keeps for up to 3 months.

Yields about 1 cup

¼ cup dried lemon zest
¼ cup dried lime zest
¼ cup dried orange zest
¼ cup dark brown sugar
1 tablespoon seasoned pepper

4 quarts water
1 cup kosher salt
1 cup dark brown sugar
½ cup lemon juice

Lemon Brine for Big Game

The simplest brine for meat is water and salt, but everyone seems to agree that a balance of sugar and an addition of flavor makes a brine just that much better. This is enough brine for a couple of birds, a couple of roasts, or a big tenderloin or two.

Combine ingredients in a container that is big enough to hold the meat you plan to brine. Brine for about 12 to 16 hours. Rinse meats in cold water to remove excess salt prior to cooking.

1 quart water
3 cups cider vinegar
½ cup kosher salt
⅓ cup dark brown sugar
1 tablespoon black
    peppercorns
1 bunch Italian parsley,
    chopped
1 onion, chopped
2 carrots, chopped
2 stalks celery, chopped

Vinegar and Salt Brine

A great brine for big game like antelope, bear, moose, sheep, and deer.

1. Combine all of the ingredients in a pot and bring to a boil. Turn off heat and let cool. Strain the liquid and toss the vegetables. Brine the big game of your choice for 12 hours to 2 or 3 days in the brining liquid in the refrigerator.

2. Rinse game to remove excess salt prior to cooking.

About Brining
Brining with water, salt, and oftentimes sugar increases the meat protein's ability to hold water. Thus, it makes a piece of meat more moist and tender. Brining is particularly effective with very lean meat, making wild game a perfect candidate. Brine recipes that have lots of additional flavorings are actually more marinade than brine, but both will add moisture, tenderness, and flavor to the meat.

Juniper–Apple Cider Brine

Pungent juniper is a wonderful flavoring for venison and elk.
Try this on sheep, bear, and javelina, too.

⌒

Yields about 5 quarts

4 quarts water
2 cups apple cider
1 cup kosher salt
½ cup sugar
12 peppercorns, crushed
12 juniper berries, crushed
12 whole cloves
1 tablespoon red pepper
   flakes
1 tablespoon ancho chile
   powder

1. Combine all of the ingredients in a large container.

2. Brine the wild game of your choice for 12 to 24 hours in the refrigerator.

3. Rinse meat to remove excess salt prior to cooking.

Apples, Onions, and Wild Game

Apples and onions are the basic fruit and vegetable recommended to stuff duck and goose "to absorb the wild flavor." Actually, they do a great job flavoring the meat. So when you have a marinade or brine to make, use up that little bit of apple juice or apple cider that's sitting in your refrigerator. It will be delicious.

Vinaigrette Marinade

This is an all-purpose vinaigrette that can be used as a marinade or salad dressing. Drizzle this over a salad topped with grilled salmon, duck breast, venison, or quail. Very versatile.

Combine all of the ingredients in a glass jar and cover with a tight-fitting lid. Keeps for up to 1 month refrigerated.

Yields 1 cup

¾ cup vegetable oil
¼ cup vinegar
1 large clove garlic, minced
4 teaspoons sugar
1 teaspoon salt

Teriyaki Marinade

Game birds, red meat, and seafood like halibut and salmon are well suited to this Asian marinade laden with citrus flavors and a bit of heat.

Combine all of the ingredients in a glass jar with a tight-fitting lid. Shake and mix well. May be stored in the refrigerator for up to 2 weeks.

Yields 1 cup

½ cup teriyaki sauce
¼ cup lime juice
2 tablespoons Chinese-style prepared mustard
2 tablespoons hoisin sauce
¼ teaspoon red pepper

Pale Ale Marinade

This is a great all-purpose beer-based marinade.
Use it for the wild game of your choice. For fun, experiment
with different kinds of beer, from pale ale to stout.

~

1. Combine all of the ingredients except the oil in a food processor or blender. Pulse to combine.

2. Slowly add the oil, pulsing and blending to emulsify.

Shrimp Boil
Try this beer-based marinade without the oil for a shrimp boil. It would work for crayfish and crab legs, too. With the oil, it is an interesting dressing for a salad of bitter greens like spinach or arugula.

Yields 2½ cups

12–14 ounces beer (pale ale)
¼ cup onion, chopped
Zest and juice of 1 lemon
Zest and juice of 1 lime
3 tablespoons Italian parsley, chopped
3 tablespoons sugar
½ tablespoon salt
½ tablespoon Worcestershire sauce
1 clove garlic, minced
1 teaspoon hot sauce
¾ cup vegetable oil

1 cup blackberry jam
½ cup white wine vinegar
½ cup olive oil
2 tablespoons Dijon mustard
4 cloves garlic, minced
½ teaspoon cinnamon
½ teaspoon allspice
1 teaspoon freshly ground
    black pepper
½ teaspoon kosher salt

Blackberry Jam Vinaigrette

This sweet, tangy berry marinade is wonderful with big game like elk and venison. Try this with steaks or duck breasts that are pan sautéed. After cooking, the pan can be deglazed with a bit of the marinade, too.

1. Place the blackberry jam in a bowl and whisk until creamy. Add the rest of the ingredients and whisk again until blended.

2. Can be made ahead and kept in a covered container in the refrigerator for several days.

Jammin' Marinades
Change this marinade by simply substituting the jams or preserves of your choice. Think of a luscious apricot vinaigrette or kicky cherry marinade. Add cranberry conserve instead of the blackberry jam for a festive holiday marinade or dressing that can dress a salad or be used as a drizzle over cooked wild game.

Espresso Joe Marinade

This is another all-purpose marinade that tenderizes big cuts of tough meat like flank steak, round steak, or roasts.

1. Combine all of the ingredients in a bowl. Whisk to blend.

2. Marinate game of your choice for 12 to 24 hours in the refrigerator. Keeps for a couple of days.

Yields 3 cups

1 cup espresso or very strong coffee
1 cup cola
½ cup vegetable oil
½ cup vinegar
3 cloves garlic, minced

Ginger-Soy Marinade and Dressing

Delicious marinade for meat, birds, or fish. Reserve some of the marinade to drizzle over a salad of mixed greens topped with sliced tenderloin or fish.

1. Combine all of the ingredients in a glass jar and secure the lid. Shake to mix well. Keeps in the refrigerator for 1 week.

2. Marinate fish for 30 minutes and meat for 1 to 4 hours.

Yields 1½ cups

½ cup orange juice
½ cup vegetable oil
¼ cup soy sauce
2 tablespoons toasted sesame oil
2 tablespoons gingerroot, grated
2 tablespoons dark honey

½ cup olive oil
½ cup white wine
½ cup whole grain mustard
¼ cup shallots, minced
2 tablespoons fresh thyme,
    chopped
2 tablespoons fresh chives,
    chopped
2 tablespoons fresh savory,
    chopped
2 tablespoons fresh oregano,
    chopped
2 tablespoons fresh lovage,
    chopped
2 tablespoons fresh lemon
    balm, chopped
3 cloves garlic, minced
Kosher salt and freshly
    ground pepper to taste

Herb Garden Marinade

*Marinate elk, venison, sheep, bear, or javelina steaks
or tenderloins in this pungent marinade.*

1. Combine all of the ingredients and mix well. Store in a glass jar with a tight-fitting lid for up to 1 week in the refrigerator.

2. Marinate fish for 30 minutes. Marinate meat or birds for several hours in the refrigerator.

Herb Gardens

Having an herb garden makes cooking with a variety of herbs an everyday luxury. A simple vinaigrette changes by adding a sprig or leaves of rosemary, basil, mint, or cilantro. Experiment with combinations to make your own signature marinade.

Rosemary-Dijon Slather

Use a pastry brush to apply this paste to fish, birds, or big game. Then broil or grill to desired doneness.

❧

1. Combine ingredients in a bowl. Stir to blend.

2. Marinate fish for 30 minutes or meat for several hours in the refrigerator. Store slather in the refrigerator in airtight container for up to 5 days.

Slathers

Thick emulsified sauces are what a slather is all about. A slather can be unadorned or used straight from the store-bought bottle. Mustard, mayonnaise, yogurt, and sour cream are all examples of products that can be slathered on a steak or breast. Then the game meat may be baked, broiled, or grilled. Adorn the plain slather by adding some seasoning or fresh herbs.

Yields about 2 cups

1 cup Dijon mustard
⅓ cup fresh Italian parsley, chopped
⅓ cup fresh rosemary, chopped
⅓ cup fresh chives, chopped
2 tablespoons white wine Worcestershire sauce
Zest and juice of 1 lemon
1 tablespoon freshly ground black pepper
1 teaspoon kosher salt

Tarragon Mustard Slather

Try slathering this mixture on fish fillets to cook on the grill. Or slather it on a burger bun with a little cranberry conserve for a divine venison burger.

❧

In a small bowl, whisk together all of the ingredients. Store in an airtight jar in the refrigerator for up to 2 weeks.

Yields about 1 cup

½ cup country-style Dijon mustard
¼ cup white wine vinegar
¼ cup olive oil
2 teaspoons fresh tarragon, snipped
Kosher salt and white pepper to taste

Sun-Dried Tomato Pesto

Yields 2 cups

5 cups water
12 ounces sun-dried
   tomatoes
8 cloves garlic, minced
1 tablespoon balsamic
   vinegar
½ cup extra-virgin olive oil
2 cups basil, firmly packed
1½ teaspoons dark honey
½ teaspoon kosher salt
½ teaspoon freshly ground
   black pepper

*When basil is plentiful, make double batches of this divine pesto.
It can be frozen in heavy-duty freezer bags and will keep for several months.
So in the dead of winter, pull a bag of this from the freezer and unleash
the flavors of summer. This is particularly good served atop a sautéed
breast of pheasant or a grilled fillet of salmon or dorado.*

1. Bring water to a boil in a saucepan. Add sun-dried tomatoes, turn down to low heat, and simmer for about 15 minutes. Drain and squeeze excess water from tomatoes.

2. Place tomatoes, garlic, and vinegar in a food processor and blend until coarsely chopped.

3. With processor running, slowly add the oil.

4. Add the basil, honey, salt, and pepper and whirl until fully incorporated.

Garlic Chive and Lemon Balm Pesto

Yields about 3 to 4 cups

2 cups garlic chives, snipped
2 cups lemon balm, firmly
   packed
1 cup pine nuts
1 cup olive oil
¾ cup Romano cheese,
   grated
Kosher salt to taste

*Pesto is usually a thick paste. By adding more oil,
you can thin it to the consistency of your choice. Then it is great
drizzled over fish and seafood or tossed with pasta.*

1. In a food processor, process the garlic chives, lemon balm, and pine nuts together until you have a smooth paste.

2. With the processor running, drizzle in the olive oil in a slow, steady stream until the pesto solidifies.

3. Add the cheese and salt to taste, just pulsing to combine.

Chapter 3

Freshwater Catch

Grilled Arctic Char
with Olive-Caper Butter

Serves 4

4 (6-ounce) char fillets
1 tablespoon olive oil
Seasoned pepper to taste
8 tablespoons butter, room
    temperature
2 tablespoons Kalamata
    olives, chopped
2 tablespoons capers, any
    size
1 clove garlic, minced

*Make extra Olive-Caper Butter. It is a wonderful alternative
to garlic bread. Spoon butter into one or two small ramekins.
Wrap them well and keep in the freezer up to 3 months.*

1. Rinse fillets and pat dry. Place on a plate and lightly coat with olive oil and season with pepper. Set aside.

2. Combine butter, olives, capers, and garlic in a bowl. Stir to blend. Spoon into a ramekin and set aside.

3. Prepare a hot fire in your grill.

4. Place fillets over the hot fire and grill for about 4 to 5 minutes per side, turning once halfway through cooking time.

5. Serve fillets with a dollop of Olive-Caper Butter.

The Rule of Thumb for Cooking Time for Fish
Timing is everything. The rule of thumb for cooking fish is 10 minutes per inch of thickness over high heat. If a fish fillet is ½ inch thick, it will grill, broil, pan sauté, fry, or bake in about 5 minutes total cooking time at a high temperature. If the temperature is medium heat, add a minute or two per inch of thickness.

Arctic Char in Parchment

Fish parcels are gifts at the table. As they are unwrapped,
their heavenly aroma wafts through the room.
Add a side of cooked rice and your meal is complete.

Serves 4

Parchment paper
4 (7-ounce) char fillets,
    skinless
2 carrots
2 zucchini
8 scallions
1-inch piece gingerroot,
    peeled
Zest and juice of 1 lime
4 tablespoons soy sauce
2 teaspoons toasted sesame
    oil

1. Preheat the oven to 425°F. Cut out four 16-inch circles of parchment paper.

2. Rinse fillets and pat dry. Place 1 fillet on each of the circles of parchment.

3. Cut the carrots, zucchini, scallions, and ginger into matchsticks. Place the ginger in a bowl and add the lime, soy, and sesame oil. Equally divide the vegetables over each fillet. Equally spoon the liquid and ginger over the top of each fillet.

4. Fold the parchment paper over the fish and seal each packet tightly. Place on a baking sheet and cook for 10 to 12 minutes or more, depending on the thickness of the fillet. Place the packets on each of four plates. Unwrap carefully as the hot steam escapes.

2 pounds bass fillets
¼ cup plus 1 tablespoon
    vegetable oil
1 tablespoon lemon pepper
1 tablespoon paprika
2 teaspoons garlic salt
2 teaspoons dried basil
2 teaspoons dried oregano
2 teaspoons red pepper
2 teaspoons freshly ground
    black pepper

Blackened Bass

*Spicy seasonings beg for something cool and refreshing like
a creamy coleslaw, a corn salad, or pickled cucumbers.*

1. Rinse fish fillets and pat dry. Place in a bowl and lightly toss with 1 tablespoon of vegetable oil. Set aside.

2. Combine lemon pepper, paprika, garlic salt, basil, oregano, red pepper, and black pepper in a bowl. Whisk to blend well. Transfer to a larger shallow bowl.

3. Add ¼ cup oil to a cast-iron skillet and place over high heat.

4. Dredge each fillet in the spice mixture, lightly coating both sides of the fillet.

5. Sear a batch of several fillets at a time in the hot skillet. Cook for about 1 to 1½ minutes per side. Fillets should be crusty. Continue cooking batches of fillets until done.

Bass

Anglers love catching the active smallmouth or largemouth bass indigenous to North America. Oftentimes they jump when hooked and they like to put up a good fight. At the table, their meat is sweet and can be prepared in foil packets, fried, broiled, and grilled.

Fried Catfish and Fried Green Tomatoes
with Cornmeal Crust

A quick aioli made with store-bought mayonnaise
adds a sophisticated twist of flavor to this dish.

~

Serves 4

¾ cup mayonnaise
Zest and juice of 1 lemon
1 clove garlic, minced
1 cup cornmeal
½ cup flour
1 teaspoon salt
1 teaspoon pepper
½ cup vegetable oil or more
2 large green tomatoes
2 pounds catfish fillets,
    skinless

1. Combine mayonnaise, lemon, and garlic in a bowl and whisk to blend. Set aside.

2. Combine cornmeal, flour, salt, and pepper in a bowl large enough for dredging.

3. Heat vegetable oil in a large skillet over medium-high heat.

4. Slice green tomatoes ½-inch thick and dredge in cornmeal mixture. Place in the skillet and cook until brown on each side, about 3 or 4 minutes per side. Remove and keep warm.

5. Dredge the catfish fillets in the cornmeal mixture. Place in the skillet and fry until golden brown, about 3 or 4 minutes per side, depending on how thick the fillets are. Add more oil as needed. Serve catfish and tomatoes with the mayonnaise sauce on the side.

2 pounds catfish fillets

1 lemon

Salt and white pepper to taste

2–3 tablespoons extra-virgin olive oil

1 cup store-bought salsa

1 tomato, chopped

1 ear of sweet corn, fresh-picked

½ cup fresh cilantro, chopped

Broiled Catfish
with Chunky Cilantro Salsa

Try this alternative to fried catfish. It gets a bit of browning from the broiler and the piquant salsa is a nice finishing touch.

1. Preheat your oven broiler to high.

2. Rinse the catfish fillets and pat dry. Squeeze lemon juice over the fillets and sprinkle with salt and white pepper.

3. Lightly oil a broiler pan and place the fillets on it. Drizzle lightly with the olive oil. Place under the broiler and cook for about 8 to 10 minutes, depending on how thick the fillets are.

4. In the meantime, combine the salsa, tomato, corn kernels, and cilantro in a bowl and mix well. Serve catfish with a dollop of salsa.

Wild Catfish

It goes without saying that the best-tasting catfish is going to come from clean streams and lakes. Because they are bottom feeders, the meat may taste muddy. It's best to fish for catfish before the water temperature gets too warm. When cleaning the fish, remove any of the meat that has blood in it, keeping only the firm white flesh.

Stir-Grilled Northern Pike

Northern pike has medium-firm flesh that holds together fairly well. This makes it a perfect candidate for grilling, and in this recipe, stir-grilling smaller chunks of the fish with fresh vegetables. This recipe could easily be adapted to a stir-fry recipe by adding oil to the wok and cooking until fish is opaque.

Serves 4

1 pound pike steak or fillets, cubed
½ pound sugar snap peas or snow peas, strings removed
12 cherry tomatoes
½ red onion, cut into small wedges
1 yellow pepper, seeded and cut into strips
½ cup soy sauce
½ cup orange juice
2 cloves garlic, minced
3 cups cooked basmati rice

1. Place fish, peas, tomatoes, red onion, and pepper in a large resealable plastic bag. Pour the soy, orange juice, and garlic into the bag. Seal the bag and shake to coat everything.

2. Prepare a hot fire in the grill. When ready to grill, set an oiled grill wok on the rack above the fire. Transfer the ingredients to the grill wok using a slotted spoon to drain the excess marinade.

3. Stir-grill until the pike is opaque, 6 to 8 minutes, using two long-handled wooden spoons to toss the mixture. Move the wok to the indirect-heat side of the grill. Close the lid on the grill and cook for another 4 to 5 minutes. Serve over the rice.

Broiled Asiago-Crusted Pike Steaks
with Peppery Couscous

*Try grilling pike with this recipe. The cooking time will be about
4 minutes per side, turning halfway through the grilling process.
The pike holds together well and the charred flavor is outstanding.*

1. Rinse the fish and pat dry. Place on a lightly oiled broiler pan. Drizzle with olive oil and sprinkle each steak with 1 teaspoon Asiago cheese.

2. Heat the chicken broth in a saucepan until it comes to a boil. Add the couscous and cover with a lid. Remove from heat and let sit for 5 minutes.

3. Preheat the oven broiler to high. When broiler is hot, place the fish in the oven and cook for about 6 to 8 minutes, until fish is opaque and cooked through.

4. Stir the couscous with a fork. Add the chopped scallions, 2 tablespoons cheese and the black pepper and stir again.

5. Divide the couscous equally among four plates. Place pike steak slanted atop the couscous.

Leftover Fish

There are many ways to use leftover cooked fish. Add chunks of fish to a vegetarian minestrone for a quick Mediterranean-style zuppa (soup). To make a fish pâté, combine 4 ounces of cooked fish, 4 ounces of cream cheese, juice from ½ lemon, and 2 chopped scallions. Stir and spoon into a ramekin. Serve with crusty toasted bread.

Pan-Fried Perch Fillets
with Whiskey Cream Sauce

Yellow perch is related to walleye and both have sweet flesh. The perch is difficult to scale and is best when served as skinless fillets. Add mashed potatoes and fresh sliced tomatoes to pair with this company-style dinner.

⌒

Serves 4

1½ pounds perch fillets
Salt and pepper to taste
1 teaspoon fresh thyme,
    chopped
4 tablespoons butter, divided
2 tablespoons vegetable oil
    or more
4 tablespoons whiskey,
    divided
½ cup heavy cream
Zest of 1 lemon

1. Rinse the fillets and pat dry. Lightly season with salt, pepper, and thyme.

2. Melt 2 tablespoons butter in a large skillet, then add oil. Over medium-high heat, sauté the fish fillets for about 2 or 3 minutes per side in batches. Remove from pan and keep warm.

3. Pour 2 tablespoons whiskey into the hot pan and light it on fire, standing back from the flame. When the flame subsides, add the remaining 2 tablespoons of butter.

4. Pour the cream into the pan and bring to a boil. Stir and reduce sauce over medium-high heat for about 3 or 4 minutes. Add the remaining whiskey and the lemon zest, stirring to blend.

5. Spoon Whiskey Cream Sauce onto each plate. Set fish fillets on top of cream and add the side dishes of your choice.

1 (2-pound) skinless salmon
    fillet
1 tablespoon olive oil
Salt and pepper to taste
1 tablespoon thyme
1 tablespoon marjoram
4 tablespoons fresh Italian
    parsley, chopped
Zest and juice of 1 lemon

Oven-Planked Herbed Salmon

The delicious fragrance of herbs makes this dish sublime. Place a baking plank in water to presoak for 30 minutes prior to baking. If you don't have a plank, simply bake the salmon in the oven at 350°F for about 12 to 15 minutes or until the salmon begins to ooze a milky white liquid.

1. Preheat oven to 350°F.

2. Rinse salmon thoroughly and pat dry with a paper towel. Place salmon on a water-soaked baking plank.

3. Lightly coat the top of the salmon with olive oil and season with salt and pepper to taste. Sprinkle the herbs over the fillet. Then sprinkle the lemon zest and drizzle the lemon juice over the fillet.

4. Place plank in the oven and bake for about 25 to 30 minutes or until salmon is opaque and begins to ooze a milky white liquid.

About Planking

Baking planks are usually 1½- to 2-inch thick planks of aromatic wood like cedar, oak, or alder. They are more expensive than the thin ¼-inch grilling planks. The theory behind the different thicknesses is that the grilling planks get heavily charred after about two or three uses and are thrown away without remorse. The more expensive baking plank may be used on the grill, but when it gets too charred to use, its price tag makes it painful to throw away. Baking in the oven keeps it at its best and it may last for several years.

Baked Salmon and Wild Rice Hot Dish

Minnesota Hot Dish is a casserole with everything in it to make a meal. Old-fashioned versions use canned soup for the sauce. Try this recipe with other fish fillets like walleye or pike or similar seafood.

~

Serves 4

½ cup long grain rice
½ cup wild rice
1 teaspoon salt
½ cup currants
1 pound salmon fillet, skinless
1 pound fresh asparagus,
   blanched
3 tablespoons butter
2 cloves garlic, minced
3 tablespoons flour
1 cup chicken stock
1 cup heavy cream
Salt and pepper to taste
½ cup Romano cheese,
   grated

1. Pour 2 cups water into a saucepan and bring to a boil. Add rice and salt and cook for 25 minutes over medium heat. Drain water and place rice in the bottom of a 2-quart casserole dish. Stir in currants.

2. Preheat oven to 425°F.

3. Cut salmon fillet into 4 equal pieces and place on top of rice. Place asparagus on top of salmon.

4. Melt butter in a skillet and sauté garlic for 1 to 2 minutes. Stir in flour to form a thick roux. Gradually add chicken stock and heavy cream. Cook over medium heat until liquid begins to thicken. Season to taste with salt and pepper.

5. Pour liquid over salmon. Sprinkle the top with cheese. Bake in oven for 20 to 25 minutes until cream is bubbling and browned on top. Serve immediately.

4 (6-ounce) salmon fillets,
    ¾ inch thick
1 tablespoon olive oil
Seasoned pepper to taste
5 tablespoons mayonnaise
2 teaspoons anchovy paste
1 clove garlic, minced
1 teaspoon Dijon mustard
1 tablespoon lemon juice
Salt and pepper to taste
1 head romaine lettuce,
    cleaned and torn
⅓ cup Romano cheese,
    freshly grated

Grillpan Salmon Caesar Salad

*Adapt this Caesar salad recipe for the fish or meat of your choice.
Or serve it as a side salad without the meat. .*

1. Rinse salmon fillets and pat dry. Place on a plate and lightly coat with olive oil and season with pepper. Set aside.

2. To make dressing, combine the mayonnaise, anchovy paste, garlic, mustard, and lemon juice in a bowl and stir to blend. Taste and add salt and pepper to your liking. Set aside.

3. Preheat a grill pan or griddle over high heat. When hot, place salmon fillets on the pan. Cook for about 4 minutes per side. Remove from pan.

4. Place the lettuce in a large bowl. Toss with dressing to lightly coat the lettuce. Add the cheese and toss again.

5. Portion out one-fourth of the lettuce on each of four plates. Top each with a salmon fillet.

Are Salmon Freshwater Fish?
Yes, even though most species spend their lives in saltwater oceans. They are born in freshwater streams and immediately make haste for the ocean. Then, when ready to spawn, they return to almost the exact spot where they were born. This process of returning to freshwater streams to spawn tags salmon and char with the term anadromous.

Smoked Salmon
with Lemon, Garlic, and White Wine

*This recipe can be used to smoke pieces of salmon fillet, too.
They will smoke much faster because they are boneless,
so adapt the time to about 1 to 1½ hours.*

Serves 4 to 6

1 lemon, sliced
6–8 sprigs fresh thyme
4 cloves garlic, sliced
1 (3- to 4-pound) salmon,
   cleaned and dressed
3 tablespoons butter
1 cup dry white wine
¼ cup lemon juice
½ teaspoon red pepper flakes

1. Place lemon slices, sprigs of thyme, and sliced garlic in the cavity of the salmon. Place the salmon in a disposable aluminum pan that will fit in your smoker or grill.

2. Melt the butter in a saucepan and add the wine, lemon juice, and red pepper flakes. Simmer for about 2 or 3 minutes. Pour the liquid over the salmon and cover tightly with foil. Let sit.

3. Prepare a 225°F fire in a smoker or grill. Place 3 chunks of wood such as oak or apple on the fire. Place the pan of salmon in the smoker or on the indirect-heat side of the grill. Close the lid.

4. Smoke for 1 hour. Then unwrap the foil on the pan and smoke for another hour, until the salmon flakes easily when pierced with a fork.

Serves 4

1 (3- to 4-pound) whole shad,
   cleaned
2 tablespoons olive oil
½ teaspoon garlic salt
1 teaspoon lemon pepper
½ cup toasted pine nuts,
   divided
4 green onions
1 lemon, halved
½ cup white wine

Baked Shad

"The shad are running," friends from the East say. But usually there is talk about eating only the delicate shad roe. That's because the shad is very bony. This is a slow method of cooking the shad to where the bones are softened, almost dissolved, and edible. Serve with Lemon Tarragon Wild Rice (page 252).

1. Preheat oven to 250°F. Lightly grease a deep disposable aluminum pan large enough to hold the shad.

2. Lightly coat shad with olive oil. Salt and pepper inside and out. Place 2 tablespoons of the pine nuts and the whole green onions in the cavity of the fish. Set in pan. Sprinkle pine nuts on top. Squeeze the juice of a whole lemon over the fish. Pour the white wine into the pan. Cover tightly with heavy-duty foil.

3. Bake in the oven for 5 hours. Serve with wine sauce spooned over each serving.

Smoked Shad

Following the preparation of the recipe above, the foil-encased shad could also be placed on a smoker at 225°F. Cook for 1 hour with the foil open so that the wood smoke can penetrate. Tightly close the foil and cook for another 4 to 5 hours.

Shad Roe

For those who enjoy roe, it doesn't get much better than this.
Serve with crusty bread to mop up any extra sauce.

Serves 4 as an appetizer

2 tablespoons unsalted butter
3 tablespoons onion, minced
2 pair shad roe (about 1½
    pounds)
1 cup dry white wine
1 bay leaf, broken in half
1 tablespoon fresh lemon
    juice
Salt and pepper to taste
1 teaspoon cornstarch
1 cup heavy cream
2 tablespoons onion chives,
    snipped

1. Melt the butter in a large skillet over medium heat. Add the onion and cook for 1 minute. Add the shad roe and sauté for 1 minute on each side. Add the wine, bay leaf, lemon juice, salt and pepper to taste. Gently simmer, uncovered, until the roe is just barely firm, about 10 minutes.

2. Remove the roe with a slotted spoon and cool. Trim off tough membrane on either end and slice the roe. Set aside.

3. Cook poaching liquid over high heat until reduced by half. Remove the bay leaf.

4. Add cornstarch to 2 tablespoons heavy cream and stir to blend. Add to poaching liquid with the rest of the cream and stir until thickened. Add chives.

5. Pour cream into a pretty shallow serving bowl and place roe in the sauce. Give everyone a plate, fork, spoon, and slices of crusty bread.

Communal Dining
Serving a large platter of appetizers communally can make for an entertaining evening. Everyone digs in and has fun. The mood is relaxed, and the stories of fishing trips or food memories from long ago make for a good time.

Serves 4

½ cup flour
1 cup saltine cracker crumbs
1 teaspoon salt
1 teaspoon black pepper
3 pounds whole sunfish,
    cleaned and scaled
½ cup vegetable oil or more,
    divided
4 tablespoons butter
3 lemons, halved
¼ cup fresh Italian parsley,
    chopped

Pan-Fried Sunfish in Cracker Crust

*Serve the fish with sautéed spinach or kale
and parsley-buttered new potatoes.*

1. Combine the flour, cracker crumbs, salt, and pepper in a bowl. Dredge the fish in the flour mixture and place in a single layer on a baking sheet.

2. Heat a large skillet with ¼ cup of the vegetable oil.

3. Over medium-high heat, sauté the fish fillets in batches for about 2 or 3 minutes per side, until golden brown. Remove from pan and keep warm. Add more oil as necessary for sautéing.

4. Drain excess oil and place skillet over medium heat. Add the butter and melt, stirring with the pan drippings until combined.

5. Plate the fish and squeeze 1 lemon over all and top with the parsley. Then drizzle the butter over all. Serve with additional lemon halves.

Barbecued Trout and Slivered Vegetables Wrapped in Foil

Ah! Fresh trout has to be one of America's favorite freshwater fish. It is as exciting to get a rainbow, brown, or cutthroat on the line as it is to eat it.

⌐

1. Prepare a hot fire in your grill or preheat the oven to 375°F.

2. Lightly oil four pieces of aluminum foil and place 1 trout on each. Place several slices of lemon in the cavity of each fish. Distribute the vegetables evenly over the trout and sprinkle ¼ teaspoon of the rosemary across the tops.

3. Whisk together the white wine and mustard. Drizzle about 2½ tablespoons over each trout. Season with salt and pepper to taste and tightly wrap the foil around the fish. Grill or bake the foil packets for about 20 to 25 minutes.

4. Place a packet on each of four dinner plates. Diners should be cautioned to open their packets carefully, as there will be a burst of hot steam.

Foil Packets

Cooking food in aluminum foil makes for very easy cleanup. This is a great way to cook on the grill, in the embers of a fire, or in the oven. You can also buy ready-made foil packets that are extra heavy duty.

Serves 4

2 tablespoons vegetable oil
4 (12-ounce) whole trout, cleaned
2 lemons, sliced
1 red bell pepper, seeded and slivered
1 yellow bell pepper, seeded and slivered
1 red onion, peeled and slivered
8 ounces mushrooms, sliced
1 teaspoon fresh rosemary leaves, chopped
½ cup dry white wine
2 tablespoons Dijon mustard
Salt and pepper to taste

1 cup orange juice
Zest and juice of 1 lime
1 bunch fresh cilantro
1 jalapeno, finely chopped
Zest of 1 lemon
4 (12-ounce) whole trout,
    cleaned
Salt and pepper to taste

Grilled Whole Trout
with Cilantro Gremolata

*Gremolata is traditionally made with Italian parsley, garlic, and lemon zest.
It is a fragrant garnish on slow-cooked Italian dishes like short ribs
and osso buco. This southwest-style version is delicious, too.*

1. Prepare a medium-hot fire in your grill.

2. Combine the orange juice and lime zest and juice in a bowl.

3. On a wooden cutting board, using a chef's knife, finely chop the cilantro, jalapeno, and lemon zest together to make the Cilantro Gremolata. Set aside.

4. Rinse the trout and pat dry. Season with salt and pepper. Place directly over the grill fire.

5. Grill until the meat is opaque and just beginning to flake when tested with a fork, 8 to 10 minutes per side, turning once about halfway through the grilling time and brushing frequently with the orange-lime baste. Serve garnished with the Cilantro Gremolata.

Citrus Zest
Whenever you use fresh-squeezed citrus, don't forget to add some extra punch by zesting the fruit first. The zest is the colored part of the rind, not the white pith. A microplane zester makes easy work of getting the zest. The zest is pungent, so you don't need lots of it. In marinades and bastes, it accentuates the final product.

Sautéed Rainbow Trout
with Lemon-Lime Drizzle

A single trout fillet makes a perfect-sized appetizer.
Serve with half a cup of dressed greens for an elegant touch.

Serves 4

8 (4- to 6-ounce) trout fillets,
    skinned and boned
Salt and pepper to taste
8 tablespoons butter
1 cup flour
Zest and juice of 1 lemon
Zest and juice of 1 lime

1. Rinse fillets and pat dry. Lightly season with salt and pepper.

2. Melt 4 tablespoons butter in a sauté pan over medium heat.

3. Lightly dredge each fillet in flour and pan sauté 2 or 3 fillets at a time for about 6 to 8 minutes, turning once. Increase heat to medium-high, but do not burn butter. Add more butter as needed with each batch. Keep warm.

4. Add any remaining butter and the zest and juices of the lemon and lime. Drizzle over the cooked fish.

Amaretto-Glazed Walleye Fillets

If you don't want to use a liqueur with this dish, substitute dark honey.

Serves 4

4 (6- to 8-ounce) skinless
    walleye fillets
Salt and pepper to taste
8 tablespoons butter
½ cup flour
2 tablespoons almonds, sliced
2 tablespoons Amaretto
    liqueur

1. Rinse fillets and pat dry. Lightly season with salt and pepper.

2. Melt 4 tablespoons butter in a sauté pan over medium heat.

3. Lightly dredge each fillet in flour and pan sauté 2 at a time for about 6 to 8 minutes, turning once. Remove from pan and keep warm.

4. Add the rest of the butter to the pan and brown the almonds. Then add the Amaretto. Drizzle over the warm walleye.

Serves 4

1 pound cooked fish
2 cups seasoned mashed
    potatoes
2–3 tablespoons milk or
    cream (optional)
1 cup flour
1 teaspoon salt
½ teaspoon pepper
¼ cup olive oil or more
2–4 tablespoons butter
1 cup sour cream
⅓ cup German-style grainy
    mustard
4 ounces arugula, cleaned
    and dried

Fish Cakes
with Mustard Cream Sauce

This is a favorite "leftover" dish because it doesn't taste left over at all.

1. Place cooked fish in a bowl. Using a fork, lightly shred the fish into small chunks. Add the mashed potatoes and stir to mix. If needed, add a little milk or cream to moisten. Make 8 equal-sized fish cakes from the mixture and set aside.

2. Combine the flour, salt, and pepper in a shallow bowl.

3. Heat olive oil and 2 tablespoons butter in a skillet over medium-high heat.

4. Combine the sour cream and grainy mustard in a bowl and set aside.

5. Sauté 4 fish cakes at a time until light golden brown on each side, turning only once. Place on a warm plate and cover to keep warm. Cook the remaining 4 cakes, adding more oil and butter if necessary.

6. Place 1 ounce of arugula on each plate; top with 2 fish cakes. Spoon 1 or 2 tablespoons of the Mustard Cream Sauce on the fish cakes and serve the remaining sauce on the side.

Bitter Greens
Europeans have had a love affair with bitter greens for years. Americans have caught on and use arugula and radicchio quite often. If the bitterness is too much for your palate, mix bitter greens with leafy green lettuces to soften the bite.

Smoked Whitefish
with Horseradish Sauce

*Horseradish sauce can be made with whipped cream,
sour cream, or yogurt with equally good results.*

Serves 4 as a main course

2 pounds whitefish fillets
½ cup heavy cream
*2–3 tablespoons prepared
    horseradish*
4 cups salad greens
1 lemon, quartered

1. Prepare a 225°F fire in a smoker or grill. Place 3 water-soaked wood chunks, maple or cherry, on the fire.

2. Place the whitefish in the smoker or on the indirect-heat side of the grill. Close the lid.

3. Smoke for 1 to 1½ hours. Whitefish should flake easily when pierced with a fork.

4. Whip the heavy cream in a bowl. Stir in the horseradish to taste. Refrigerate until ready to use.

5. To serve, place a fish fillet over 1 cup of the greens on each serving plate. Spoon a little of the horseradish sauce over each fillet and garnish with a lemon quarter. Serve remaining sauce in a dish on the side.

Smoked Whitefish

Even though excellent smoked whitefish is available at supermarkets, grocery stores, and upscale gourmet shops, making your own is a delicacy. Whitefish is an oily fish so it takes to smoking well. You may marinate the fish prior to smoking or sprinkle a pepper rub on it for something a little bit different.

4 (7-ounce) whitefish fillets
½ cup sun-dried tomatoes,
   chopped
½ cup cured olives, chopped
¼ cup fresh basil, chopped
2 tablespoons extra-virgin
   olive oil
1 lemon, quartered

Baked Whitefish Fillets
with Sun-Dried Tomato Relish

*The contrast of dark red, green, and black in the relish pairs
beautifully with any white-fleshed fish.*

1. Preheat oven to 350°F.

2. Rinse fish and pat dry. Place fillets in a casserole dish.

3. Combine sun-dried tomatoes, olives, basil, and olive oil in a bowl. Stir to blend. Spread about 2 to 3 tablespoons of the relish over each fish fillet.

4. Cover the casserole with foil and bake in the oven for about 15 minutes. Uncover and bake for another 5 minutes or until fish is done (when it just begins to flake when touched with a fork). Serve fillets with any extra relish and a wedge of lemon.

Quick Condiments
Almost all grocery stores and specialty food shops carry delicious and interesting prepared relishes, mustards, pestos, flavored oils and vinegars, and sauces. Buy an assortment to add to your pantry. Then use them!

Sautéed Frog Legs
with Garlic and White Wine

Simple ingredients often make for the tastiest meals.

~

Serves 4 to 5

2 pounds frog legs
Salt and pepper to taste
1 cup flour
8 tablespoons butter
2 cloves garlic, minced
1 lemon
1 cup dry white wine
1 tablespoon capers
    (optional)
¼ cup fresh Italian parsley,
    chopped
1 loaf crusty bread

1. Season the frog legs with salt and pepper and lightly dredge in flour. Place on a baking tray.

2. Melt the butter in a skillet and sauté frog legs over medium-high heat until golden brown and tender, about 6 to 8 minutes.

3. Add the garlic to the butter in the pan and cook for a minute.

4. Squeeze lemon juice over the legs. Add wine and capers (optional). Simmer for a few minutes more. Sprinkle with chopped parsley.

5. Serve with crusty bread and a glass of the dry white wine.

Start with a Simple Recipe
This classic recipe is full of flavor and very easy to execute. If you want to embellish, try adding fire-roasted red peppers or tomatoes for a Mediterranean-inspired meal.

6 pounds live crawfish
4 cloves garlic, sliced
1 stalk celery, cut in half
1 carrot, cut in half
1 onion, quartered
Hot sauce to taste
Creole seasonings to taste
2 cups dry white wine
Salt to taste

Crawfish Boil

*This is a bit messy, so make sure everyone knows it's a casual supper.
Serve with crusty bread, a green salad, and hand towels.*

1. Bring a big pot of water, large enough to hold the crawfish, to a rolling boil. Add garlic, celery, carrot, and onion and boil for 20 minutes.

2. Add hot sauce, Creole seasonings, white wine, and salt to taste; cook for another 15 minutes.

3. Add live crawfish and boil for about 5 to 8 minutes, until crawfish turn red. Use a long-handled spoon to stir crawfish from the bottom to the top halfway through cooking.

4. Ladle crawfish into 4 or 6 bowls. Ladle broth into bowls.

How to Eat Crawfish

Pull the heads off and suck the juices from the head if you desire. Press the sides of the top of the tail. The shell will give a little and crack; then you can pull out the meat with your front teeth.

Chapter 4

Saltwater Catch

2–3 pounds barracuda fillets
⅓ cup olive oil
⅓ cup fresh lemon juice
1 tablespoon Dijon mustard
2 cloves garlic, minced
1 teaspoon dried basil
1 teaspoon salt
1 teaspoon ground black
    pepper

Grilled Mustard Herb Barracuda

Citrus and Dijon mustard marry well with fish. Grouper, dorado, salmon, swordfish, and just about any other fish will work in this recipe.

1. Place the fish in a shallow pan. In a bowl, mix together the olive oil, lemon juice, mustard, garlic, basil, salt, and pepper. Pour half of the marinade over the fish, reserving the remaining marinade. Let stand at room temperature for 30 minutes.

2. Heat the grill, and when it is hot, grill the fish directly over the flames for about 4 to 5 minutes per side or 10 minutes per inch of thickness of the fillet. Turn only once, halfway through grilling. Serve at once, drizzled with the reserved marinade.

Barracuda

The legendary barracuda has a reputation for sharklike terror in the water, but on the grill, it's delicious. Moderately firm, textured, and medium flavored, barracuda can stand up to assertive flavors.

Bass Baked in Salt

Salt crust should be used only for whole fish, not fillets or steaks.

Serves 2

1 (2-pound) sea bass
4 pounds coarse sea salt
1 lemon, halved

1. Clean and gut the sea bass, but do not scale it. Rinse and pat dry.

2. Preheat the oven to 400°F.

3. Pour half of the salt into a rectangular glass casserole dish that is large enough to hold the whole fish. Set the fish on the salt. Then pour the rest of the salt over the fish to completely cover it, and pat the salt down.

4. Bake in the hot oven for 30 to 35 minutes. Remove from the oven. Carefully break the salt off of the fish, removing as much salt as you can. Serve immediately, squeezing lemon juice over the fish.

Stripers

Black sea bass are striped bass, more commonly known to fishermen as stripers. They have thick bodies and make excellent thick fillets that are not very bony.

1 quart water
⅓ cup honey or maple syrup
¼ cup kosher salt
1 tablespoon Dijon mustard
1 teaspoon red pepper flakes
1 sprig rosemary
1 tablespoon coarse black
   pepper
2–3 pounds fresh bluefish
   fillets
Olive oil for brushing

Grilled Bluefish in Rosemary Honey Brine

*Brining improves the taste and texture of saltwater fish. As the
brine moves into the fish, it brings the flavor with it. You can substitute
other oily fish, such as mackerel or sardines, for bluefish.*

1. Combine the water, honey, salt, mustard, red pepper flakes, rosemary,
   and black pepper in a deep nonreactive pan. Add the bluefish fillets,
   cover, and refrigerate for 8 hours or overnight.

2. Remove the fish from the brine and rinse under cold, running water.
   Pat dry. Brush the fillets with olive oil.

3. Heat the grill, and when it is hot, grill the fish directly over the flames
   for about 4 to 5 minutes per side or 10 minutes per inch of thickness of
   the fillet. Turn only once, halfway through grilling. Serve at once.

Plank-Baked Bonito
with Lemon Herb Butter and Arugula

This tunalike fish is very meaty.

Serves 4

4 (5- to 6-ounce) bonito
   steaks, ½ inch thick
6 tablespoons butter
2 tablespoons lemon juice
1 tablespoon chives, snipped
1 tablespoon basil, chopped
5 cups arugula or other
   greens
1 cup cherry tomatoes,
   halved
¼ red onion, slivered

1. Soak a wooden (oak, cedar, or alder) baking plank in water for 30 to 60 minutes. Then preheat the oven to 350°F.

2. Place the fish steaks on the water-soaked plank.

3. In a small saucepan, melt the butter. Add the lemon juice, chives, and basil. Pour the sauce over the fish. Bake for 20 minutes in the preheated oven.

4. Arrange arugula on a platter. Place the fish steaks down the center of the platter, overlapping slightly. Arrange the halved tomatoes and onion slivers around the fish. Spoon the sauce over all and serve at once.

Baking Planks

Wood planking adds an aromatic wood flavor dimension to fish that is divine. Wood planks for grilling are usually flat pieces of wood ³⁄₈ to ¾ inch thick. Baking planks are heftier pieces of wood that are 1½ to 2 inches thick, with a slightly hollowed out center that is perfect for holding fish or meat with a sauce. They can be purchased at grill or gourmet shops.

Serves 8

8 ears of corn, unshucked
8 pounds steamer clams,
   rinsed under running
   water
1 pound unsalted butter,
   melted
1 teaspoon liquid smoke
   flavoring
2 teaspoons barbecue
   seasoning
2 pounds new potatoes,
   parboiled, threaded onto
   metal skewers

Old-Fashioned Clambake

A traditional clambake is held on or near a beach, with clams, corn on the cob, and new potatoes cooked over an open fire, then drizzled with butter. If you don't live on or near a beach, you can still enjoy a clambake, courtesy of your grill.

1. Heat the grill, and when it is hot, grill the corn directly over the flames for about 3 to 4 minutes per side or 8 minutes total. Turn only once, halfway through grilling. Remove and keep warm.

2. Place the clams on the grill rack, discarding any that have opened. Close the lid and grill until the clams have opened, about 10 minutes. Discard any clams that have not opened. Remove and keep warm.

3. In bowl, stir together the melted butter, smoke flavoring, and barbecue seasoning. Brush the potato skewers with the mixture, reserving the remaining butter mixture. Arrange the skewers on the grill rack, close the lid, and grill for 4 to 5 minutes per side or until done.

4. To serve, shuck the corn and place the corn, clams, and potato skewers on a platter. Drizzle the corn and clams with the butter mixture and serve.

Fresh-Caught Crab Gazpacho

*Once you've caught your own crabs, brought them safely home,
then cooked and picked the meat out, you understand
why crabmeat is so expensive at the store!*

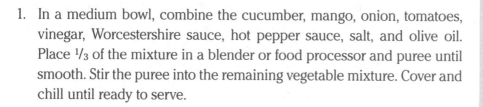

Serves 8

1 medium cucumber, peeled,
    seeded, and diced
1 medium mango, seeded,
    diced, and peeled
1 medium red onion, peeled
    and diced
2 large beefsteak tomatoes,
    diced
3 tablespoons red wine
    vinegar
1 tablespoon Worcestershire
    sauce
1 teaspoon hot pepper sauce
1 teaspoon salt
½ cup extra-virgin olive oil
8 blue crabs, steamed and the
    meat picked out, or about
    1 pound lump crabmeat

1. In a medium bowl, combine the cucumber, mango, onion, tomatoes, vinegar, Worcestershire sauce, hot pepper sauce, salt, and olive oil. Place ⅓ of the mixture in a blender or food processor and puree until smooth. Stir the puree into the remaining vegetable mixture. Cover and chill until ready to serve.

2. To serve, spoon the gazpacho into parfait glasses or bowls and top with the crabmeat.

Baja Gazpacho Condiment Bar
Seaside restaurants on the Baja Peninsula serve a bowl of tomato puree when someone orders gazpacho. At first look, it seems disappointing. But wait until the condiments come, served on the side. There are chopped onions, chopped tomatoes, chopped peppers, chopped herbs, grated goat cheese, shrimp, and so on. Diners make their soup as thin or as chunky as they want, with whatever ingredients they choose.

3 cups mashed potatoes,
   warm
½ cup heavy cream
2 cups cooked fish, such as
   cod, salmon, or halibut
8 green onions, chopped
¼ cup Italian parsley,
   chopped
½ teaspoon kosher salt
¼ teaspoon white pepper
3 eggs, beaten
1 cup Asiago cheese, grated

Seafood Soufflé

Cook and serve in a pretty baking dish with a green salad on the side.

1. Heat the oven to 350°F. Butter a large baking dish and set aside.

2. In a large bowl, mix the warm mashed potatoes with the heavy cream so that the potatoes are fluffy. (Add additional cream if they need more moisture.) Flake the fish and add to the bowl. Add the onions, parsley, salt, white pepper, and eggs and gently mix together.

3. Pour into the buttered baking pan. Sprinkle the top with Asiago cheese. Place in the oven and bake for about 30 minutes. If you'd like a browned topping, turn on the broiler to high and broil until bubbling, about 3 to 4 minutes. Serve immediately.

Seafood Soufflés

Soufflés, or puffs as they are sometimes referred to, are fishing villages' versions of comfort food, like macaroni and cheese. They are a wonderful way to spin a new dinner from leftover fish and mashed potatoes.

Pistachio-Crusted Corbina

Serve this with steamed asparagus and Olive Oil Smashed Potatoes (page 96).

Serves 4

1 tablespoon olive oil
4 (6- to 7-ounce) corbina
    fillets, 1 inch thick
4 tablespoons pistachios,
    finely chopped
4 tablespoons unsalted butter

1. Lightly oil the fish fillets and dredge in the pistachios.

2. Sauté in butter over medium-high to high heat. Cook for 4 to 5 minutes per side, turning only once. Serve at once, drizzled with the pan drippings.

Corbina/White Sea Bass

Corbina is a popular sports angler fish that is also known as white sea bass. It's a relative of the croaker and drum families.

Rockin' Rockfish

If you're in the mood for rockfish but they aren't biting, substitute other moderately firm, moderately flavored saltwater fish such as barracuda, bonito, sablefish, or sea bream in this dish.

Serves 4

2 tablespoons dried lemon
    peel
1 tablespoon dried basil
1 tablespoon dried tarragon
1 teaspoon garlic powder
1 teaspoon ground white
    pepper
1 teaspoon sea salt
1 teaspoon red pepper flakes
4 whole rockfish, cleaned
¼ cup olive oil

1. Preheat the oven to 450°F.

2. In a bowl, combine the lemon peel, basil, tarragon, garlic powder, white pepper, salt, and red pepper flakes. Set aside.

3. Rinse the rockfish under cold, running water and pat dry. Place the fish in a deep, shallow pan. Sprinkle the fish, inside and out, with the spice mixture. Drizzle the fish with the olive oil.

4. Bake the fish for 18 to 22 minutes, or until the fish begins to flake when tested with a fork in the thickest part. To serve, fillet and remove the skin.

1½ pounds dorado
(mahimahi) fillets
4 tablespoons spicy barbecue
seasoning
2 cups Napa cabbage, cored
and shredded
1 cup assorted tender greens
¼ cup tarragon vinegar
¼ cup sour cream
Juice of 2 lemons
8 green onions, finely
chopped
½ teaspoon salt
8 flour tortillas

Dorado Fish Tacos

*Delicious fish tacos are brilliant because there are so many
fish that can be used in this recipe. Try substituting catfish,
halibut, grouper, haddock, and even salmon.*

1. Sprinkle the dorado with the barbecue seasoning and set aside.

2. Combine the cabbage and greens in a large bowl.

3. In a small bowl, combine the vinegar, sour cream, lemon juice, green onions, and salt to make the dressing. Set aside.

4. Heat the grill, and when it is hot, grill the fish directly over the flames for about 4 to 5 minutes per side or 10 minutes per inch of thickness of the fillet. Turn only once, halfway through grilling. Place cooked fish on a plate and cut into bite-sized chunks. (Fillets may be pan sautéed.)

5. Pour the dressing over the cabbage mixture and toss to blend just before assembling. To make the tacos, place 3 ounces of grilled fish chunks on the tortilla. Top with about ⅓ cup of the cabbage slaw and roll up.

Dorado/Mahimahi
Dorado is the regional name for mahimahi, which is actually a dolphin-fish part of the mackerel family. Be careful not to confuse dolphinfish, which is a fish, with dolphin, which is a mammal.

Baked Flounder in Parchment

Individual servings of fish baked in parchment paper are like presents at the table. The paper keeps the fish nice and hot. Diners carefully open the paper to a waft of aromatic heat. Warn them to be careful. Serve with a nice salad and crusty bread to soak up the sauce.

Serves 4

4 (6- to 8-ounce) flounder
    fillets
Parchment paper
1 large beefsteak tomato,
    chopped
1 bunch green onions,
    chopped
½ cup Kalamata olives,
    halved
1 teaspoon anchovy paste
¼ cup extra-virgin olive oil
2 tablespoons lemon juice
¼ teaspoon kosher salt
¼ teaspoon freshly ground
    black pepper

⌁

1. Preheat the oven to 350°F.

2. Place a serving of fish in the center of each of four 8-inch square pieces of parchment paper. Place one-fourth of the chopped tomato, green onions, and olives on top of each fish fillet.

3. In a small bowl, combine the rest of the ingredients and whisk to blend. Spoon about 1½ tablespoons of the sauce over each fish fillet. Fold the parchment paper to enclose the fish and hold in the vegetables and sauce.

4. Place on a baking sheet and cook in the preheated oven for about 15 minutes. Carefully set each parchment packet on a dinner plate and serve at once.

Sautéed Grouper
with Citrus Butter

Serves 4

6 tablespoons unsalted butter
4 (6- to 8-ounce) grouper
    fillets
Zest and juice of 1 lemon
½ teaspoon hot sauce

To put a different spin on this recipe, substitute the lemon with orange, grapefruit, lime, or a combination of any of these citrus fruits.

1. Melt butter in a skillet and sauté grouper over high heat for about 4 to 5 minutes per side. Place grouper on individual plates.

2. Add lemon zest and juice to the skillet and heat until bubbly. Add the hot sauce and stir. Drizzle over the fish and serve.

Poached Halibut
with Red Pepper Aioli

Serves 4

2 cups dry white wine
4 (7- to 8-ounce) halibut fillets
1 cup mayonnaise
2 cloves garlic
½ cup roasted red peppers
    from a jar
Lemon juice to taste
Italian parsley to garnish,
    chopped

Strain and freeze the poaching liquid to use in seafood soups or sauces later on.

1. Simmer the wine over medium heat. Add halibut, cover, and gently poach for 10 minutes or until the fish begins to flake when tested with a fork.

2. Make the Red Pepper Aioli by combining mayonnaise, garlic, and roasted red peppers in a food processor or blender. Puree, then add lemon juice to taste.

3. To serve, arrange a halibut fillet on each plate and top with a dollop of aioli. Sprinkle with parsley.

Mesquite-Grilled Kingfish
with Avocado Corn Salsa

*The sportsman's favorite from the drum family. If you can't catch or
find kingfish at the store, you can substitute another moderately firm,
full-flavored fish such as amberjack, mackerel, mullet, or wahoo.*

Serves 4

1 cup mesquite chips
2 large, ripe avocados
1 cup fresh corn kernels or
    thawed frozen corn
¼ cup green onion, chopped
2 cloves garlic, minced
2 tablespoons cilantro,
    chopped
1 teaspoon bottled chipotle
    pepper sauce
Juice of 1 lime
Kosher salt to taste
4 (6- to 8-ounce) kingfish
    fillets
Olive oil for brushing
Freshly ground black pepper
    to taste

1. Soak a handful of mesquite chips in water for 30 minutes.

2. In a bowl, combine the avocados, corn, green onion, garlic, cilantro, chipotle pepper sauce, lime juice, and salt to taste. Stir to blend and set aside.

3. Brush the fish with olive oil and season with kosher salt and freshly ground pepper to taste.

4. Heat the grill, and when it is hot, throw the mesquite chips on the coals. Grill the fish directly over the flames for about 4 to 5 minutes per side or 10 minutes per inch of thickness of the fillet. Turn only once, halfway through grilling. Serve, topped with the salsa, at once.

Metal Smoker Boxes

Metal smoker boxes have small holes all over the box so that maximum smoke is emitted. Since smoker boxes are made especially for gas grills (so wood chip residue does not fall through the grates and clog the gas jets), give them a try. Place the box over the hot fire and close the lid for 10 to 15 minutes. When smoke is coming from the box, then start cooking.

6 (6- to 7-ounce) mackerel
steaks or fillets
Olive oil for drizzling
Kosher salt and freshly
ground black pepper to
taste
8 ounces medium-size shell
pasta, cooked al dente
1½ cups brine-cured Nicoise
or Kalamata olives,
drained, pitted, and
chopped
1 (16-ounce) can chopped
fire-roasted tomatoes
(Muir Glen brand)
2 teaspoons fresh thyme
leaves, chopped
⅔ cup Parmesan or Asiago
cheese, freshly grated

Mediterranean Grilled Mackerel and Pasta

*This ultimate Mediterranean macaroni and cheese
accompanies grilled fish in style.*

1. Prepare a hot fire in the grill. Preheat oven to 300°F.

2. Lightly drizzle fish with olive oil and season to taste with salt and pepper. Set aside.

3. Place pasta in a large bowl. Drizzle with olive oil. Stir in the olives, tomatoes, and thyme and blend well. Stir in the cheese. Season to taste with salt and pepper. Put in a baking dish and cover with foil. Set in the oven for not more than 20 minutes.

4. Grill the fish over a hot fire for 10 minutes per inch of thickness, turning once, halfway through cooking.

5. Plate the pasta and serve the grilled fish on top.

Barbecue Rubbed Permit

Grilling limes or lemons looks pretty and results in a juicier fruit from the warmth. Serve with sliced tomatoes and White Cheddar Coleslaw (page 247).

2–3 tablespoons olive oil
4 (6- to 8-ounce) permit fillets
2–3 tablespoons Chile Pepper
   Rub for Fish and Game
   (recipe below)
2 limes, halved

1. Prepare a hot fire in the grill.

2. Lightly oil the fish and sprinkle the Chile Pepper Rub on both sides. Lightly oil the lime halves.

3. Grill fish for 10 minutes per inch of thickness over a hot grill fire, turning only once. Grill the limes, cut-side down, for 2 or 3 minutes.

4. Serve fillets with grilled lime halves on the side.

Chile Pepper Rub for Fish and Game

Combine all the following ingredients in a large glass jar with a tight-fitting lid: 2 tablespoons each chili powder, ancho chili pepper, chipotle chili pepper, lemon pepper, sweet Hungarian paprika, dill weed, granulated onion, celery seed, and dark brown sugar. Secure the lid and shake to blend. Will keep in the cupboard for several months.

4 (6- to 8-ounce) redfish fillets
5 tablespoons blackened or
    Cajun seasoning mixture
Olive oil for spraying
½ cup (1 stick) unsalted
    butter, softened

Grilled Blackened Redfish

A delicious dish that gets very smoky when cooked indoors.
This grilled version lets the fish sizzle outdoors on a grill. Instead of
redfish, you could use red snapper or orange roughy.

1. Rinse the redfish under cold, running water and pat dry. Sprinkle blackened seasoning on both sides of each fillet, using 4 tablespoons. Spray each fillet with olive oil.

2. In a bowl, mix the softened butter with the remaining 1 tablespoon blackened seasoning mixture and set aside.

3. Heat the grill, and when it is hot, grill the fish directly over the flames for about 4 to 5 minutes per side or 10 minutes per inch of thickness of the fillet. Turn only once, halfway through grilling. Serve at once with a dollop of the seasoned butter.

Paul Prudhomme's Blackened Redfish

Paul Prudhomme is the creator of the blackened redfish craze in Louisiana. The redfish is traditionally sprinkled with a hot peppery seasoning (Cajun) and cooked indoors in a red-hot skillet. It became so popular in the 1980s that redfish was put on the endangered list and couldn't be fished. Luckily, with good game management, the Gulf is teaming with redfish again.

Baked Herbed Shark

Shark steaks are very lean. Pair this dish with something rich and creamy like Baked Risotto with Sun-Dried Tomatoes (page 253).

Serves 4

4 (6- to 7-ounce) shark steaks
1 tablespoon olive oil
4 tablespoons thyme
4 tablespoons marjoram
8 tablespoons parsley flakes
1 teaspoon red pepper flakes
1 tablespoon dried lemon
   peel
½ teaspoon salt

1. Rinse shark thoroughly and pat dry with a paper towel. Lightly coat with olive oil. Place shark in a glass baking dish.

2. Combine the dried herbs, red pepper flakes, dried lemon peel, and salt in a glass jar. (This makes about 1 cup of Spicy Herb Rub, which may be stored in a tightly covered glass jar for several weeks.) Sprinkle several tablespoons of herb mix on both sides of the shark, lightly patting to distribute herb mix evenly. Shark may be cooked immediately or refrigerated for 30 minutes to allow for greater penetration of herb flavors.

3. Preheat oven to 350°F. Place shark in glass baking dish into the oven. Bake for about 10 to 12 minutes or until shark is opaque and begins to ooze a milky white liquid.

Shark

This is one of the fish that breaks the "cook over high heat for 10 minutes per inch thickness" rule. Instead, a 1-inch-thick shark steak cooks in about 7 to 8 minutes over high heat and 10 to 12 minutes over medium heat. Buy pure white steaks without any dark meat, which is unpleasant.

Pompano with Spring Vegetables
in Parchment Paper

Serves 4

(12 x 18-inch) sheets parchment paper or aluminum foil
4 (6-ounce) pompano fillets
Kosher salt and ground white pepper to taste
16 thin asparagus spears, trimmed
½ cup green onion, chopped
½ cup mushrooms, sliced
4 tablespoons unsalted butter
4 tablespoons fresh lemon juice

Packet cooking is a great way to get a moist, aromatic result with fish, and it's easy cleanup, too. You can find parchment paper at better grocery stores or gourmet shops, or just use aluminum foil.

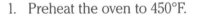

1. Preheat the oven to 450°F.

2. Arrange the sheets of parchment or foil on a flat surface and place a pompano fillet in the center of each one. Sprinkle each fillet with salt and ground white pepper and top with 4 asparagus spears and a fourth of the green onion and mushrooms. Place 1 tablespoon of butter on each and drizzle with 1 tablespoon of lemon juice. Seal each packet and place on a baking sheet.

3. Bake for 18 to 22 minutes or until the fish begins to flake when tested with a fork.

Roasted Red Snapper
on a Bed of Onions, Tomatoes, Olives, and Herbs

Serves 4

2 large red onions, peeled and sliced
½ cup mixed herbs, chopped (chives, basil, tarragon, thyme, etc.)
1 cup fresh or canned tomatoes, chopped
½ cup Nicoise or Kalamata olives, pitted
1 large whole red snapper, about 2 pounds, cleaned
½ cup olive oil

This is a whole-fish dish that is fragrant, flavorful, and beautiful. Serve it on a platter for presentation.

1. Preheat the oven to 450°F.

2. In a casserole or gratin dish large enough to hold the fish, arrange the onions, chopped herbs, tomatoes, and olives.

3. Rinse the snapper under cold, running water and pat dry. Place the snapper on top of the onion mixture and drizzle with olive oil.

4. Tent the fish with aluminum foil and roast for 20 to 22 minutes or until the fish begins to flake when tested in the thickest part.

Pan-Cooked Snook
with Lemonata Sauce

If you catch a snook (or two or three), you deserve a treat, and this recipe is it.
Sauté the fillets in oil, then make a Lemonata Sauce to pour over the fish.

Serves 4

2 tablespoons olive oil
4 (6- to 8-ounce) snook fillets
½ cup seasoned all-purpose
flour
½ cup dry white wine
¼ cup chicken broth
½ cup (1 stick) unsalted butter
2 tablespoons fresh lemon
juice, or to taste
2 tablespoons capers, drained

1. Heat the oil in a large nonstick skillet over medium-high heat.

2. Rinse the fish under cold, running water and pat dry. Dredge the fish in the flour.

3. Sauté the fish until golden on both sides. Transfer to a warm plate.

4. Pour the wine and chicken broth into the skillet, turning the heat to high. Let reduce until about ¼ cup liquid remains.

5. Reduce the heat to medium and whisk the butter into the reduced liquid, 1 tablespoon at a time, until you have a smooth sauce. Whisk in lemon juice to taste, then the capers. Serve each fillet drizzled with the Lemonata Sauce.

Sautéed Fish in a Skillet
Baked, broiled, grilled, smoked, and poached fish are all delicious. However, if there was only one way to prepare fish for the rest of eternity, sautéed in a skillet would win. Everybody has a skillet. And a skillet can be used indoors or outdoors. The skillet's high heat gives fish a nice sear and a teeny bit of a crust that contrasts with the tender, delicate interior. Best of all, a skillet can hold all kinds of delicious sauces.

1 (7.5-ounce) can of salmon,
    drained
1 cup Cheddar or pepper jack
    cheese, grated
¼ cup green onion, chopped
6 leaves fresh basil, chopped
½ roasted red pepper, sliced
2 eggs
1 cup half-and-half
¼ teaspoon kosher salt
Freshly ground black pepper
    to taste
¼ cup Romano or Asiago
    cheese, grated

Crustless Salmon Quiche

*Oftentimes, salmon fishermen will have some of their catch canned.
It is a special treat when it's chinook, the most colorful and highest in good
omega-3 fatty acids. The great thing about canned fish is that it makes
easy preparation for burgers, and serving it from tin to table as
part of a salad is nutritious and delicious.*

1. Heat oven to 350°F. Grease an 8" square baking dish (or pie plate).

2. Flake salmon and arrange on the bottom of the baking dish. Sprinkle evenly with 1 cup of cheese and the chopped green onion. Then sprinkle with the basil and arrange the strips of red pepper attractively.

3. In a small bowl, beat the eggs; then add the half-and-half, salt, and pepper and mix well. Pour over the salmon. Top with the Romano or Asiago and bake in the preheated oven for about 45 minutes or until the middle of the mixture doesn't jiggle and is set.

4. Let rest for 5 minutes before serving.

Apple Smoked Steelhead

Serve this as an entree hot or cold. If there are any leftovers, combine with cream cheese, sour cream, lemon juice, and capers to make a wonderful appetizer served on toasted bread or crackers.

Serves 4 to 6

3–4 pounds steelhead
    salmon fillet
4 tablespoons butter
½ cup dry vermouth
Zest and juice of 1 lemon
Zest and juice of 1 lime
1 tablespoon Dijon mustard
½ teaspoon hot sauce
2 tablespoons capers
1 clove garlic, minced

1. Prepare a smoker with an indirect 225°F fire. Add 3 wood chunks or 1 cup wood chips, soaked in water for 30 minutes, to the fire.

2. Place the fish in a disposable aluminum pan.

3. In a small saucepan, melt the butter. Add the rest of the ingredients and heat through. Pour the sauce over the salmon.

4. Place the pan of salmon with sauce in the smoker and cook for 1 hour, until opaque and the fish begins to flake when tested with a fork. Serve warm or chilled.

Electric Smokers

One of the easiest smokers to use is the electric water smoker. They are shaped like a bullet and usually have two or three compartments. The electrical coil is at the base, and this is where wood chunks are added. The next compartment holds the water bowl. The food racks are above the water bowl. Then the lid is placed on top to close the unit. Smoking usually takes about 20 to 30 minutes per pound of food on the smoker.

1 cup bottled Italian
  vinaigrette
2 pounds swordfish steaks,
  cut into 1-inch pieces
16 (12-inch) bamboo skewers,
  soaked for 30 minutes in
  water
½ cup mayonnaise
1 teaspoon sweet Hungarian
  or smoked paprika
2 cloves garlic, minced
Lemon juice to taste

Tapas-Style Swordfish Skewers

Tapas, or "little bites," is a great way to entertain. You can serve these skewers hot, room temperature, or cold with the dipping sauce.

1. Place the vinaigrette and the swordfish in a large, sealable plastic bag and let marinate in the refrigerator for ½ hour.

2. Remove the swordfish from the marinade and thread onto the skewers.

3. In a bowl, mix together the mayonnaise, paprika, garlic, and lemon juice. Cover and chill until ready to serve.

4. Heat the grill, and when it is hot, grill the fish skewers directly over the flames for about 4 to 5 minutes per side or until done. Turn only once, halfway through grilling. Serve at once, accompanied by a bowl of the flavored mayonnaise.

Skewers

Skewers come in all sizes, shapes, and materials. There are round skewers that fit perfectly on a round plate. Long flat metal skewers keep food from spinning. Wooden skewers must be soaked in water so that they don't burn up on the grill. Double wooden skewers keep food from spinning. Woody herbs like rosemary make fragrant skewers. Sugar cane is great for fruit on the grill.

Grilled Ahi Tuna
with Sesame-Soy Dipping Sauce

Ahi tuna is so meaty and tender, it deserves to be treated like the finest steak. So grill this to medium-rare at most.

〜

1. Rinse the tuna under cold, running water and pat dry. Brush with olive oil, and season with salt and pepper.

2. In a bowl, mix the rice vinegar, soy sauce, garlic, sesame oil, and ginger together. Divide the mixture among 4 ramekins.

3. Heat the grill, and when it is hot, grill the tuna steaks directly over the flames for about 2 to 3 minutes per side or until medium-rare. Turn only once, halfway through grilling. Serve at once, sliced on the diagonal, accompanied by the ramekin of dipping sauce.

Serves 4

4 ahi tuna steaks
Olive oil for brushing
Kosher salt and freshly
  ground black pepper to
  taste
$2/3$ cup rice vinegar
$1/3$ cup soy sauce
2 cloves garlic, minced
2 teaspoons toasted sesame
  oil
1 tablespoon ginger, freshly
  grated

Serves 4

4 tuna steaks

Olive oil for brushing

Kosher salt and cracked black
pepper to taste

1 pound new potatoes,
cooked and cut in half

2 beefsteak tomatoes, cut
into wedges

4 hard-boiled eggs, sliced

½ cup Nicoise or Kalamata
olives, pitted

1 cucumber, sliced thinly

1 cup Mustard Vinaigrette
(recipe below)

Grilled Tuna Nicoise Salad

*A very refreshing dish for a hot summer day. Even better
when you serve it al fresco with a chilled bottle of rose wine.
Grill the tuna a little more done for this salad.*

1. Rinse the tuna under cold, running water and pat dry. Brush with olive oil and season to taste with salt and pepper.

2. Heat the grill, and when it is hot, grill the tuna directly over the flames for about 3 to 4 minutes per side or until medium-well. Turn only once, halfway through grilling.

3. Remove the tuna to a cutting board and cut into 1-inch pieces. Divide the tuna among four plates. Arrange the new potatoes, tomatoes, hard-boiled eggs, olives, and cucumber around the tuna. Drizzle with the vinaigrette and serve.

Mustard Vinaigrette

Adding 1 or 2 teaspoons of mustard to a vinaigrette helps it to hold together and adds extra creaminess and extra tang, too. In a small bowl, place ⅓ cup white wine or red wine vinegar, 1 tablespoon honey, and ½ teaspoon kosher salt and whisk together. Add ⅔ cup vegetable or olive oil and whisk some more. Then add 1 to 2 teaspoons prepared mustard, preferably Dijon or German mustard, and whisk until creamy.

Chapter 5

Elk, Deer, Antelope, Caribou, & Moose

2 pounds ground meat
(venison, buffalo, bear,
etc.)
½ cup seasoned bread
crumbs
1 onion, finely chopped
2 cloves garlic, minced
1 cup Italian cheeses,
shredded
½ teaspoon red pepper flakes
2 tablespoons barbecue
sauce
2 eggs, beaten
2 cups spicy barbecue sauce
1 teaspoon liquid smoke
½ teaspoon ground chipotle
pepper

Smoky Spicy Meatballs in BBQ Sauce

*Make plenty of this recipe. After the meatballs are cooked,
freeze them on a baking tray and then place in a plastic freezer bag.
The meatballs will be individually frozen and can be used as
needed for "party" meatballs, spaghetti, or sandwiches.*

1. Preheat oven to 375°F.

2. Combine meat, bread crumbs, onion, garlic, cheese, red pepper flakes, 2 tablespoons barbecue sauce, and beaten eggs. Roll into 1-inch meatballs and place on a baking sheet. Bake for 45 to 60 minutes until well browned.

3. Combine 2 cups spicy barbecue sauce, liquid smoke, and chipotle pepper. Heat in a chafing dish and add meatballs and serve as an appetizer.

Smoked Meatballs

Cooking them with wood smoke gives these meatballs added character. Prepare an outdoor grill or smoker for indirect cooking. Place water-soaked wood chunks or chips directly on a charcoal fire. For a gas grill, place the wood in a metal box or place in a foil boat. Place meatballs on an aluminum tray and smoke over indirect heat at 225°F for about 1½ to 2 hours.

Venison, Apple, and Cheddar Plait

As tasty as they are pretty, these savory puff pastry plaits are multipurpose—good for brunch, lunch, or dinner. The recipe makes two plaits.

Serves about 12

½ pound ground venison
½ pound Italian sausage or venison
1 large yellow onion, chopped
2 large tart apples, peeled, cored, and chopped
1 cup cooked wild rice
1 pound sharp Cheddar cheese
1 teaspoon salt
½ teaspoon freshly cracked black pepper
2 eggs
2 sheets frozen puff pastry, thawed

1. Preheat oven to 400°F. Lightly butter 2 large baking sheets and set aside.

2. Brown meat in a skillet over medium-high heat. Add onion and cook until soft. Transfer to a large bowl, draining off any liquid. Add apples, rice, cheese, salt, and pepper. Beat 1 of the eggs and stir into meat mixture to bind.

3. On a lightly floured work surface, roll out each of the 2 puff pastry sheets to a 14" × 18" rectangle. Spoon half of the mixture down the center of each rectangle, starting 3 inches from the top and ending 3 inches from the bottom. Fold the top and bottom edges of the pastry over the filling. Then cut the pastry on either side of the filling into diagonal strips about ½ inch wide. Braid the strips, alternately from each side, over the filling. Cut off any excess dough. Repeat with the other pastry.

4. Place each pastry on a baking sheet. Beat the remaining egg and brush over both pastries. Bake for 30 minutes or until pastry is puffed and golden brown.

Serves 8

2 pounds ground game meat
(venison, bear, antelope)
Coarse kosher salt and freshly
cracked black pepper to
taste
8 or 10 buns, buttered and
toasted
1 head romaine lettuce,
washed and torn
1 red onion, thinly sliced
2 beefsteak tomatoes, thinly
sliced
2 avocados, peeled and sliced
1 cup Kalamata olives,
chopped
Assorted cheeses, crumbled,
sliced, or shaved (Boursin,
Cheddar, blue, pecorino,
goat, Monterey jack, etc.)
1 pound bacon, fried crisp
Assorted spreads: mustard,
mayonnaise, ketchup,
barbecue sauce, etc.

Grilled Game Burgers
with Condiment Bar

These game burgers are sensational and easy to make. Buy good-quality bakery buns or an assortment of breads and buns. Have all of the goodies on the side as the condiment bar. Sides to serve include Layered Spinach Salad (page 246), Herbed German-Style Potato Salad (page 267), and Texas-Style Baked Pinto Beans (page 269).

⟶

1. Form meat into 8 to 10 ¾-inch-thick patties. Place on a baking sheet. Sprinkle with coarse salt and cracked pepper to taste. Turn patties over and repeat the seasoning. Refrigerate for an hour so the meat will hold together on the grill. (Variation: For pan searing, burgers do not need to be refrigerated.)

2. Place breads and buns in a basket.

3. Arrange lettuce, onion, tomatoes, avocados, olives, sliced cheeses, and bacon on a platter. Place crumbled and shaved cheeses in bowls. Set spreads out in the bottles for a casual get-together or transfer to serving bowls for a fancier party.

4. Prepare a hot fire in the grill. Sear burgers over high heat for about 2 or 3 minutes per side for medium-rare. Cook longer for more well-done. Place on a platter and serve with all the fixings.

Wild Ground Meat
Ground venison and other big game fills a hunter's freezer. Thankfully, it is delicious. It is also very lean, depending on how much fat is added during the butchering process. Meatloaf, hamburgers, soups, and chilies are all the better when made with ground game.

Johnny Marzetti

Also known as slumgullion, this dish was a low-budget recipe that could feed a big family. The original called for several canned items. This version uses more fresh vegetables and is brighter in flavor, but still homey and comforting.

⁓

1. Preheat oven to 325°F. Grease a large baking dish and set aside.

2. Cook pasta according to package directions. Drain (reserving 1 cup of pasta water) and place in a large bowl. Pour tomatoes over pasta and let sit.

3. In a heavy skillet, brown the meat. Add pepper and onion. Sauté another 4 to 5 minutes. Add Worcestershire sauce, Bloody Mary mix, parsley, oregano, and salt and pepper to taste.

4. Stir meat mixture into pasta and tomatoes. If mixture isn't juicy enough, add some of the reserved pasta water. Pour into the baking dish. Sprinkle the top with cheese. Bake for 45 minutes until bubbly and hot.

Cheesy Elk Dip

So simple to make and hearty, too. Combine 1 pound browned ground elk or other big-game meat with 1 can (10-ounces) Ro-Tel Original Diced Tomatoes and Green Chilies in a saucepan and bring to a boil. Lower heat and stir in 16 ounces of cubed pasteurized process cheese such as Velveeta. When cheese is melted, serve with corn chips.

Serves 8 to 10

1 (8-ounce) package elbow macaroni

1 (28-ounce) can chopped fire-roasted tomatoes

1½ pounds ground big-game meat

1 green pepper, chopped

1 onion, chopped

2 teaspoons Worcestershire sauce

1½ cups spicy Bloody Mary mix or tomato juice

1 tablespoon fresh Italian parsley, chopped

1 tablespoon fresh oregano, or 1 teaspoon dried oregano, chopped

Kosher salt and freshly ground black pepper to taste

2 cups sharp Cheddar cheese, shredded

Serves 6

1½ pounds ground game
    meat
1 pound ground Italian or
    game sausage, mild or
    spicy
1 onion, finely chopped
1 cup cooked white rice
2 eggs, beaten
½ teaspoon nutmeg, freshly
    ground
Kosher salt and freshly
    ground pepper to taste
12 large cabbage leaves
1 cup chicken broth
6 tablespoons dry white wine
1 tablespoon shallots, finely
    minced
½ teaspoon kosher salt
10 tablespoons unsalted
    butter, chilled

Cabbage Rolls
with Beurre Blanc

This wonderful old-fashioned recipe is worth the effort. But why not make a double recipe and invite company? It takes about the same amount of time to assemble and can be prepared a day ahead, prior to baking. It's served with a classic white butter sauce. Nice accompaniments include carrots, spinach, beans, and sourdough dinner rolls.

1. Preheat oven to 350°F.

2. In a large bowl, combine the meats, onion, rice, eggs, nutmeg, and salt and pepper to taste. Set aside.

3. Place the cabbage leaves in a large bowl and pour boiling water over to cover. Let stand for about 4 to 5 minutes. Remove from water and dry with a towel.

4. Divide meat mixture into 12 portions. Place a portion in the center of each cabbage leaf. Fold over the sides and roll. Fasten with a toothpick. Arrange the cabbage rolls in a covered roasting pan. Add the chicken broth, cover, and bake for 45 minutes, turning once, halfway through cooking.

5. To make beurre blanc, bring white wine, shallots, and salt to a boil and reduce by half. Lower heat and add butter, 1 tablespoon at a time, whisking until each piece has almost dissolved before adding the next. The sauce will be slightly thick and ivory colored.

Beurre Blanc
A beurre blanc is a delicate hot butter sauce that is delicious over fish, shellfish, chicken, and vegetables or vegetable dishes. To add another dimension to the sauce, add chopped fresh herbs, finely diced sun-dried tomatoes, or even caviar at the finish.

Slow-Cooker Venison Stew

If the butcher doesn't wrap up packages of stew meat, then use a small roast cut into 2-inch cubes for this recipe.

~

1. Brown venison in oil in a large Dutch oven. Combine beef bouillon, beer, gravy mix, oregano, bay leaf, garlic, and onions. Bring to a boil, cover, and reduce heat to a simmer for 1 hour.

2. Peel and cut up potatoes and carrots. Add to stew and simmer for another 30 minutes or until vegetables are fork tender.

3. Remove bay leaf. Serve in bowls with rustic bread on the side to sop up all of the wonderful broth.

Serves 6 to 8

3 pounds venison stew meat
4 tablespoons olive oil
5 cups beef bouillon
1 cup beer
2 envelopes peppercorn
     gravy mix
2 teaspoons oregano
1 bay leaf
2 cloves garlic, minced
2 cups pearl onions
4 potatoes
6 carrots
1 loaf rustic bread

Venison Meatloaf Italiano

Save the extra spaghetti sauce to serve warmed on the side or spooned over individual slices of meatloaf. Serve with cooked spaghetti tossed with olive oil and Parmesan or Romano cheese.

~

1. Preheat oven to 350°F.

2. Combine ground meat, eggs, cracker crumbs, cheese, onion, ⅓ cup spaghetti sauce, herbs, salt, and pepper. Shape into a rectangle and place in a shallow baking dish.

3. Bake for 45 minutes. Pour ⅔ cup spaghetti sauce over top and bake 15 minutes longer. Serve hot or cold.

Serves 6 to 8

2 pounds ground meat
     (venison, buffalo, bear,
     etc.)
2 eggs
1 cup cracker crumbs
1 cup Romano cheese, grated
1 cup onion, chopped
⅓ cup spaghetti sauce
2 teaspoons dried Italian
     herbs
1 teaspoon salt
1 teaspoon seasoned pepper
⅔ cup spaghetti sauce

1 tenderloin of wild big game
    like venison, antelope, or
    moose
1 quart Vinegar and Salt
    Brine (page 24)
½ cup (1 stick) butter, melted
2 cloves garlic, minced
1 tablespoon soy sauce

Vinegar and Salt Brined Rotisserie Tenderloin

*Invite a crowd over for this delicious meat that is slow cooked
on a motorized spit. Figure ½ pound meat per person.*

1. Place tenderloin in brine mixture and refrigerate 10 to 15 hours. Remove from marinade, rinse well, and pat dry.

2. Follow manufacturer's rotisserie directions: secure clamp and fork at one end of rotisserie rod; slide rod through center of meat. Attach the other fork and secure clamp. Make sure meat is balanced. Tie-up loose pieces of meat with string. Rotisserie cook at 350°F over a pan of water with the lid closed.

3. Combine melted butter, garlic, and soy sauce. Baste tenderloin every 15 minutes. Cook until rare or medium-rare for best juiciness and tenderness. Let meat rest 15 minutes, then slice and serve. (Variation: tenderloin may be grilled directly over the fire, turning every 5 to 7 minutes to sear all over until desired doneness.)

Internal Meat Temperatures

Use a meat thermometer to ensure perfectly cooked meat. Most game has less fat than domesticated animals do. Lean tender cuts become dry and tough if overcooked. Cook tenderloins for about 12 to 15 minutes per pound. Most game hunters and eaters prefer rare to medium-rare for optimum tenderness and juiciness: 125°F for rare, 130°F–140°F for medium-rare, 145°F–155°F for medium, and 160°F for well-done.

Grilled Venison Chops or Steaks
with Béarnaise Butter

Have game steaks cut about ½ to ¾ inch thick.
They will cook quickly and be less chewy.

Serves 4

2 tablespoons olive oil
4 venison chops or steaks, or
    other big game
2 tablespoons Coarse Kosher
    Salt and Freshly Cracked
    Pepper Rub (page 21)
Béarnaise Butter (page 15)

1. Prepare a hot fire in the grill.

2. Rub olive oil on meat and sprinkle with salt and pepper rub. Set aside.

3. Make the Béarnaise Butter and spoon into a ramekin. Set aside.

4. Grill meat for about 3 to 4 minutes per side for rare to medium-rare. Serve with a pat of the Béarnaise Butter on top.

Sautéed Cube Steaks
with White Wine Reduction Sauce

Cube steaks, also known as minute steaks, are also great for grilling over a hot fire. They'll be done in 1 or 2 minutes, thus the name.

Serves 6

6–8 venison cube steaks
1 cup seasoned flour
3 tablespoons olive oil
2 tablespoons butter
1 tablespoon onion, finely
    chopped
⅔ cup white wine
1 tablespoon Dijon mustard

1. Dredge cube steaks in flour and pan sauté in hot oil for about a minute per side. Set on a plate and keep warm.

2. Add butter and 1 tablespoon finely chopped onion to pan and sauté for a minute. Pour wine into pan and cook over high heat until reduced by half. Stir in mustard and spoon an equal amount of sauce over each steak.

Tenderizing Wild Game Steaks

When butchering elk, venison, or other big game, have the round steak, skirt steak, or flank steak cut into small (4- to 6-ounce) portions and run through the meat cuber once or twice to tenderize. The meat will be very tender and tasty and will cook in a jiffy.

1 venison tenderloin, about 5
  pounds
3–4 tablespoons olive oil
Kosher salt and seasoned
  pepper to taste
¼ cup cognac or brandy
3–4 tablespoons shallots,
  chopped
1 clove garlic, minced
2–3 tablespoons unsalted
  butter
1 cup red wine
1 cup beef consommé
¼ cup sun-dried tomato
  paste
½ teaspoon Maggi or
  Worcestershire sauce

Venison Burgundy

*The delicious red wine sauce with this is killer. It is best when
mixed with pan juices and drippings from the meat, which is best
accomplished by roasting in a pan in the oven. However, if grilling
the meat, the red wine sauce alone is very good, too.*

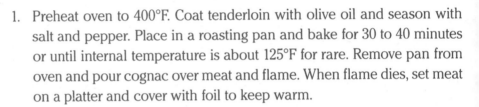

1. Preheat oven to 400°F. Coat tenderloin with olive oil and season with
   salt and pepper. Place in a roasting pan and bake for 30 to 40 minutes
   or until internal temperature is about 125°F for rare. Remove pan from
   oven and pour cognac over meat and flame. When flame dies, set meat
   on a platter and cover with foil to keep warm.

2. Sauté shallots and garlic in butter. Add red wine and boil until reduced
   to ¼ cup. Add 1 cup beef consommé and bring to a boil. Add sun-dried
   tomato paste and Maggi. Pour red wine sauce into the pan with meat
   drippings and cognac. Bring to a boil, then simmer for 5 minutes. Whisk
   in butter and season to taste with salt and pepper.

3. Slice tenderloin into ½- to ¾-inch-thick slices and spoon some sauce
   over the meat. Serve additional sauce on the side.

Removing Fat from Venison
*The fat is what has the distinct wild flavor that many people find
unpleasant. Once the fat is removed, most claim that the wild game
meat tastes better than any beef ever tasted. The silver skin needs to be
cut from the tenderloin before preparing it for cooking. Also, any bits of
fat are best removed from steaks. Roasts taste better with much of the
fat removed, too.*

Big Game Roast Sauerbraten-Style

*A German-style feast that begs for mashed potatoes or
fried potato cakes and braised red cabbage.*

———

Serves 6 to 8

1 (5-pound) big-game roast
Kosher salt and cracked
    pepper to taste
2 cups white vinegar
2 cups water
1 onion, sliced
8 whole cloves
8 peppercorns
2 bay leaves
2 tablespoons oil
2 tablespoons all-purpose
    flour
2 cups Gingersnap Sauce
    (page 14)

1. Place roast in a large bowl and season to taste with salt and pepper.

2. Combine vinegar, water, onion, cloves, peppercorns, and bay leaves
   and bring to a boil. Let cool and pour over roast. Cover roast and refrigerate for 2 days, turning meat twice a day.

3. Remove roast from marinade and pat dry. Strain marinade and
   reserve.

4. Heat oil in a Dutch oven. Dust roast with flour and brown on all sides.
   Remove roast and set aside. Add reserved marinade to the pot and
   bring to a boil. Add roast and cover tightly, lowering to a simmer. Cook
   slowly for about 2½ hours or until meat is fork tender. Turn meat every
   half hour while cooking.

5. Make Gingersnap Sauce using pan juices. Slice meat and serve with
   sauce on the side or poured over all.

Sauerbraten

*This German recipe usually features a beef roast. The meat marinates
2 to 3 days, refrigerated, then cooks slowly in the sweet-and-sour mixture until it is fork tender. It is traditionally served with parsleyed dump-
lings, noodles, or boiled potatoes.*

Serves 4

8 elk or deer tenderloin
    steaks, ½ inch thick
Coarse kosher salt
Freshly cracked black pepper
2 tablespoons olive oil
2 tablespoons unsalted butter

Salt and Pepper Elk Steaks

*Simplicity lets the flavor of the food shine. Try this recipe with
the meat pan sautéed or seared over a hot charcoal fire.*

1. Season the steaks with salt and pepper to taste.

2. Heat oil and butter in a heavy skillet over medium-high heat. Place
    4 steaks in the hot skillet at a time. Sear for about 2 minutes per side,
    turning only once. Repeat and cook the remaining steaks. Serve hot.

Serves 4 to 6

1 (5- to 6-pound) venison
    roast
1 tablespoon German-style
    grainy mustard
1 teaspoon garlic salt
1 teaspoon freshly ground
    black pepper
1 beer (wheat or pale ale)

Beer-Braised Venison Roast

*Think outside of the box when it comes to braising liquids. Instead of beer
or red wine, try cranberry juice, apple cider, or even cola.*

1. Preheat oven to 350°F.

2. Rub roast with mustard and sprinkle with garlic salt and pepper. Place
    in a roasting pan and bake, uncovered, for ½ hour. Add the beer and
    cover the pan. Lower the heat to 275°F and baste every 20 minutes.
    Cook for about 3 or 4 hours or until meat is tender and done to your
    liking.

Venison Daube in Dijon and White Wine

This white wine daube is a bit lighter than the classic red wine version.

~

1. Heat oil in a large Dutch oven. Season meat with salt and pepper. Brown in three or four batches to avoid crowding the pan. Brown meat on all sides, about 10 minutes per batch. Set meat aside.

2. Pour off any excess oil. Add wine and bring just to a boil. Lower heat to a simmer and cook, uncovered, for about 10 minutes. Whisk in the mustard. Add the meat, onions, tomatoes, garlic, fresh herbs, and bay leaves. Cover and simmer for about 2 to 3 hours, until meat is fork tender. Remove bay leaves and serve hot.

Daubes

A daube is a French pot roast of sorts. Usually made with red wine and vegetables, with each region in France stamping its personal touch to it by adding garlic, mustard, cream, anchovies, and so forth. A daubiere, the traditional cooking vessel, has a long neck to keep the liquid from readily evaporating.

Serves 8

3 tablespoons olive oil

1 (3-pound) venison roast, cut into 3-inch cubes

Kosher salt and freshly ground black pepper to taste

4 cups white wine

2 tablespoons grainy Dijon mustard

4 onions, peeled and sliced thin

1 (28-ounce) can fire-roasted tomatoes

4 cloves garlic, minced

1 tablespoon Italian parsley, chopped

1 tablespoon tarragon, chopped

2 bay leaves

1½ pounds elk or venison
    liver
8 strips bacon
2 onions, sliced

Sautéed Liver, Onions, and Bacon

Try this recipe with fresh elk or other game liver. It's easy to prepare by campfire in a heavy skillet. If the liver is frozen and makes its way to a kitchen, it will still be quite good.

1. Slice liver very thin. Keep refrigerated until ready to use.

2. Fry bacon until crispy and brown. Set aside.

3. Sauté onions in bacon grease until wilted and slightly browned. Remove with a slotted spoon and drain on paper towels.

4. Sauté liver slices over high heat, searing for about a minute or less on each side.

5. Serve liver topped with onion and 2 slices of bacon per person.

Elk and Deer Liver

Liver is very perishable. It needs to be eaten fresh or packed in ice and frozen to eat another time. Slice the liver into 1- or 2-pound pieces so that a very large piece of liver (3 or 4 pounds for a medium-sized deer and 6 or more pounds for a medium-sized elk cow) does not go to waste.

Venison Stuffed Pepper Boats

Any other ground game meat can be substituted for the venison in this recipe. This makes heaping pepper boats. If you are serving these as appetizers, add 1 more pepper to the recipe.

~

1. Preheat oven to 350°F. Prepare couscous according to package directions. Place in a large bowl.

2. Stem, seed, and halve bell peppers. Place the peppers skin-side down on a baking tray.

3. Sauté venison and onion until meat is browned and onion is soft. Add spicy tomato juice and heat until bubbling. Pour mixture into the bowl of couscous. Add 8 ounces of the feta, olives, parsley, and seasoned pepper, stirring to combine well. Divide mixture into sixths and fill each pepper half. Top with the remaining crumbled feta cheese.

4. Bake for about 20 to 30 minutes. Serve as an appetizer or as a main course.

Yields 6 pepper boats

1 (6-ounce) package couscous
1 large red pepper
1 large yellow pepper
1 large green pepper
1 pound ground venison
1 cup onion, chopped
1½ cups spicy tomato juice
12 ounces feta cheese, crumbled and divided
1 cup Kalamata olives, chopped
½ cup fresh Italian parsley, finely chopped
1 teaspoon seasoned black pepper

Serves 4

4 antelope steaks or chops
2 tablespoons extra-virgin
    olive oil, and extra for
    drizzling
Kosher salt and freshly
    cracked black pepper to
    taste
¼ cup shallots, finely
    chopped
¼ cup Italian parsley, finely
    chopped
¼ cup thyme, finely chopped

Sautéed Antelope Steaks or Chops

Most game steaks are about ½ to ¾ inch thick.
They cook quickly. Many people like the meat rare to medium-rare
simply because it gets dry and tough when overcooked.

1. Lightly coat the steaks or chops with olive oil. Sprinkle both sides with salt and pepper to taste. Set aside.

2. Combine the shallots, parsley, and thyme in a small bowl and set aside.

3. Heat a heavy sauté pan or iron skillet over high heat. When hot, sear the steaks or chops for about 2 or 3 minutes per side or until desired doneness.

4. Sprinkle the herb mixture over each steak while hot. Finish with a drizzle of extra-virgin olive oil.

Olive Oil Smashed Potatoes

Place 4 to 6 potatoes, peeled or not, in a saucepan and cover with water. Cook over high heat for 20 to 25 minutes. When potatoes are fork tender, drain the water well. Smash the potatoes with a masher, just a couple of times. Drizzle with olive oil and sprinkle with salt and pepper to taste. Serve hot and lumpy.

Spicy Sausage and Antelope Brunch Dish

If your butcher makes game breakfast sausage, then just use it for this recipe. Or use ground game and spice it up with fennel, red pepper flakes, and assorted herbs like oregano and basil. This casserole is easy to assemble at the last minute and holds well on a buffet. Oh! It's delicious, too.

~

1. Preheat oven to 350°F. Grease a large baking dish and set aside.

2. Brown meat and place evenly in the baking dish. Season to taste with salt and pepper. Sprinkle green chilies, then cheese, evenly over meat.

3. With the back of a spoon, slightly hollow 12 places for the eggs (away from the edge of the baking dish). Break eggs into the indentations and lightly break yolks with a fork. Pour milk over all and bake for about 30 to 40 minutes, just until set.

4. Serve with salsa, sour cream, and chopped green onions on the side.

Serves 8 to 10

½ pound ground antelope or venison
½ pound spicy breakfast sausage
Kosher salt and freshly ground pepper to taste
2 (4-ounce) cans green chilies, chopped
1 cup Monterey jack cheese, shredded
12 eggs
1½ cups whole milk
Salsa, sour cream, and chopped green onions

1 (5- to 7-pound) big-game
  tenderloin
2 tablespoons olive oil
Kosher salt and cracked black
  pepper to taste
4 tablespoons butter
3 shallots, finely chopped
3 tablespoons hoisin sauce
2 tablespoons Dijon mustard
½ teaspoon freshly ground
  black pepper
1 cup sherry

Turn-off-the-Oven Tenderloin

This turn-off-the-oven method of cooking works quite well for other large cuts such as rib roasts. About twice the time is required for a bone-in roast in the turned-off oven . The temperature of the oven varies the cooking time, too. If the beginning temperature is 500°F, then the cooking time will be shorter versus a preheated 375°F oven.

1. Preheat oven to 500°F.

2. Coat tenderloin with oil and liberally sprinkle with salt and cracked pepper. Place in a shallow pan and roast for 5 minutes per pound. Then turn off oven, but do not open the oven door. Keep in the oven for 10 minutes per pound for rare tenderloin (i.e., 50 minutes for a 5-pound tenderloin, and 70 minutes for a 7-pound tenderloin). If meat is too rare, turn the oven on to 375°F and cook for another 15 to 20 minutes to desired doneness. Let rest for 10 minutes.

3. In a saucepan, melt the butter and sauté the shallots. Add the rest of the ingredients. Bring to a boil and reduce heat to a low simmer to keep warm. Spoon over carved tenderloin and serve extra on the side.

Big-Game Tenderloins and Roasts
The size of big-game tenderloins and roasts can be quite large. Have the butcher cut large tenderloins in half or to desired weight for cooking smaller portions and to avoid any waste. Keep tenderloins and roasts to 4 to 5 pounds for best results in roasting, grilling, and braising.

Braised Venison Roast
with Mushrooms and Root Vegetables

*All that's needed with a delectable roast like this is a great loaf of bread
and butter, for dipping into the wonderful meat juices.*

~

1. Sprinkle roast with Citrus Rub. Wrap in plastic wrap and place in a
   bowl. Refrigerate 8 to 12 hours or overnight.

2. Preheat oven to 350°F.

3. Brown the roast in hot oil. Set aside. Add the mushrooms and garlic to
   the pan. Sauté for 3 or 4 minutes. Add the rest of the ingredients and
   bring to a boil. Add roast, cover, and place in the oven. Cook for about
   1 hour or until meat is fork tender. Serve hot.

Serves 8

1 (3- to 4-pound) venison
    roast or butt
¼ cup Citrus Rub (page 23)
3–4 tablespoons olive oil
8 ounces mushrooms, sliced
2 cloves garlic, minced
2 turnips, peeled and roughly
    chopped
3 carrots, peeled and
    chopped
2 potatoes, peeled and
    chopped
8 ounces pearl onions
1 can dark beer
1 (10-ounce) can beef
    consommé
Kosher salt and freshly ground
    black pepper to taste

Barbecued Tenderloin and Mushroom Skewers

*Make this meal a summer treat! Serve the skewers with a sliced tomato salad,
garlic bread, and Rhubarb, Peach, and Wild Berry Crisp (page 290) for dessert.*

~

1. Soak 8 wooden skewers in water for 20 to 30 minutes.

2. Melt butter in a saucepan and sauté garlic. Add barbecue sauce, wine,
   and toasted sesame oil. Keep warm.

3. Prepare a hot fire in the grill.

4. Cut tenderloin into 2-inch cubes. Alternately thread skewers with about
   3 pieces of meat and 2 mushrooms. (Do not pack too tight or meat will
   not cook evenly.)

5. Grill skewers for 2 minutes per side of cubed meat, turning 4 times until
   browned and medium-rare in the center. Serve 2 skewers per person.

Serves 4

4 tablespoons butter
2 garlic cloves, minced
1 cup barbecue sauce
1 cup white wine
1 tablespoon toasted sesame
    oil
1½ pounds venison
    tenderloin
16 medium-sized mushrooms,
    portabellas or porcini

1 (5- to 7-pound) top or
    bottom round roast of
    caribou or other venison
2 tablespoons olive oil
Kosher salt and seasoned
    pepper to taste
1 cup dry red wine
1 cup beef consommé
1 bay leaf
3 cups cherry or grape
    tomatoes, quartered
1 cup Kalamata olives, sliced
1 cup (1 ear) fresh corn
    kernels
3 tablespoons vinegar
6 tablespoons olive oil
2 cloves garlic, minced
½ teaspoon salt
½ tablespoon sugar

Caribou Pot Roast
with Fresh Summer Vegetables

*Use a good-quality top or bottom round roast for this dish rather
than a tougher cut of meat. The vegetables are spooned in between the
slices of caribou and the heat of the meat "cooks" the vegetables.
This technique would be wonderful with a tenderloin, too.*

1. Preheat oven to 350°F. Rub roast with oil and season to taste with salt and pepper.

2. Place a Dutch oven over high heat and brown the meat on all sides. Add the wine, beef consommé, and bay leaf and bring to a boil. Transfer to the oven, cover, and bake for about 2½ hours until meat registers 145°F to 150°F, basting several times.

3. Combine tomatoes, olives, and corn in a bowl.

4. In a jar, combine vinegar, oil, garlic, salt, and sugar. Cover with lid and shake to combine. Pour over vegetables and let sit while roast is cooking.

5. When roast has rested for about 10 minutes, cut ½-inch slices about three-quarters of the way through the roast. Spoon vegetable mixture in between slices. Place a piece of foil around the roast to hold the meat and vegetable mixture together. Let stand at room temperature for about 20 minutes. Serve a slice with vegetables per person.

Venison

*North American antlered animals whose meat is referred to as venison
include elk, moose, whitetail deer, blacktail deer, mule deer, and caribou. Antelope is also considered a venison, though antelope don't have
antlers and are technically more closely related to goat than deer.*

Crock-Pot Roast of Moose

This tender treatment of venison is perfect for making venison French dip sandwiches. Pile pulled meat onto a hoagie-style bun that has been buttered and toasted. Serve a small bowl of the hot au jus on the side for dipping. If there is not enough au jus, add 1 can of beef consommé to the juice and heat.

~

1. Preheat oven broiler to high. Make small slits over roast and insert slices of garlic. Season with salt and pepper to taste. Broil for about 10 to 15 minutes.

2. Place one-third of the onion slices in the bottom of a Crock-Pot. Cover with roast. Add remaining ingredients. Cover and cook on low for about 10 to 12 hours or until meat is fork tender.

3. Serve pieces of roast with au jus.

Serves 8 to 10

1 (5- to 6-pound) moose or other venison roast
3–4 cloves garlic, sliced
Kosher salt and freshly ground black pepper to taste
3 onions, peeled and thickly sliced
3 bay leaves
3 whole cloves
3 whole peppercorns
1½ cups hot water
1 tablespoon Worcestershire sauce
1 tablespoon soy sauce

Steak Soup

This is a simple soup that comes together fairly quickly. As with most soups or stews, it tastes better the second day, when the flavors have had time to blend. Serve with Buttermilk Biscuits (page 260) or corn bread.

~

1. Brown ground meat in a large pot. Add butter and melt. Stir in flour and cook over medium-high heat for about 5 minutes. Slowly add beef consommé, stirring to keep smooth.

2. Put onion, carrots, and celery in a food processor and pulse until finely chopped. Pour into the pot and bring to a boil. Reduce heat to a simmer, cover, and cook for 30 minutes. Add the rest of the ingredients and simmer for another 30 minutes. Season to taste with salt and pepper.

Serves 8

1 pound ground game meat
½ cup (1 stick) unsalted butter
½ cup all-purpose flour
4 (10-ounce) cans beef consommé
1 onion, peeled and quartered
3 carrots, peeled and chunked
2 stalks celery, chopped
1 cup canned tomatoes, chopped
1 (15-ounce) can creamed corn
½ cup frozen peas
2 teaspoons Kitchen Bouquet
1 beef bouillon cube
Kosher salt and freshly ground black pepper to taste

8 tablespoons unsalted
    butter, divided
1 large shallot, finely chopped
½ pound mushrooms, sliced
½ cup beef consommé
1 cup heavy cream
4 (6- to 8-ounce) moose
    steaks, ½ inch thick
½ cup seasoned flour
2 tablespoons olive oil

Moose Steaks
with Mushroom Sauce

*Serve these steaks with Olive Oil Smashed Potatoes (page 96)
and sautéed fresh spinach on the side.*

1. Melt 4 tablespoons butter in a skillet. Sauté shallot and mushrooms for about 4 to 5 minutes over medium-high heat. Add beef consommé and bring to a boil. Add cream and bring to a boil. Reduce heat and simmer until slightly thickened, about 10 minutes. Cover and remove from heat.

2. Lightly dredge steaks in seasoned flour. Heat 2 tablespoons olive oil and remaining 4 tablespoons of butter in a large sauté pan. Sauté steaks over high heat for about 2 to 3 minutes per side. Place on a platter and keep warm.

3. Pour the sauce into the sauté pan and scrape the drippings on the bottom. When hot, ladle sauce over the steaks, reserving some to serve on the side.

Moose
The moose weighs up to 1,600 pounds and is the largest member of the deer family, followed next by the elk. Both meats are exceptional in flavor, with most wild-game aficionados considering the meat from either of these animals to surpass the flavor of the best beef.

Moose Daube
with Cabernet Sauvignon

This daube is best made 2 days ahead, marinated overnight the first day, cooked the second day, then cooled and refrigerated. Heat the third day and serve with crusty bread and butter, and a hearty glass of red wine.

Serves 8 to 10

4–5 pounds moose or other venison roast
4–5 onions, thinly sliced
5 whole cloves
5 whole allspice
5 bay leaves
5 sprigs thyme
5–6 cups cabernet sauvignon or other dry red wine
3–4 tablespoons olive oil
Kosher salt and freshly ground black pepper to taste
1 (28-ounce) can fire-roasted whole tomatoes
1 (15-ounce) jar roasted red peppers, drained and chopped
4 cloves garlic, minced
2 tablespoons capers

1. Cut roast into 3-inch cubes of meat. Place meat in a large stainless steel bowl. Cover with onions and add cloves, allspice, bay leaves, and thyme. Pour 5 to 6 cups cabernet sauvignon over all to cover. Cover bowl and refrigerate for about 1 day, 20 to 24 hours.

2. When ready to cook, strain the onions and meat from the pan, reserving the pan marinade. Remove bay leaves.

3. Heat oil in a Dutch oven; sauté onions for 10 minutes. Remove from pan and set aside. Add more oil if necessary, and brown meat in three or four batches over medium to medium-high heat. Do not overcrowd the pan. Do not scorch the meat, simply brown it well. Season the meat with salt and pepper and remove from pan.

4. Pour the marinade into the pan and bring to a boil, lower heat, and add tomatoes and juice, drained peppers, garlic, capers, onions, and meat. Simmer for 2 to 3 hours or until meat is fork tender. Remove lid and let cool for about an hour or more. Then re-cover and refrigerate overnight. Reheat the next day and serve in bowls.

3 pounds stew meat, a
combination of big-game
meat

8 tablespoons butter, divided

1 pound game sausage or
Italian sausage, sliced
into 1-inch pieces

2 onions, chopped

8 ounces porcini mushrooms,
sliced

3 cups green cabbage,
shredded

3 carrots, peeled and finely
chopped

1 (28-ounce) can fire-roasted
tomatoes, chopped

1 pound cooked ham, diced

4 (10-ounce) cans chicken
stock

½ cup Madeira

Kosher salt and freshly
ground black pepper to
taste.

Rocky Mountain Hunter's Stew

*Hunter's stew was typically made with a hodgepodge of leftover
game meat. So if one's refrigerator or freezer has any leftover cooked
game, add it to the pot. To heighten and brighten the flavor of
soups and stews, add some lemon zest and juice.*

1. Trim excess fat off of stew meat. Sauté in melted butter in two batches
   to sear and lightly brown. Set stew meat aside. Add game sausage and
   heat through. Set aside.

2. Add 4 more tablespoons butter to pot. Sauté onions and mushrooms
   for 3 or 4 minutes. Add the rest of the ingredients and bring to a boil.
   Reduce heat, cover, and simmer for 1½ to 2 hours, stirring occasionally.
   If stew is too thick, add 1 or 2 cups of water to thin down.

Rocky Mountains

*The soaring range known as the Rocky Mountains stretches from
western Canada into New Mexico. It is abundant with wildlife, especially big game. The conservation folks do a splendid job overseeing
the management of the wild game, which includes keeping the game
numbers in control and the animals safe from disease.*

Big Sky Killer Chili

Big game like buffalo, elk, deer, moose, antelope, and bear all work well with this chili. If this recipe makes more than you need, it freezes well. Serve with toasted slices of Jalapeno Cheddar Beer Bread (page 259).

(page 259)

1. After soaking overnight, rinse beans well and set aside.

2. Brown meat in a large pot over medium-high heat. Add onions and garlic and cook until soft, about 7 to 8 minutes. Add can of tomatoes and cider vinegar.

3. Finely chop the chipotle pepper and add to the pot. Add adobo sauce, chili powder, and cumin and season with salt and pepper to taste. Stir well and bring to a boil. Add 2 or 3 cups of water if chili is too thick; readjust seasonings. Turn heat down to a simmer and cover. Cook for 30 minutes or longer.

4. Set cheese, red onion, and herbs in separate bowls for garnishing. Then serve chili.

Chipotle Peppers in Adobo Sauce

This is a marvelously smooth and hot product. The only problem is it's an 11-ounce can filled with 10 or 12 chipotle peppers and almost ½ cup adobo sauce. Most recipes call for only 1 or 2 peppers. Place the peppers on parchment paper on a tray and freeze them individually so the rest of the can does not go to waste.

Serves 6 to 8

2 cups dried pinto beans, soaked overnight
3 pounds ground big-game meat
2 onions, chopped
3 cloves garlic, minced
1 (28-ounce) can fire-roasted tomatoes
2 tablespoons cider vinegar
1 chipotle pepper from a can of chipotle peppers in adobo sauce
1 teaspoon adobo sauce
3 tablespoons chili powder
1 tablespoon ground cumin
Kosher salt and freshly ground black pepper to taste
2 cups sharp Cheddar cheese, shredded
1 red onion, diced
1 cup mixed fresh herbs, chopped (parsley, cilantro, and chives)

2 pounds meaty soup bones
6 whole cloves
6 allspice berries
1 teaspoon black peppercorns
1 onion, roughly sliced
2–3 carrots, roughly chopped
1 teaspoon salt
6 tablespoons butter
7 tablespoons all-purpose
    flour
3 cups beef stock or
    consommé
1 (28-ounce) can diced fire-
    roasted tomatoes or
    stewed tomatoes
Zest and juice of 1 small
    lemon
Kosher salt and freshly
    ground black pepper to
    taste.
¼–½ cup Madeira wine, or
    to taste

Rich Velvety Big Game Soup

*Make this soup once and then never forget to have the butcher save some
meaty soup bones to make this wondrous potion. Serve it as a main-course
soup with salad and bread. Or, it's a tasty appetizer served in mugs to sip by
the fire. Because this soup takes lots of time, consider doubling the recipe and
freezing half of it to serve at another time. Another tip is to start the soup a
day ahead of time. After it has cooked until the meat is tender and pulls off the
bone, let it cool and refrigerate it. Then finish it the next day from step 2 on.*

1. In a large stockpot, place the soup bones, cloves, allspice, peppercorns,
   onion, carrots, and 1 teaspoon salt. Fill with 3 quarts of water and bring
   to a boil. Lower heat to a simmer and cook, uncovered, until meat is
   tender, 4 to 6 hours. Do not stir. Remove meaty soup bones. When cool,
   pick the meat from the bones, dice, and set aside. Place picked bones
   back into the stock.

2. Bring stock to a boil and cook over high heat until it is reduced to about
   1 quart.

3. Strain stock into another bowl or pan and let cool. Discard spices, vegetables, and bones.

4. In the large pot, melt the butter and stir in the flour to make a roux.
   Cook over medium heat for about 7 to 8 minutes to brown. Slowly pour
   in the beef stock or consommé and stir well to blend with the roux. Add
   the game stock, diced meat, tomatoes and juice, and lemon zest and
   juice. Cook over medium heat until hot. Season to taste with salt and
   pepper. Stir in the wine to taste, just before serving.

Chapter 6

Wild Pig, Wild Boar, Javelina, Buffalo, Bear, Mountain Goat, & Sheep

Serves 6

2 tablespoons brown sugar, packed

1 tablespoon coarse kosher salt

1 tablespoon red pepper flakes

1 tablespoon fresh cracked black pepper

½ teaspoon ground cloves

4 cloves garlic, minced

3–4 tablespoons olive oil

6 apples, crisp and tart varieties like Jonagold

6 wild pig chops or steaks

Grilled Wild Pig Chops
with Stir-Grilled Apples

Make this recipe in the fall when apples are freshly picked. Try several different varieties for this recipe. The wild pig is delicious and succulent. Substitute wild pig for wild boar or domestic pork in any recipe.

1. Prepare a hot fire in a grill. Grease a grill wok.

2. Combine brown sugar, salt, pepper flakes, cracked black pepper, and cloves, whisking to combine. Stir in garlic and olive oil.

3. Core and quarter the apples. Mix together with one-third of the brown sugar mixture.

4. Coat the chops with the rest of the brown sugar mixture.

5. Grill chops to 125°F for rare and 135°F for medium-rare. While chops are grilling, place apples in a grill wok. Toss with wooden spoons until apples are a bit browned and warmed through. Serve chops in the center of a platter surrounded by the apples.

Cooking Apples
Here's a short list of apples that are tart and crisp and perfect for cooking on the grill: Jonathan, Jonagold, Snow Apple, Honey Gold, Honeycrisp, Northern Spy, and Golden Delicious.

Shredded Wild Boar over Polenta

Boar can weigh in at several hundred pounds. It is always best when it is a young animal, two years old or less. Boar may be substituted in any of the venison recipes for daubs, stews, or braised roasts.

Serves 8 to 10

1 (4- to 5-pound) boar
  shoulder roast
½ recipe Juniper–Apple Cider
  Brine (page 25)
3–4 tablespoons olive oil
2 onions, thinly sliced
5 cloves garlic, minced
3 tablespoons white wine
  vinegar
2 cups dry white wine
1 (28-ounce) can fire-roasted
  tomatoes, chopped
1 sprig fresh rosemary
Zest and juice of 1 lemon
2 cups quick-cooking polenta
  or yellow cornmeal
1½ teaspoons kosher salt
Freshly ground black pepper
  to taste

1. Cut roast in half and place both pieces in a large stainless steel bowl. Pour ½ recipe of the Juniper–Apple Cider Brine over meat. Cover and refrigerate for 1 to 2 days, turning twice a day.

2. Remove roast from brine and rinse extremely well; pat dry. Throw the brine away.

3. Heat oil in a Dutch oven. Sauté onions and garlic until light golden brown. Add meat and brown on all sides over medium-high heat. Add white wine vinegar and white wine. Bring to a boil, then reduce heat and simmer for 30 minutes. Add tomatoes, rosemary, lemon zest, and juice. Bring to a boil, reduce heat, and simmer for another 2 hours or until meat is fork tender. If sauce is too thick, add ¼ to ½ cup water to thin down. With a fork and knife, shred meat. Keep warm in the tomato sauce.

4. In a large saucepan, bring 7 cups water to a boil. Slowly add the polenta, stirring constantly. Add the salt and lower heat to a simmer, stirring until polenta is the consistency of thick oatmeal.

5. Spoon polenta onto each plate and top with a serving of the boar stroganoff. Season to taste with pepper.

Wild Boar Butt
with Barley and Sauerkraut

1 (3- to 4-pound) wild boar
butt
1½ quarts sauerkraut, rinsed
and drained
2 onions, thinly sliced
½ cup pearl barley, rinsed
and drained
2 bay leaves
½ teaspoon freshly ground
pepper
2 bottles beer, wheat or pale
ale
¼ cup German-style mustard
2–3 cups water

Big game loin roast or chuck steak can be substituted for the butt. Serve this with some additional German-style grain mustard and crusty rye bread.

1. Preheat oven to 350°F.

2. Place boar in a Dutch oven. Top with sauerkraut, onions, and barley. Tuck in bay leaves and grind pepper over top. Pour beer over boar, then stir in the mustard. Add water to the top of the sauerkraut (about 2 to 3 cups) and cover.

3. Bake for 3 hours. Remove boar, slice, and serve on a platter surrounded with the sauerkraut and barley.

Wild Pigs or Feral Hogs
Runaway domestics are what these animals are. They are also known as razorbacks because they developed razor tusks and hair on their backs after reproducing in the wild for several generations. They are much smaller and tastier than a big old boar. The best-tasting animals weigh around 40 and up to 80 pounds. Avoid anything larger if possible.

Mesquite-Grilled Javelina Steaks
with Rosemary-Dijon Slather

Small tenderloins may be cooked whole. For steaks, try cutting them 2 inches thick, then butterfly them for a large steak. It looks nicer on the plate and is easier to handle on the grill. The slather can be a serving sauce as well as a slather applied prior to cooking.

Serves 4

6–8 javelina fillets, 2 inches thick
2 tablespoons olive oil
Coarse kosher salt and freshly ground black pepper to taste
Rosemary-Dijon Slather (page 31)

1. Prepare a hot fire in the grill with mesquite charcoal or a combination of charcoal and mesquite wood.

2. Butterfly the steaks by cutting them from the side, almost to the other side, but not all the way through. They will lay flat and be double in size. Coat with oil and season with salt and pepper.

3. Grill the steaks for 2 to 3 minutes per side for rare to medium-rare. Serve with Rosemary-Dijon Slather spooned over the top.

Javelina
Javelinas are much smaller than wild boars and domestic pigs. They usually weigh between 30 and 60 pounds. Their meat is a little darker than boar but twice as delicious. Grilling tenderloins and steaks gives excellent results.

2 javelina tenderloins
Ginger-Soy Marinade and
    Dressing (page 29)
2 tablespoons olive oil
4 tablespoons unsalted
    butter, divided

Pan-Seared Javelina Tenderloin

*Serve the javelina with Smoked Gouda Grits (page 255). Spoon grits
onto each plate. Slice tenderloin into 1-inch-thick slices and arrange beside
the grits. Pour the pan drippings over the meat. Serve a fruity salad like the
Mandarin Orange and Blue Cheese Salad (page 245) or a variation of it with
strawberries, raspberries, and blueberries instead of the oranges. The
remaining Ginger-Soy Marinade and Dressing can dress the salad.*

1. Marinate tenderloins in ¾ cup (half) of the marinade for 30 to 60 minutes, refrigerated.

2. Remove tenderloins from marinade (discard used marinade) and pat dry. Heat olive oil and 2 tablespoons butter in a skillet and sear tenderloins for about 1½ minutes per side, turning a quarter at a time until rare. Set aside and keep warm.

3. Add 2 tablespoons of the reserved marinade to the pan and heat until bubbly. Add the remaining 2 tablespoons butter to make the sauce. Serve as described above.

Beer-Braised Buffalo Rib Roast

*This recipe is savory and earthy. Use this marinade
with other roasts or tenderloins.*

Serves 8 to 10

1 (8- to 9-pound) buffalo rib
   roast
3 cups dark beer, divided
½ cup dark honey
½ cup balsamic vinegar
2 tablespoons grainy
   German-style mustard
Zest and juice of 1 lime
3 cloves garlic, minced
1 tablespoon kosher salt
1 tablespoon lemon pepper

1. Trim all fat from rib roast and place in a large resealable plastic bag. Combine 1 cup beer, honey, vinegar, mustard, lime zest and juice, garlic, salt, and lemon pepper. Reserve ½ cup of marinade in a covered jar. Pour rest of marinade over rib roast and seal the bag shut. Refrigerate 12 to 16 hours or overnight.

2. Preheat oven to 475°F. Remove roast from marinade and place in a roasting pan. Discard used marinade. Place rib roast in oven and bake for 15 minutes to sear. Add remaining 2 cups of beer to pan. Baste the roast with the ½ cup reserved marinade. Lower heat to 350°F. Continue cooking for about 1 to 1½ hours or until internal temperature registers 130°F for medium-rare.

3. Let roast rest for 10 to 15 minutes. Bring pan juices to a boil. Season to taste with additional salt and pepper. Carve roast and ladle warm pan juices over each slice.

Internal Cooking Temperatures for Buffalo

Buffalo is extremely lean. If overcooked, it is dry and chewy. For optimum results, cook buffalo 120°F for rare, 130°F for medium-rare, and 140°F for medium. Overcooked buffalo is inedible.

Serves 12 to 14

2 tablespoons coarse kosher
   salt
6 tablespoons cracked black
   pepper
1 (8-pound) buffalo
   tenderloin
9 tablespoons unsalted butter
3 tablespoons olive oil
1 cup brandy

Peppered Buffalo Tenderloin

*A large animal has a large tenderloin. This makes a lot
and is great for a crowd. But the leftovers are wonderful to
make a salad or sandwich for noshing on the weekend.*

1. Evenly press salt and pepper all over tenderloin.

2. In a large (flat surface) roasting pan, heat the butter and oil and sauté
   the tenderloin over high to medium-high heat. Cook for about 20 to
   30 minutes, searing on all sides until cooked rare or medium-rare.

3. Place tenderloin on a cutting board to rest. Heat juices in roasting pan
   and add brandy. Bring to a boil and simmer over medium heat for
   5 minutes.

4. Slice tenderloin in ½-inch-thick slices. Arrange on a platter and pour
   warm pan juices over all.

Buffalo

*Though wild until it was near extinction in the late 1800s, there are
some free-ranging herds in protected parks. The buffalo that graces
one's table is domestically raised. The animals are hardy and are usually not given any hormones or antibiotics. The meat has half the cholesterol of beef.*

Grilled Buffalo Steaks
with Caesar Butter

This lean cut of steak is enhanced with a pat of melting Caesar Butter. It's a must to add a Caesar salad to this simple and sophisticated dinner. The leftover butter (or make a double recipe) can be wrapped tightly in a log and frozen. Then just cut off the pats of butter as needed.

Serves 4

½ cup (1 stick) unsalted butter, softened

2 tablespoons chives, snipped

2 tablespoons Romano cheese

1 tablespoon anchovy paste

1 teaspoon Dijon mustard

Zest of 1 lemon

½ teaspoon Worcestershire sauce

1 clove garlic, minced

4 buffalo steaks

1 tablespoon olive oil

Coarse kosher salt and freshly ground black pepper to taste

1. In small bowl, stir together butter, chives, cheese, anchovy paste, Dijon mustard, lemon zest, Worcestershire sauce, and garlic. Place butter on a piece of waxed paper. Roll into a log 1½ to 2 inches thick. Refrigerate. (Caesar butter can be made ahead. It will keep for 2 weeks refrigerated and for several months frozen.)

2. Prepare a hot fire in the grill. Brush both sides of steaks with oil; sprinkle with salt and pepper to taste. Grill for 2 or 3 minutes per side or until rare or medium-rare. Serve steaks with a pat of Caesar butter on top.

Serves 8 to 10

2 pounds ground buffalo
    meat
1 onion, chopped
2 tablespoons chili powder
2 (19-ounce) cans black beans
    with liquid
2 cups fresh or frozen corn
    kernels
2 (10-ounce) cans Ro-Tel
    Original Diced Tomatoes
    and Green Chilies
Kosher salt and freshly
    ground black pepper to
    taste
8 or 10 small round loaves of
    bread, hollowed out
1 cup sour cream
1 cup green onions, chopped
1 cup fresh cilantro, chopped

Buffalo Black Bean Chili in a Bread Bowl

Ground meat or stew meat can be used in this chili. The ground meat cooks faster. The stew meat needs to cook at a slower temperature and simmer longer so that it gets tender. The presentation in the bread bowls makes for the whole meal. As the chili is eaten, so is the bread bowl.

1. Brown meat in a large pot. Add onion and sauté until soft. Add chili powder, black beans, corn, and Ro-Tel. Stirring, bring to a boil. Cover and turn heat down, simmering for 1 to 2 hours. Add water to thin chili if it is too thick. Season to taste with salt and pepper.

2. To serve, ladle chili into bread bowls. Garnish with sour cream, green onions, and cilantro.

Chili Mac, Taco Salad, and More
Instead of chili in bread bowls, serve it ladled over a plate of macaroni, known as chili mac. For a buffalo taco salad, chili works just as well as seasoned ground meat. Place crushed taco chips on each plate, a couple of spoonfuls of chili, crisp torn lettuce, cheese, olives, peppers, onions, and more chili, and serve with salad dressing on the side. Hot dogs or game dogs, if your processor makes these, are delicious topped with chili. Some people like chili burgers, too.

Buffalo Meatloaf with Merlot

Meatloaf fit for company. Serve this with a Caesar salad and garlic mashed potatoes. Don't forget to fill the wineglasses with the remaining merlot.

⌒

1. Preheat oven to 400°F.

2. In a large bowl, combine the meat, cheese, bread crumbs, crushed Italian herb seasoning, red pepper, onion, beaten eggs, and ½ cup spaghetti sauce. Season to taste with salt and pepper. Form into a loaf and place in a baking dish.

3. Pour wine and remaining 1 cup spaghetti sauce over meatloaf. Bake at 400°F for 30 minutes. Lower heat to 350°F and bake for 30 minutes more. Spoon the sauce over the meatloaf several times while cooking. Let rest for about 10 to 15 minutes before slicing.

Serves 8 to 10

2 pounds ground buffalo meat
1 pound ground sirloin
1 cup ricotta cheese
¾ cup Italian-style bread crumbs
2 tablespoons Italian herb seasoning, crushed
1 cup roasted red pepper, chopped
1 onion, chopped
2 eggs, beaten
1½ cups spaghetti sauce, divided
Kosher salt and seasoned pepper to taste
½ cup merlot

½ cup (1 stick) unsalted
    butter, softened
2 green onions, chopped
2 tablespoons
    parsley, chopped
2 teaspoons fresh tarragon,
    chopped
2 teaspoons tarragon vinegar
Seasoned pepper to taste
6 hamburger buns
1½ pounds ground big-game
    meat like buffalo or
    venison
Kosher salt and pepper
1 cup Cranberry and Golden
    Raisin Relish (page 19)

Skillet Burgers
with Tarragon Butter and Cranberry Relish

*Serve burgers on good-quality bread like kaiser rolls, focaccia, ciabatta,
or crusty bakery rolls. Don't forget to shape the burgers to fit the buns.*

1. Combine butter, onions, parsley, fresh tarragon, tarragon vinegar, and seasoned pepper to taste. Butter the hamburger buns and set aside.

2. Form ground meat into 6 patties to fit hamburger buns. Salt and pepper both sides of each burger.

3. Heat a heavy-duty skillet over high heat. Place burgers in skillet and sear over high heat for about 3 minutes per side for rare, 4 minutes per side for medium, and 5 to 6 minutes per side for well-done.

4. While the burgers are cooking, broil or toast the hamburger buns. Serve burgers on buns with a spoonful of Cranberry and Golden Raisin Relish atop the burgers.

Cast-Iron Skillets
Nothing beats the high heat retention of an old-fashioned iron skillet. They are the perfect choice for searing burgers and steaks. Blackened seasoned foods rely on the sear and quick cooking of an iron skillet, too.

Bear Steaks

Just like most of the wild big game, younger bear is more tender and desired for recipes using steaks. Since older meat is tougher, it is often made into ground meat, stew meat, or roasts that need to be slowly braised and cooked until fork tender and well-done.

Serves 4

4 (6- to 8-ounce) bear steaks
1 cup seasoned flour
3–4 tablespoons vegetable oil
2 tablespoons shallots, finely
    chopped
1 teaspoon ground thyme
1 clove garlic, minced
½ cup dry red or white wine
2 tablespoons heavy cream
2 tablespoons unsalted butter

1. Tenderize the bear steaks with a meat mallet or by running them through a cuber once or twice to ⅜ inch thick. Dredge the meat in seasoned flour.

2. Heat oil in a large sauté pan over high heat. Add the meat and cook for about 2 to 3 minutes on each side until browned and the internal temperature is at least 140°F. Place steaks on a plate and keep warm.

3. Add the shallots, thyme, and garlic to the pan and sauté for 2 or 3 minutes.

4. Add wine to deglaze pan by cooking for 2 or 3 minutes, until reduced by half. Finish with cream and butter, heating through. Serve steaks with sauce spooned over the top.

1 (5- to 6-pound) bear roast
¼ cup grainy German-style
    mustard
Coarse kosher salt and freshly
    cracked pepper to taste
2 cups beef bouillon
1 cup red wine
2 tablespoons soy sauce
Zest and juice of 1 lemon
4 cloves garlic, minced
1 tablespoon gingerroot,
    shredded

Brisket-Style Bear Roast

The cooking time of a bear roast or other wild game fluctuates greatly depending on the age of the animal. Younger animals will be more tender and will cook more quickly. Older animals need more liquid for brining or braising and may require marinating for 1 or 2 days, refrigerated.

1. Preheat oven to 275°F.

2. Place roast in a large pan. Spread with mustard and sprinkle with salt and pepper.

3. Combine beef bouillon, red wine, soy sauce, lemon zest and juice, garlic, and gingerroot. Pour over roast. Place in the oven and bake, uncovered. Baste with sauce every 20 to 30 minutes until well glazed. After 3 hours, cover tightly with heavy-duty foil and bake for an additional 2 to 3 hours or until meat is well-done and fork tender.

Precaution on Cooking Bear

Take caution in cooking bear; it is known to carry the parasite that causes the illness trichinosis. Freezing does not kill the parasite. Cooking bear meat to an internal temperature of at least 140°F is the safest way to ensure that the parasite is killed. Many prefer bear cooked well-done for safety's sake.

Baked Mountain Goat
with Artichokes, Tomatoes, and Fresh Herbs

Mountain goat is a strong-flavored animal. If too old, it's tough and stringy. So cook goat when you have access to young meat or brine the older meat prior to cooking. However, a baked stew of sorts is an excellent way to get good results from this animal. Serve with cooked rice.

1. Preheat oven to 350°F.

2. Cut the meat into 1½-inch cubes. Coat with olive oil and salt and pepper to taste. Sauté for about 3 to 4 minutes, until lightly browned. Remove meat from skillet and place in a covered baking dish or Dutch oven.

3. Place artichokes and tomatoes in the skillet and heat until bubbling. Stir in the garlic, parsley, oregano, and lemon zest and juice. Season to taste with salt and pepper. Pour over the meat.

4. Bake for 45 to 60 minutes covered, until meat is fork tender. Garnish with torn basil leaves.

Serves 4

2 pounds wild goat tenderloin or round steak
2 tablespoons olive oil
Kosher salt and freshly ground black pepper to taste
1 cup artichoke hearts
1 (28-ounce) can whole tomatoes
2 cloves garlic, minced
2 tablespoons fresh parsley, chopped
1 tablespoon fresh oregano, chopped
Zest and juice of 1 lemon
4–6 basil leaves, torn for garnish

1 (6- to 7-pound) leg of sheep
1 pound spinach leaves,
    roughly chopped
3 garlic cloves, finely chopped
2 tablespoons olive oil
½ cup fresh bread crumbs
¼ cup golden raisins
¼ cup toasted pine nuts
¼ cup fresh basil, chopped
3 ounces soft goat cheese
Kosher salt and freshly
    ground black pepper to
    taste

Leg of Wild Mountain Sheep

Any lamb recipe can be used for mountain sheep.

1. Preheat oven to 350°F.

2. Bone, trim, and butterfly the leg of wild mountain sheep. Lay out flat.

3. Sauté spinach and garlic in oil over high heat for about 2 to 3 minutes. Place in a bowl and stir in the rest of the ingredients. Spread the mixture over the meat. Roll up lengthwise and tie with kitchen twine at 1-inch intervals.

4. Place meat on a baking sheet and roast for about 1 hour to desired doneness. Let rest for 10 minutes. Slice and serve.

Rocky Mountain Bighorn Sheep

Mountain sheep is a game meat prized for its tenderness and sweetness. The meat has a bit more fat marbled throughout it compared to other wild game of this sort. The Rocky Mountains are home to many of these sheep. It is an incredible climber and difficult to hunt. Good luck.

Shepherd's Pie

Leftover stew makes a perfect quick Shepherd's Pie. Simply pour the stew into the baking dish and cover with the topping of choice. Bake at 350°F for about 30 minutes or until bubbly and hot.

1. Preheat oven to 450°F. Grease a 2-quart baking dish.

2. Sauté ground meat in olive oil until cooked through and browned. Transfer meat to baking dish. Add 1 more tablespoon oil to pan if needed and sauté garlic, onion, red pepper, and mushrooms until tender, 4 or 5 minutes. Spoon over meat in baking dish.

3. Pour off excess oil from pan. Melt butter and add flour to form a roux. Cook for about 3 or 4 minutes over medium-high heat. Slowly add the chicken broth, stirring to keep smooth. Cook until bubbly and slightly thickened. Remove from heat and add Worcestershire sauce. Season to taste with salt and pepper. Pour over meat and vegetables.

4. Roll out pastry crust to fit over casserole dish. Crimp edges to seal. Prick with a fork to allow steam to escape. Bake until crust is well browned, about 20 to 30 minutes. Serve hot.

Savory Pie Toppings

There are so many toppings for a pot pie. The traditional pastry crust is used in this recipe. Other topping choices include mashed potatoes, puff pastry, buttered bread crumbs, and phyllo dough. Biscuit dough makes a good topping, too. Try Buttermilk Biscuits (page 260) or Dropped Herbed Rolls (page 260).

Serves 6 to 8

2 pounds ground sheep or other big-game meat
2–3 tablespoons olive oil
2 cloves garlic, minced
1 onion, chopped
1 red pepper, chopped
½ cup mushrooms, sliced
4 tablespoons unsalted butter
4 tablespoons all-purpose flour
2 cups chicken broth
2 teaspoons Worcestershire sauce
Kosher salt and pepper to taste
1 (9-inch) unbaked pastry crust

CHAPTER 6: WILD PIG, WILD BOAR, JAVELINA, BUFFALO, BEAR, MOUNTAIN GOAT, & SHEEP

123

Chapter 7

Small Game: Rabbit, Hare, Squirrel, Raccoon, Woodchuck, Beaver, Opossum, & Muskrat

Serves 6

¼ cup butter
1 (3-pound) rabbit, cut into
 pieces
1 cup seasoned flour
2 cups onion, chopped
2 cups dry white wine
½ cup whipping cream
¼ cup grainy mustard
2 tablespoons capers
Kosher salt and freshly
 ground pepper to taste

Rabbit in Mustard Caper Cream Sauce

This is a divine dish and it's all because of the wonderful flavor bestowed by the grainy mustard. Serve a fresh green salad with a light vinaigrette along with the rabbit and cream sauce spooned over biscuits, pasta, or rice.

1. Melt the butter in a large skillet. Dredge the pieces of meat in seasoned flour and brown in the skillet until golden brown on all sides. Remove from the skillet and set aside.

2. Add the onion to the skillet and sauté for about 5 to 7 minutes, until wilted. Add the wine and bring to a boil. Add the browned pieces of meat and lower the heat to a simmer. Cover and cook for 30 minutes. Remove the lid and cook for another 30 minutes, continuing at a simmer.

3. Add the whipping cream, mustard, and capers and simmer for 15 minutes. Taste and adjust seasonings.

Slow Cooker Rabbit Stew

*Serve the fall-off-the-bone meat and sauce over rice
or noodles or a toasted piece of Italian bread.*

1. Fry bacon in a large skillet until crisp and set aside. Dredge pieces of meat in seasoned flour. Sauté in 3 to 4 tablespoons oil or bacon grease over medium-high heat until well browned. Place pieces of meat in a slow cooker.

2. Sauté onion and garlic in skillet for about 4 to 5 minutes over medium heat. Spoon into slow cooker. Add the parsley, tomatoes and juice, herbs, and port and season to taste. Cook over low heat for 6 to 8 hours. Serve hot.

The Peter Rabbit Syndrome

The rabbit is the most widely hunted small animal in the United States. Its meat is versatile and can be prepared as many ways as chicken can. Its texture and flavor are similar to chicken's. But Americans don't eat nearly as much rabbit as their European counterparts do. This is probably due to childhood memories of sweet little Peter Rabbit or the Easter Bunny.

Serves 4 to 6

3 slices bacon
1 (2- to 3-pound) rabbit, cut into pieces
1 cup seasoned flour
3–4 tablespoons vegetable oil or bacon grease
1 onion, sliced
1 clove garlic, minced
4 sprigs Italian parsley, chopped
1 (8-ounce) can chopped tomatoes, preferably Italian Roma
1 teaspoon dried basil
1 teaspoon dried oregano
¼ cup port
Kosher salt and freshly ground pepper to taste

Serves 8 to 10

2 pounds rabbit meat, diced

½ pound ham, diced

2 boiled potatoes, peeled and diced

3 cooked carrots, peeled and diced

Kosher salt and freshly ground black pepper to taste

¼ cup brandy

1 pound liver pâté

1 teaspoon fresh thyme, chopped

2–4 tablespoons heavy cream, if needed

1 pound bacon

Terrine of Rabbit

Liver pâté is available fresh or in tins in gourmet stores. Or make the Goose Liver Pâté recipe on page 219.

1. Place diced rabbit meat, ham, potatoes, and carrots in a large bowl. Season to taste with salt and pepper. Add brandy and stir to mix. Cover and refrigerate for 2 hours.

2. Preheat oven to 300°F.

3. Remove rabbit mixture from refrigerator and combine with liver pâté and thyme. (If the liver pâté is not creamy, stir in 2 to 4 tablespoons of heavy cream or more, as needed.)

4. Line a terrine or loaf pan with slices of bacon. Spoon mixture into the pan. Cover with bacon. Cover the pan and place in a water bath. (Set the terrine or loaf pan in a large pan, then pour 1 inch of water into large pan.) Bake for 1½ hours or until the juices simmering in the terrine are completely clear.

5. Let cool to room temperature. Take off the cover and place a small board on the terrine, topped with a ½-pound weight. Refrigerate. Serve from the terrine.

Rabbit Pie with Dropped Herbed Rolls

This is a great way to use leftover rabbit or other small game. Vegetables added to this dish can be fresh, frozen, or from a jar or can. It's a homey dish for a winter night by the fire and a game of cards or Scrabble.

Serves 6

3 cups cooked rabbit, chopped
1 onion, chopped
4 tablespoons unsalted butter
8 ounces mushrooms, sliced
3 tablespoons all-purpose flour
2 cups chicken broth
1 (16-ounce) bag frozen mixed vegetables, thawed
Kosher salt and seasoned pepper to taste
Dropped Herbed Rolls (page 260)

1. Preheat oven to 350°F. Butter a baking dish. Spread cooked rabbit in the dish.

2. Sauté onion in butter for 3 or 4 minutes. Add mushrooms and cook for 3 or 4 minutes, stirring. Sprinkle with flour and stir to blend. Slowly add the chicken broth, stirring to combine. Cook until beginning to boil; add vegetables. If mixture is too thick, add ¼ to ½ cup hot water to thin. Season to taste with salt and pepper. Pour mixture over rabbit.

3. Make recipe for Dropped Herbed Rolls. Drop spoonfuls of the dough over the rabbit pie. Bake for 20 to 25 minutes, until mixture is bubbly and rolls are slightly brown. (If there is extra dough, make more rolls and bake in the oven with the pie.)

Save Leftover Rabbit and Squirrel
Savory pot pie–style recipes are especially easy if one thinks ahead. Double the recipe for the Rabbit in Mustard Caper Cream Sauce (page 126). Serve half over buttered noodles and use the other half to make a rabbit pie.

Serves 6 to 8

2–3 rabbits (6 pounds each),
    cut up
1 cup seasoned flour
4 bacon strips
2 tablespoons butter
2 onions, chopped
3 carrots, chopped
12 ounces mushrooms, sliced
2 cups chicken broth
1 tablespoon fresh parsley,
    chopped
1 tablespoon fresh thyme,
    chopped
½ cup heavy cream
¼ cup dry vermouth
Kosher salt and freshly
    ground black pepper to
    taste

Rabbit Baked in a Clay Pot

The unglazed earthenware, which is a clay pot, gives this dish a depth of flavor. Serve with Buttermilk Biscuits (page 260).

1. Preheat oven to 350°F. Dredge rabbit in flour and set aside.

2. Fry bacon in a skillet, and when it is almost crisp, remove it with a slotted spoon and set aside in a bowl.

3. Over medium-high heat, brown a few rabbit pieces at a time in the bacon grease. Place browned pieces in a large clay casserole (unglazed earthenware).

4. Melt butter in the skillet with the bacon grease. Sauté onions and carrots for 5 to 7 minutes. Add mushrooms and sauté for 2 or 3 minutes. Add chicken broth, bacon (crumbled into bits), and herbs. Bring to a boil and pour over rabbit.

5. Bake, uncovered, for 45 to 60 minutes. Stir in heavy cream and dry vermouth and bake for another 10 to 15 minutes, or until rabbit is fork tender. Season to taste with salt and pepper.

Juniper Marinated Hare

A jug of wine, a loaf of bread, and a bowl of Juniper Marinated Hare.

~

1. Place cut-up hare in a large stainless steel bowl. Pour Juniper–Apple Cider Brine over hare. Refrigerate, covered, for 2 to 3 days.

2. Remove hare from marinade, pat dry, and dredge in seasoned flour. Discard the marinade.

3. Heat oil in a large skillet and fry hare to a golden brown. Set meat aside and sauté the onions, carrots, celery, and garlic. Sprinkle 4 tablespoons of seasoned flour over vegetables and stir to make a roux. Slowly stir in the chicken broth and bring to a boil. Add the wine, juniper berries, sun-dried tomato paste, and hare. Lower heat to a simmer and cook slowly for 3 or more hours until the meat is fork tender. Ladle into a bowl to serve.

Hares

Hares are related to rabbits and are considered the "wild" larger cousin, growing to as big as 15 or so pounds. Game hunters often prefer the richer, darker meat of the hare, which has a more pronounced "wild" flavor. The best eating hares are the smaller (5 to 6 pounds) and younger ones. Most common preparation of hare includes marinating in red or white wine or buttermilk for 1 to 4 days in the refrigerator.

Serves 4

1 (5-pound) hare, cut up
½ recipe Juniper–Apple Cider Brine (page 25)
1 cup seasoned all-purpose flour, 4 tablespoons reserved
½ cup vegetable oil
2 onions, slivered
4 carrots, chopped
4 stalks celery, sliced
2 cloves garlic, minced
2 cups chicken broth
1 cup white wine
6 juniper berries
2 tablespoons sun-dried tomato paste

4–5 pounds rabbit or hare,
    cut up
1½ cups red wine
1½ cups cider vinegar
2 onions, quartered
2 bay leaves
6 whole cloves
1 tablespoon dried thyme
1 tablespoon dry mustard
½ tablespoon kosher salt
⅛ teaspoon ground mace
½ cup seasoned flour, 3–4
    tablespoons reserved
5 tablespoons bacon
    drippings or butter
¾ cup red currant jelly
1 pound noodles, cooked and
    buttered

Hasenpfeffer

*A German preparation of rabbit or hare similar to sauerbraten,
also known as jugged hare. The hare is refrigerated for at least 24 hours
in a red wine marinade. Red currant jelly is one of the distinctive flavor
choices for the finishing sauce. In one word: delicious.*

1. Place rabbit pieces in a large stainless steel bowl. Add red wine, vinegar, onions, bay leaves, cloves, thyme, mustard, salt, and mace. Stir, cover, and refrigerate for 24 to 48 hours, turning rabbit pieces.

2. Remove rabbit from marinade and pat dry. Remove onion from marinade and let drain, then pat dry. Reserve the marinade. Dredge rabbit in flour.

3. Preheat oven to 350°F. Melt bacon drippings or butter in a skillet. Sauté rabbit over medium-high to high heat until golden brown. Place pieces in a Dutch oven. Sauté onion for 5 to 7 minutes and place on top of rabbit.

4. Add 3 to 4 tablespoons of the seasoned flour to the skillet and cook for 2 or 3 minutes to form a roux. Strain the marinade and add 1 cup at a time, stirring to blend. Bring to a boil. Add the jelly and whisk to melt and combine.

5. Pour sauce over rabbit. Cover and bake in the oven for 1½ hours, until the rabbit is fork tender. Serve with buttered noodles.

Golden-Fried Squirrel or Rabbit

A heavy skillet is a must to make really good fried fare. The best choice is an iron skillet. The oil in the pan should be hot but not smoking. As pieces of food are placed in the skillet, the temperature of the oil will decrease. Adjusting the temperature gauge is a must. So raise the heat, then lower it a bit. Next batch, raise the heat again, then lower a little bit again.

Serves 4 to 6

2 squirrels or rabbits, cut into
   pieces
2 cups seasoned flour
4 eggs
½ cup whole milk
1 cup vegetable oil for frying,
   or more

1. Clean and rinse pieces of meat. Place in a large pot and fill with salted water to cover. Refrigerate for 2 hours or overnight.

2. When ready to fry, remove from salted water and pat dry.

3. Place seasoned flour in a large bowl. Combine eggs and milk in another large bowl and beat.

4. Dip each piece of meat first in the egg mixture and then in the flour mixture, then dip in the egg and flour again. Set on a platter.

5. In the meantime, heat the oil in a large skillet until hot. Fry several pieces of the meat at a time, making sure not to crowd the skillet. Fry meat, turning several times until meat is cooked through, tender, and golden brown, about 12 to 15 minutes for small pieces of meat and 16 to 18 minutes for larger pieces. Serve hot.

Soaking Squirrels and Rabbits in Saltwater or Milk
Small game and birds can all take a bit of soaking. The simplest soak is a big bowl of cold water plus 2 or 3 tablespoons of salt. The saltwater can be changed several times until it runs clear, without a trace of blood. If soaking in milk, refrigerate for 2 or 3 hours, then rinse in water.

Butterflied Grilled Squirrel
with Peanut Butter Dipping Sauce

*Red or fox squirrels are larger than gray squirrels, weighing in
at 1 pound dressed. Three will feed four people. The smaller grays
weigh about ¾ pound dressed and feed one person each.*

Serves 4

*4 whole small squirrels,
    flattened in half
Kosher salt and freshly
    ground black pepper to
    taste
Zest and juice of 1 lime
⅓ cup sherry
⅓ cup heavy cream
¼ cup creamy peanut butter
¼ cup chili sauce
½ cup (1 stick) unsalted butter*

1. Prepare a hot fire in the grill. Sprinkle squirrels with salt and pepper to taste.

2. Combine lime zest and juice, sherry, heavy cream, peanut butter, and chili sauce in a saucepan. Simmer for 10 minutes, stirring. Season to taste with salt and pepper. Keep warm.

3. Melt butter in a saucepan and take out to the grill. Baste squirrels with butter and grill over medium-high heat for about 15 to 20 minutes or until leg meat pulls away from the bone.

4. Serve with individual bowls of peanut butter dipping sauce and plenty of hand towels.

Barbecued Squirrel

This can be cooked outside like the Butterflied Grilled Squirrel, but the barbecue sauce should be applied the last 5 to 10 minutes of grilling. Serve with fresh corn on the cob, sliced tomatoes, and slaw.

～

1. Preheat oven to 350°F.

2. Lightly coat squirrel pieces with olive oil and sprinkle with the Spicy Chipotle Rub (or rub of your choice). Lay squirrel pieces in a single layer in a baking pan. Bake for 30 minutes.

3. Combine the barbecue sauce, garlic, and sesame oil. Liberally or to taste, brush on meat. Continue to bake for 30 to 60 minutes more, or until meat is fork tender and pulling from the bone. Baste with additional barbecue sauce to taste.

Serves 4

4 whole small squirrels, cut up
2–3 tablespoons olive oil
4 tablespoons Spicy Chipotle Rub (page 23)
2 cups barbecue sauce
3 cloves garlic, minced
1½ teaspoons toasted sesame oil

Raccoon Sautéed in Bacon Drippings
with Peppers, Tomatoes, and Onions

As with most game, smaller, younger animals yield a tastier dish. Raccoons are best when at 6 pounds or less dressed.

～

1. Place raccoon meat in a large pot and fill to cover with water. Add celery, onion, and bay leaves. Bring to a boil, then lower heat and simmer for about 1 hour.

2. Remove meat from pot, let cool, and debone. Sprinkle meat with salt and pepper. Set aside.

3. In a large skillet, sauté bacon and onion until just beginning to brown. Add meat and sauté until lightly browned. Add pepper, tomatoes, and red wine. Simmer for about 20 to 30 minutes, until meat is fork tender.

Serves 4

1 (3- to 4-pound) raccoon, cut into pieces
3 stalks celery, roughly chopped
1 onion, quartered
2 bay leaves
Kosher salt and freshly ground black pepper to taste
4 strips bacon, chopped
1 onion, slivered
1 green bell pepper, cut into strips
4 Roma tomatoes, chopped
½ cup red wine

Serves 6 to 8

3 squirrels, cut up
6 cups chicken broth
2 strips bacon, diced
1 onion, chopped
2 potatoes, peeled and
    chopped
2 cups baby lima beans
2 cups corn kernels
1 (28-ounce) can whole
    tomatoes, drained
1 tablespoon brown sugar
1 tablespoon Worcestershire
    sauce
Salt and pepper to taste

Brunswick Stew

This is the real Brunswick stew. Try it, then make it with a bit of sherry and a bag of frozen mixed vegetables for convenience's sake.

1. Place the squirrel pieces in a large pot and fill with chicken broth. Bring to a boil, reduce heat, and simmer for about 60 to 75 minutes or until meat begins to fall off the bone. Set meat aside to cool, then debone.

2. Skim fat off the top of the broth. Add meat, bacon, onion, potatoes, lima beans, corn, tomatoes, brown sugar, and Worcestershire sauce to broth. Bring to a boil, reduce heat, and simmer for 30 minutes, until vegetables are tender. Season to taste with salt and pepper.

Brunswick Stew

This famous stew originated in Brunswick County, Virginia, in 1828. Comprising squirrel, onion, potatoes, lima beans, and corn, it is equally good with rabbit.

Braised Woodchuck Stew
with Root Vegetables

Use whichever root vegetables look good in the store—potatoes, yams, winter squash, onions, turnips, rutabagas, or carrots. Think color, too.

Serves 6 to 8

1 (about 6 pounds)
    woodchuck, cut into
    pieces
Water to cover
1 cup cider vinegar
1 cup seasoned flour
¼ cup vegetable oil
2 onions, quartered
3 cloves garlic, minced
3 carrots, peeled and
    chopped
3 turnips, peeled and
    chopped
1 small butternut squash,
    peeled and chopped
2 cups chicken broth, or more
    as needed
Kosher salt and freshly
    ground black pepper to
    taste

1. Place woodchuck pieces in a large pot, cover with water, and add cider vinegar. Refrigerate for 12-plus hours or overnight in the refrigerator.

2. Remove meat, pat dry, and dredge in flour. Discard the water.

3. Heat oil in a heavy pot or Dutch oven. Sauté meat in batches over medium-high to high heat until golden brown. Place onions and garlic on the bottom of pot. Lay meat over onions. Add carrots, turnips, butternut squash, and chicken broth. Bring broth to a boil. Reduce heat and simmer for 1½ to 2 hours or until meat is fork tender and vegetables are done. Season to taste with salt and pepper.

Woodchuck, Groundhog, or Whistle Pig?

They are one and the same. These small mammals spend most of their days sunning on big rocks beside streams or rivers and eating in preparation for a long winter hibernation. They are the bane of farmers because they love to dine on young sprouts, and they ruin many gardens, too. On February 2, they're coaxed to awaken by some nutty humans who think the little creatures can predict the weather.

Serves 8

1 (4- to 5-pound) beaver
    roast(s)
4–5 cloves garlic, minced
Kosher salt and freshly
    ground black pepper to
    taste
3 onions, sliced and divided
6 whole cloves
2 cups hot water
1 (16-ounce) bottle of spicy
    barbecue sauce
8 sandwich buns, kaiser rolls,
    or hoagie rolls

Crock-Pot Barbecued Beaver

This is a double-cooked slow-cooker recipe. Do the first cooking overnight, which cooks the meat until tender. The next day, remove fat and bones (if any). The lean meat is put back to simmer in the barbecue sauce. Yummy!

1. Rub roast with garlic and season with salt and pepper to taste.

2. Place one-third of the onion slices in the bottom of a Crock-Pot. Cover with roast. Place one-third of the onions on top of the roast. Add cloves and water. Cover and cook on low for about 10 to 12 hours or until meat is fork tender.

3. Place meat on a baking sheet and remove fat and any bones. Empty the Crock-Pot.

4. Place one-third of the onions on the bottom of the Crock-Pot. Add cleaned meat and barbecue sauce. Cook on low for 4 to 8 hours or cook on high for 1 to 3 hours.

5. Toast buns and serve with barbecued meat.

Doctored-Up BBQ Sauce

Make gourmet barbecue sauce by doctoring up store-bought sauce. Begin with 1 cup of a favorite sauce and add a few goodies. For Asian-style sauce, add 1 teaspoon each sesame oil and freshly grated ginger; for citrus-flavored sauce, add zest and juice of 1 orange; for Southwestern-style sauce, add 1 to 2 teaspoons ancho chile pepper and lime zest and juice; for Southern-style sauce, add 1 teaspoon smoked hickory salt and 2 tablespoons cider vinegar.

Roast Opossum
with Sauerkraut

Serve this dish with extra mustard and thick slices of rye or pumpernickel bread and butter. Don't forget the beer.

Serves 3 or 4

1 small opossum, dressed out
  and whole
1 (28-ounce) jar or can of
  sauerkraut
1 beer, light or dark
2 tablespoons or more
  German-style grainy
  mustard
Kosher salt and freshly
  ground black pepper to
  taste

1. Place opossum in pot of salted water and bring to a boil. Lower heat and simmer for 1 hour, until slightly tender. Remove from pot and while warm, scrape off all the fat. Empty the water from the pot.

2. Place opossum back in the pot and add sauerkraut, beer, mustard, and salt and pepper to taste. Simmer for about an hour or until meat falls from the bones. Serve in shallow bowls.

Muskrat Dredged
in Mustard and Cracker Crumbs

This recipe works when there is a nice-sized tenderloin from any small critter such as muskrat, rabbit, possum, or beaver. Remove silver skin and any fat for optimum flavor.

Serves 4 to 6

4–5 pounds muskrat pieces
2 cups Dijon mustard
4 cups crushed saltine
  crackers

1. Soak meat in salted water overnight.

2. Preheat oven to 350°F.

3. Coat meat in mustard, then dredge in cracker crumbs. Place on a baking sheet (do not crowd). Bake for 1½ to 2 hours, until meat is fork tender and beginning to pull away from the bone.

1 (6- to 8-pound) muskrat,
    cut into pieces
Vinegar and Salt Brine
    (page 24)
6 strips bacon, chopped
1 onion, sliced
1 cup seasoned all-purpose
    flour
1 cup beef consommé
1 cup sour cream

Dutch Oven Muskrat

*This is similar to a stroganoff, but the meat is still on the bone.
Serve with buttered egg noodles and crusty bread. Also add a plate
of fresh tomatoes in the summer or stewed tomatoes in the winter,
both perked up with fresh basil leaves.*

1. Soak muskrat pieces in a bowl of Vinegar and Salt Brine overnight.

2. Remove meat and throw brine away. Remove as much fat from meat as possible and set meat aside.

3. Fry chopped bacon in a Dutch oven until beginning to brown. Add onion and cook for 3 or 4 minutes.

4. Dredge meat in flour and brown over medium-high to high heat with the bacon and onion. Brown in two batches to avoid crowding the pan. When browned, place all meat back in the pan. Add beef consommé and simmer for about an hour or until meat is fork tender. Add the sour cream and warm through.

Calling All Small Young Animals
When a game cookbook calls for a small animal, it means an animal two years old or younger. These young small animals are tender and usually not strong flavored. Older small animals are almost not worth messing with. Their strong flavor and tough, stringy meat are best not set on the table.

Small Critter Casserole

Serve this easy-to-make dish with crusty bread or spoon it over egg noodles or cooked rice. Tailor the vegetables to suit your own taste. Fancy it up with fresh mushrooms. A tablespoon or two of chopped fresh tarragon or thyme would be a nice addition, too. If it needs some extra zip, add a squeeze of fresh lemon juice and a pinch of red pepper flakes.

Serves 8

2 pounds small game meat, cut into 2-inch chunks

1 cup seasoned flour

¼ cup vegetable oil, more if needed

1 (16-ounce) bag frozen mixed vegetables

1½ cups artichoke hearts, chopped

8–10 green onions, chopped

2 cups chicken stock

1 12-ounce can cream of celery soup

Kosher salt and freshly ground pepper to taste

1. Dredge meat in seasoned flour and brown in a skillet with ¼ cup vegetable oil. Brown in two batches so the pan is not overcrowded. Add more oil, if needed.

2. Add vegetables, artichoke hearts, green onions, chicken stock, and celery soup. Cook over medium-high heat, stirring occasionally, until it just comes to a boil, about 12 to 15 minutes. Lower heat to a simmer, cover, and cook until meat is tender. Season to taste with salt and pepper.

3. Serve from the pot or transfer to a pretty serving bowl to serve family-style at the dinner table.

Appalachian Mountains

Framing the Great Plains from the east, the grand old Appalachians stretch from Newfoundland through Georgia. The early settlers hunted an abundant variety of wildlife here and learned to hunt and cook many dishes from the Native Americans. The hills are yet filled with the bounty of wild game.

Serves 8

2–3 pounds rabbit, squirrel, or other small game

2 tablespoons oil

Kosher salt and freshly ground black pepper to taste

1 pound spicy sausage (Italian, andouille, or game)

4 tablespoons unsalted butter

2 onions, chopped

1 green bell pepper, chopped

3–4 stalks celery, chopped

8 ounces fresh mushrooms, sliced

2 cloves garlic, minced

6 tablespoons all-purpose flour

8 cups chicken broth, divided

1 cup fire-roasted red pepper, chopped

½ teaspoon red pepper flakes

1 teaspoon dried thyme

2 bay leaves

Small Wild Game Sausage Gumbo

A gumbo is an ongoing work of art. Use this recipe as a base and add other vegetables or game meat, beef consommé or broth, herbs, and lace with sherry or other wine to taste.

1. Preheat the oven to 400°F. Cut small game into pieces. Rub the meat with 2 tablespoons oil and season with salt and pepper. Place in a roasting pan and cook for about 45 to 60 minutes, or until tender. Remove, let cool, and pick meat off the bones and set aside.

2. Brown sausage in a large pot or Dutch oven over medium-high heat. Add butter, onions, pepper, celery, mushrooms, and garlic. Sauté for about 10 to 12 minutes, stirring slowly. Stir in flour to form a roux and cook for about 3 or 4 minutes. Slowly add 2 cups of the chicken broth, stirring to combine; then add the rest of the broth, red peppers, red pepper flakes, thyme, bay leaves, and game meat.

3. Bring the mixture to a gentle boil, lower the heat, and simmer, uncovered, for 2 hours. If mixture is too thick, add 1 or 2 cups of water or additional chicken broth. Season to taste with salt and pepper. Remove bay leaves before serving.

Chapter 8

Upland Game Birds: Pheasant, Quail, Partridge, Prairie Chicken, & Ptarmigan

2 (2½ pounds each)
    pheasants
2 oranges, halved
Kosher salt and freshly
    ground black pepper
    to taste
1 apple, quartered
1 onion, quartered
2 bay leaves
2 sprigs rosemary
2 tablespoons olive oil
8 slices bacon
1 cup chicken bouillon
½ cup cream sherry

Roast Pheasant

Roast pheasant is best prepared with young cocks or tender hens. Since hens are very limited to hunt, depending on the laws of each state, the young cock is most likely the choice for this recipe. The birds have strong, wiry legs. This makes it difficult to cook the bird's legs until tender without drying out the lean breast meat. So covering the breast meat with bacon is the answer.

1. Preheat oven to 350°F.

2. Rinse and dry pheasants. Squeeze oranges all over birds and inside the cavities, too. Season with salt and pepper. Place a half-squeezed orange, 2 apple quarters, 2 onion quarters, 1 bay leaf, and 1 sprig of rosemary in each cavity. Brush each bird with 1 tablespoon olive oil.

3. Place the pheasants in a roasting pan and lay 4 slices of bacon over the breast of each bird. Pour the bouillon and sherry into the pan.

4. Bake for 1½ hours, basting every 20 minutes with pan juices. Remove bacon and cook for another 15 to 20 minutes to brown the breast a bit. Pheasant is done when a meat thermometer registers 160°F to 170°F in the breast. To serve, carve meat and spoon with pan drippings.

Juggling When Breast Meat Is Done vs. Leg Meat

When roasting a pheasant, the breast meat gets done before the legs can get tender. So cut off the legs and place in the pan juices, covered, and cook for an additional 30 to 60 minutes or until the meat falls off the bone. Keep the breast meat warm or reheat in the oven just before serving.

Pheasant Breast Mornay

Mornay sauce is velvety and creamy. It goes well with any poultry and fish or shellfish. Chicken or fish stock can be added as part of the liquid to complement what is being served.

Serves 4

*3–4 tablespoons olive oil
4 boneless, skinless pheasant breast halves
1 cup seasoned flour, 4 tablespoons reserved
4 tablespoons butter
1¼ cups whole milk
¼ cup Parmesan, grated or Swiss cheese, shredded
⅓ cup chopped Italian parsley to garnish*

1. Preheat oven to 350°F. Lightly grease a baking dish and set aside.

2. Heat oil in a large skillet. Dredge pheasant breasts in seasoned flour and sauté until brown for about 3 to 4 minutes each side, turning once. Place breasts in an oiled baking dish and place in the oven. Lay a piece of foil on top of baking dish but do not crimp or cover tightly. Bake for about 15 minutes or until meat is cooked through.

3. While pheasant is baking, make a white sauce. Melt butter in a saucepan. Stir in 4 tablespoons of the seasoned flour, and cook over medium heat to lightly brown and incorporate the flour. Slowly add the milk, stirring over medium heat until thickened. Stir in the cheese.

4. Plate the pheasant, spoon 2 tablespoons sauce over each breast, and sprinkle with parsley. Serve the remaining sauce on the side.

What's the Difference Between a White Sauce and a Béchamel Sauce?

Nothing. This classic sauce is called a béchamel sauce in French, a balsamella in Italian, and a white sauce in English. It is made by pouring milk into a roux, a heated mixture of equal parts butter and flour. A thin sauce is made with 1 tablespoon each of butter and flour to 1 cup milk. Increase the butter and flour to make a thicker sauce. Add Parmesan or Swiss cheese to make it a Mornay sauce.

3–4 tablespoons olive oil

4 boneless, skinless pheasant
breast halves

1 cup seasoned flour

1 egg with ½ teaspoon water,
beaten

½ cup onion, chopped

½ cup dry white vermouth

¼ cup pimiento-stuffed green
olives, chopped

3 tablespoons butter

Pheasant French

A fly-fishing guide described a dish called chicken French as boneless, skinless chicken breasts dredged in flour, then dipped in egg, sautéed, baked, and finally sauced. Here is a version for pheasant that is very tasty.

1. Preheat oven to 350°F. Lightly grease a baking dish and set aside.

2. Heat oil in a large skillet. Dredge pheasant breasts in seasoned flour, then dip in beaten egg mixture. Place breasts in hot oil and sauté until brown for about 3 to 4 minutes each side, turning once. Place breasts in oiled baking dish and place in the preheated oven. Lay a piece of foil on top of baking dish but do not crimp or cover tightly. Bake for about 12 to 15 minutes.

3. While pheasant is baking, sauté onion in the skillet for 3 or 4 minutes. Carefully add vermouth and turn heat to high and reduce by half. Add olives and butter. Place baked pheasant breasts in the skillet and cook over medium heat for about 5 minutes or until meat thermometer registers about 160°F to 165°F. Spoon sauce over breasts while cooking. Skillet may be lightly covered.

4. Serve warm. May also be made ahead and refrigerated overnight and reheated. If doing so, do not overcook the pheasant on the first go-round.

Kiss of Smoke Brie-Stuffed Pheasant Breast

*The key to smoking is not looking. When the lid is opened to take a peek,
the little bit of low heat escapes and another 5 to 10 minutes will be needed to
compensate. The smoke also escapes—so don't peek.*

Serves 4

4 boneless, skinless pheasant
    breast halves
4 ounces Brie
8 basil leaves
4 slices prosciutto
2 tablespoons olive oil

1. Prepare a water smoker by adding 3 or 4 chunks of water-soaked wood (like oak, apple, or pecan) to the fire. Maintain a 225°F temperature during the smoking.

2. Flatten pheasant breasts with a meat mallet until ½-inch thick. Place 1 ounce of sliced brie and 2 basil leaves in the middle of the breast meat. Fold the sides over to enclose the cheese, tucking a little bit of the ends inward, too. Wrap a slice of prosciutto around the rolled meat. Lightly coat with olive oil.

3. Place meat on an aluminum pan and set in the smoker. Close lid and smoke for about 45 to 55 minutes. Pheasant is done when internal temperature is about 160°F to 165°F. Remove from smoker and let rest for 10 minutes.

4. Serve the stuffed breast by slicing into ¾-inch slices to show off the stuffing.

Wood Smoking

Most gas or charcoal grills come with directions for smoking or indirect cooking. Every unit is different, so follow the manufacturer's directions. Simple smoking is attained by cooking indirectly from the heat source. So a charcoal grill is prepared by banking the coals to one side, adding the wood, and adding a water pan above the fire. The food is placed on the other side of the grill, the indirect-heat side. On a gas grill, have the burner on low, with a wood box filled with dry wood chips above it. Preheat the grill so that the wood begins to smolder. Place a water pan above the flame, and the food on the other side of the grill, the indirect-heat side.

Serves 4

4 boneless, skinless pheasant
    breast halves
2 cups flour
2 eggs
1 cup buttermilk
¼ cup butter
½ cup Madeira
1 cup porcini mushrooms,
    sliced
¼ cup artichoke hearts,
    chopped
3 cups chicken stock
1 cup heavy cream

Pheasant Madeira

This is a brilliant dish. The pheasant breasts' coating puffs, turning a golden brown. Go all out and serve with Cranberry and Golden Raisin Relish (page 19) and Lemon Tarragon Wild Rice (page 252).

1. Dredge pheasant breasts in flour. Combine eggs and buttermilk. Dip pheasant into egg mixture. Dredge again.

2. Melt butter in a large skillet and sauté pheasant over medium heat. Cook for about 4 to 5 minutes on each side. Keep warm in the oven.

3. In a small saucepan, bring Madeira to a boil and add the mushrooms. Reduce wine by half. Add artichokes, chicken stock, and heavy cream. Reduce by half or until thick and creamy.

4. Place a pheasant breast on each plate and pour about ¼ cup of the sauce and mushrooms over each.

Serving Wine with Upland Game Birds
The Madeira sauce is divine and goes well with a bottle of white Riesling or sauvignon blanc. For broiled or smoked dishes, try a white burgundy or chardonnay. Also, a simple voignier goes with any of the game birds. Enjoy!

Asiago-Crusted Pheasant Breast Bake

This dish may be prepared with boneless, skinless breasts, too. Just bake for 10 or 15 minutes less. Other cheese may be substituted for the Asiago, like Romano, Parmesan, Cheddar, or Monterey jack. Serve this with Creamed Spinach (page 264) and a platter of fresh sliced tomatoes, red onions, and green peppers for color.

1. Preheat oven to 325°F. Grease a baking dish.

2. Rinse pheasant breasts well and pat dry. Coat each breast with olive oil, cheese, bread crumbs, and salt and pepper to taste. Place pheasant in baking dish and bake for about 35 to 40 minutes, until golden brown and internal temperature registers 165°F.

Serves 4

4 pheasant breasts, bone in
2 tablespoons olive oil
4 tablespoons Asiago cheese, freshly grated
2 tablespoons toasted bread crumbs
Kosher salt and freshly ground pepper to taste

Scaloppini of Pheasant
with White Wine Caper Sauce

Thinly sliced meat cooks very quickly. It is important to have all of the ingredients portioned out and ready at the cooking station (mise en place). Serve salads and side dishes that can be assembled and set on the table prior to cooking the pheasant, like Tomato Salad with Pesto Vinaigrette (page 248). Side dishes that make up ahead and simply pull out of the oven work well, too, like Herbed Cheese Soufflé (page 257).

1. Carefully slice partially frozen pheasant breasts into thin cutlets. Dredge in seasoned flour.

2. Heat oil in a large skillet. Sauté cutlets over high heat for about 30 seconds per side. Set on a plate and cover to keep warm.

3. Add garlic and pour in white wine, standing back in case the wine flames. Cook over high heat until reduced by half. Stir in capers and butter to finish the sauce. Serve 2 or 3 cutlets per plate and top with the sauce.

Serves 2 to 3

2 boneless, skinless pheasant breast halves, slightly frozen
½ cup seasoned flour
3–4 tablespoons olive oil
1 clove garlic, minced
1 cup white wine
1½ tablespoons capers
2 tablespoons butter

Serves 6

⅔ cup artichoke hearts,
   chopped
⅔ cup mayonnaise
⅔ cup Parmesan cheese,
   finely grated
6 boneless, skinless pheasant
   breast halves

Parmesan Artichoke Pheasant Casserole

*Bone-in pheasant breast also can be used for any of the boneless,
skinless breast recipes. The cooking time will just take longer, about
10 to 15 minutes more should do it. The breast meat's internal temperature
should be about 160°F to 165°F. After it is removed from the oven, it
will continue to rise another 5 degrees or more.*

1. Preheat oven to 350°F. Grease a baking dish.

2. In a medium-sized bowl, combine the artichoke hearts, mayonnaise,
   and Parmesan cheese.

3. Place the pheasant breasts in the baking dish. Spoon about 4 tablespoons of the artichoke mixture over each breast. Spread it evenly
   to coat all over. Dollop the rest of the mixture (if any) on top of the
   breasts.

4. Place the pheasant in the oven and bake for about 25 to 35 minutes,
   until brown and bubbly. Internal temperature of breast meat should
   register 160°F to 165°F.

Parmesan Artichoke Dip
*How easy and tasty this baked dip is. The proportions are basically
equal measurements of chopped artichoke hearts, mayonnaise, and
grated Parmesan. But variations that are delicious include adding ½
cup drained cooked chopped spinach or finely chopped roasted red peppers or sun-dried tomatoes.*

Dutch Oven Fall-off-the-Bone Pheasant Legs

Dark-meat lovers will rave over this meal. There's so much rich gravy from this dish, be sure to serve rice, noodles, mashed potatoes, or the Corn Bread and Italian Sausage Stuffing (page 256). The Freshly Grated Carrot Salad (page 247) would be a nice light side for contrast.

Serves 4

8 pheasant or partridge or ptarmigan legs
1 cup seasoned flour
4–6 tablespoons unsalted butter
2 onions, chopped
4–5 carrots, chopped
1–2 teaspoons dried oregano
1 cup chicken stock
1 cup white wine
1 cup heavy cream, more or less
Kosher salt and freshly ground pepper to taste

1. Preheat oven to 325°F. Dredge pheasant legs in the seasoned flour.

2. Heat butter in a Dutch oven and brown 3 or 4 legs at a time. Set legs aside.

3. Add onions and sauté for 3 or 4 minutes. Add carrots and sprinkle with oregano. Place legs in pot. Add chicken stock, wine, and heavy cream, not quite covering the legs. Season with salt and pepper to taste. Cover and bring to a boil. Turn off heat and place heavy foil over pot, then place the lid on top to cover tightly. Place in the oven and bake for about 2 to 3 hours until meat falls from the bone.

4. Alternatively, continue to simmer on top of the stove with the tightly covered foil and lid, for the same length of time.

Game Bird Legs

Tough old pheasant legs can be chewy and unappetizing. However, slow cooking or braising them in liquid is the ticket. The taste of a fall-off-the-bone pheasant leg is excellent. The dark meat has a rich flavor and melts in your mouth. There are lots of slender bones in pheasant and other game-bird legs. So eat carefully and use fingers to pull the bones out of the way. Serve these meals with fingertip towels instead of napkins.

Serves 8 to 10

2 pheasants, cut into breasts,
    legs, and thighs
1 cup seasoned flour
4–6 tablespoons vegetable oil
1½ pounds sauerkraut, rinsed
    and drained
Kosher salt and freshly
    ground pepper to taste
1–2 cans good beer
1–2 tablespoons grainy
    German-style mustard

Peasant Pheasant and Sauerkraut

*Slow-cooking recipes are simple to prepare and just take time on the
cooking end. Since it takes a while, why not cook more and invite friends or
family over for this delicious simple meal? Serve with a green salad, Baked
Applesauce (page 242), sourdough or rye bread for sopping up the liquid,
and extra mustard on the side. This is an excellent way to cook the
tougher legs of pheasant, partridge, and ptarmigan.*

1. Dredge pheasant pieces in the seasoned flour.

2. Heat oil in Dutch oven and brown 3 or 4 pieces of meat at a time. Drain oil, but not crusty browned bits.

3. Place ½ pound sauerkraut on the bottom of the pot. Lay pheasant pieces on top, and lightly salt and pepper to taste. Then lay another ½ pound sauerkraut over the pheasant. Pour in the beer to almost cover. Stir in the mustard and simmer for about 2 hours. Stir in the rest of the sauerkraut and cook for another ½ hour or until leg meat falls off the bone.

4. Serve on a platter, with pheasant pieces atop the sauerkraut, and more German-style mustard on the side.

Smothered Quail, Onions, and Mushrooms

Smothering is simply covering with liquid. In this recipe, the liquid is a canned soup and milk. For a lighter sauce, use chicken broth. For pure decadence, cover with heavy cream. Serve with salad and garlic mashed potatoes.

Serves 4

8–10 quail
1 cup seasoned flour
2–3 tablespoons oil
*2–3 tablespoons unsalted
    butter*
2 onions, chopped
8 ounces mushrooms, sliced
*1 (10-ounce) can Campbell's
    Golden Mushroom Soup*
2 cups whole milk

1. Dredge quail in flour.

2. Heat oil and butter in a large skillet. Sauté the quail on both sides for about 3 or 4 minutes per side, until golden brown and crispy. Set aside.

3. Add onions and mushrooms to skillet and cook over medium heat for 3 or 4 minutes. Stir in soup and milk and bring to a boil. Add quail and cover. Reduce heat to a simmer and cook for 1 hour or until leg bones pull off the bird.

Quail on Toast
Hopefully there are a couple of leftover quail from the recipe above. Pull the meat from the bones prior to refrigerating the leftovers. Combine the meat and the remaining sauce and refrigerate. Reheat the following day for a decadent breakfast or easy supper, and serve the quail and sauce over buttered toast.

6–8 quail
1 cup seasoned flour
3–4 tablespoons unsalted
    butter
2 shallots, finely chopped
¼ cup brandy
2 cups chicken stock
¼ cup almonds, sliced
1 cup sour cream
2 tablespoons horseradish
Kosher salt and freshly
    ground pepper to taste

Brandied Casserole of Quail

Quail are such small birds that one per serving will do when there are several side dishes and salad to go with it. For simpler meals where a green salad and one side are served, allow two quail per person. The brandy-and-sour-cream sauce begs for dinner rolls, homemade or store bought, whichever suits the cook.

1. Dredge quail in flour.

2. Heat butter in a large skillet. Sauté the quail on both sides for about 3 or 4 minutes per side along with the shallots until quail is golden brown and crispy.

3. Add ¼ cup brandy and ignite, standing back until flame subsides. Add chicken stock and almonds and bring to a boil. Cover tightly and lower heat to a simmer. Cook for about 1 hour or until leg bones pull off the bird.

4. Stir in the sour cream and horseradish. Simmer for another 15 minutes. Add salt and pepper to taste, if needed. Serve hot.

Why Heavy Cream and Game?

Good question. Because game is so lean and what little fat is present is usually removed, it needs to have some fat and/or moisture added while cooking. Recipes that call for chicken stock or milk often require finishing a sauce or dish with butter. Heavy cream has the components of water, milk, and butter all rolled into one. Just use it sparingly.

Sautéed Quail and Corn Salad

*Serve this salad during the summer, when good fresh corn is plentiful.
Grilled or broiled quail works well for this recipe, too.*

Serves 4

2 strips bacon
1–2 ears fresh corn
1 head butter lettuce
4 quail
1 cup seasoned flour
4 tablespoons oil, or more as needed
1 cup Vinaigrette Marinade (page 26)
2 cups cherry or grape tomatoes, halved
Kosher salt and seasoned pepper to taste

1. Fry bacon until crisp. Set aside. Cut corn kernels off cob and set aside.

2. Clean lettuce and tear off the leaves, leaving them whole. Pat dry and arrange on four plates.

3. Dredge quail in seasoned flour and sauté in bacon drippings for about 15 minutes over medium-high heat, turning every 2 or 3 minutes. When golden brown and the legs begin to fall apart from the body, quail is tender and done.

4. Drain oil from pan and add ⅓ cup of the Vinaigrette Marinade. Heat over medium-high heat and add corn kernels. Sauté for about 3 or 4 minutes. Add ⅓ cup more of the vinaigrette and warm through.

5. Place a quail on the bed of lettuce on each plate. Crumble bacon and scatter tomatoes on each salad. Spoon warmed vinaigrette and corn evenly among the plates. Serve additional vinaigrette on the side. Season to taste with salt and pepper.

8 quail
1 pheasant, halved
Teriyaki Marinade (page 26)
12 bacon strips
3–4 water-soaked wood
    chunks like apple,
    mesquite, or hickory

Bacon-Wrapped Smoked Quail and Pheasant

These fragrant smoked birds are tender and juicy. Serve them with Texas-Style Baked Pinto Beans (page 269) and Grilled Asparagus (page 261).

1. Place quail and pheasant in a large resealable plastic bag. Pour 1 cup Teriyaki Marinade over birds, seal, and refrigerate for 8 to 10 hours.

2. Remove from marinade and wrap each quail with 1 slice of bacon. Wrap pheasant halves with 2 strips of bacon each.

3. Prepare a charcoal grill for indirect cooking. Add the wood chunks directly to the charcoal fire. Over the hot fire, sear pheasant for about 4 minutes per side and quail for about 2 minutes per side. Move pheasant, bone-side down, to the indirect-heat side of the grill. Stack quail on top of pheasant. Cover grill with lid and cook for 30 to 45 minutes. Game birds are done when the leg joints move easily. Remove from grill and serve hot.

Ideas for Wrapping Skinless Birds
Quail and pheasant are commonly field dressed by skinning and gutting them. Without the protection of their skin, these tender birds need to have their exposed meat covered to keep the breasts from drying out. Bacon, prosciutto, and thinly sliced ham all work as protective coatings. Some unusual but easy wraps to consider are fresh and dried corn husks and grape leaves.

Quail en Croute with Liver Pâté

This is an inviting way to serve quail as a first course.

❧

1. Preheat oven to 325°F. Dredge quail in flour.

2. Melt butter over medium-high heat and sauté the quail for about 4 or 5 minutes on each side until golden brown. Set aside.

3. Cut the top off the loaf of bread and reserve. Hollow out the bread until there is room for the quail. Spread liver pate on the inside of the bread. Place the quail in the bread. Put the lid on the bread. Wrap in foil and place in the oven for 30 minutes. Open the foil and cook for another 10 minutes to crisp the bread.

4. Serve communal style, with the quail-stuffed loaf of bread in the middle of the table. Everyone tears into the bread and takes 1 quail per person.

Serves 4 to 6

4–6 quail
½ cup seasoned flour
3–4 tablespoons butter
1 large round loaf of rustic French or Italian bread
8 ounces creamy liver pâté, available at upscale gourmet shops

Thimble of Quail Livers, Gizzards, and Hearts

This recipe is for those who love liver, pâté, gizzards, and such. Make this only when fresh game is cleaned while still warm. It is a very small appetizer, thus not recommended as a company dish.

❧

1. Clean liver, gizzards, and hearts well and rinse in water several times until water runs clean. Pat dry and dredge in flour.

2. Heat oil and butter in a small skillet. Sauté over medium-high heat for about 3 to 4 minutes. Serve with buttered sour dough toast points.

Serves 2

Livers, gizzards, and hearts from 8 quail
½ cup seasoned flour
2 tablespoons oil
2 tablespoons butter
2 pieces buttered sourdough toast, cut in fourths

Serves 4

2½ cups Sour Cream
Mushroom Sauce
(page 16)
4 boneless, skinless prairie
chicken breast halves
2 tablespoons olive oil
Kosher salt and freshly
ground black pepper to
taste

Grilled Prairie Chicken
with Sour Cream Mushroom Sauce

*Olive oil, salt, and pepper are the mantra for preparing foods
for the grill. It's simple and good. A dry rub sprinkled on lightly oiled
game can be quite tasty. Try Herb Rub for Birds (page 22) or
Spicy Chipotle Rub (page 23) with this recipe, too.*

1. Make the Sour Cream Mushroom Sauce and keep warm or at room temperature.

2. Prepare a hot fire in the grill.

3. Flatten prairie chicken breasts with a meat mallet until ½ inch thick. Lightly coat with olive oil and season to taste with salt and pepper.

4. Grill over a hot fire for about 1½ to 2 minutes per side.

5. Serve each grilled breast with several spoonfuls of the Sour Cream Mushroom Sauce.

Prairie Chicken

This bird is abundant in the Flint Hills of Kansas on into Oklahoma. Prairie chickens fly in set patterns at the same time every day. Hunters often stalk them by being in position for fly-over time. The smart birds continue to fly at the same time; however, they reposition themselves 50 feet away from the pattern of the day before, just out of reach of the hunters' guns.

Prairie Chicken Parmesan in Lemon and Cream

*When a game dinner needs to be stretched, this is a
good way to do it. Instead of serving a half breast per person,
cut the breast meat into strips or cubes. Serve this creamy dish
over the rice, accompanied by steamed or grilled broccoli.*

1. Preheat oven to 350°F. Grease a baking dish.

2. Cut breast meat into strips. Dredge in flour.

3. Melt 4 tablespoons butter in a skillet and sauté breast meat for about
   6 minutes, turning once, until golden brown. Transfer meat to the baking dish.

4. Add white wine to the hot pan and deglaze, scraping loose any pan
   drippings. Add the lemon zest and juice. Slowly add the cream, stirring
   to incorporate, and cook until bubbling. Pour over chicken. Top with
   Parmesan cheese. Broil for about 5 to 8 minutes, until golden. Serve
   over rice.

Serves 6

3 boneless, skinless prairie
    chicken breast halves
1 cup seasoned all-purpose
    flour
½ cup butter, divided
2 tablespoons white wine
Zest and juice of 1 lemon
1¼ cups heavy cream
½ cup Parmesan cheese,
    grated
3 cups cooked rice

Serves 4

8 boneless, skinless partridge
breast halves
6 tablespoons olive oil,
divided
Kosher salt and freshly
ground black pepper to
taste
3 garlic cloves, minced
1 cup Kalamata olives, sliced
1 cup cherry or grape
tomatoes, halved
1 red bell pepper, cut into
strips
1 yellow bell pepper, cut into
strips
1 green bell pepper, cut into
strips
2 tablespoons capers
4 tablespoons fresh basil,
chopped, 4 sprigs for
garnish
½ cup chicken broth
1 pound orzo, cooked

Partridge, Pasta, and Tri-Colored Peppers

*Colorful vegetables invite the eye to dine as well as the palate. This dish
views well. Use it as an example when preparing other dishes.*

1. Lightly coat partridge breasts with 2 tablespoons oil and season to taste
   with salt and pepper. Pan sauté, grill, or broil the breasts for about 4 to
   5 minutes per side or until 155°F internally.

2. Heat remaining 4 tablespoons of oil in a pan. Sauté garlic for 1 minute.
   Add olives, tomatoes, and peppers. Cook over high heat for 3 to 5 minutes, or until heated through and still crisp. Add capers and basil and
   toss. Pour into a bowl and set aside.

3. Heat broth in pan. Add orzo to reheat until hot and most of the broth
   has been absorbed.

4. Spoon orzo equally onto four plates. Place breasts atop the orzo. Spoon
   the vegetables over all. Garnish with additional basil.

Partridge

*Partridge tend to be an in-between size. A whole bird weighs under 1
pound. When serving a whole bird, it is a hefty serving. But half a bird
is a bit on the skimpy side, thus the quandary. So serve 1 whole breast
(2 halves) for a serving. When serving half a bird, have plenty of side
dishes to round out the meal.*

Partridge and Warm Pear Salsa

A sweet mild partridge paired with onion and garlic in a savory wine sauce is complemented with fresh pear and dried fruit. An Herbed Cheese Soufflé (page 257) pops into the oven while the rest of the meal cooks on the stove. Perfect!

~

1. In a large skillet, brown partridge in the oil over high heat. Remove to a platter. Add the onions and garlic and sauté for about 5 minutes, until garlic is lightly browned. Add the bay leaf, wine, and sherry. Bring to a boil. Add partridge and season to taste with salt and pepper. Cover and lower heat to a simmer. Cook for about 60 minutes or until meat is tender.

2. Just before serving the partridge, prepare the pear salsa. In a smaller pan, melt the butter. Add the sliced pears, golden raisins, and black walnuts, sautéing for 3 or 4 minutes. Sprinkle the lime juice and red pepper flakes over all. Crumble gorgonzola cheese on top of salsa. Serve ½ partridge with ¼ of the salsa per person.

Serves 4 to 6

2 whole partridges,
    split in half
2–3 tablespoons olive oil
2 onions, sliced
6–8 garlic cloves, halved
1 bay leaf
1¼ cups white wine
¼ cup sherry
Kosher salt and freshly
    ground black pepper
    to taste
2 tablespoons unsalted butter
2 ripe pears, peeled and sliced
¼ cup golden raisins
¼ cup toasted black walnuts
    or English walnuts
2 teaspoons fresh lime juice
1 teaspoon red pepper flakes
2 ounces Gorgonzola cheese

4 game-bird breast halves
1 cup seasoned flour
4 tablespoons olive oil
½ pound ham, cubed
½ cup Italian parsley,
    chopped
½ cup green onions, chopped
12 ounces mushrooms, sliced
½ cup brandy
1 cup chicken broth
2–3 sprigs thyme
Kosher salt and freshly
    ground black pepper
    to taste
1 sheet of puff pastry

Partridge or Pheasant Pot Pie

*Pop this pie into the oven when you want home-cooking
aromas wafting throughout the house.*

1. Preheat oven to 400°F. Butter a baking dish.

2. Cut breast meat into 1-inch-thick strips and dredge in the seasoned flour. Heat the oil in a large skillet and add the breast meat. Sauté quickly for about 2 or 3 minutes. Do not crowd the pan. Set aside.

3. Place the cubed ham on the bottom of the greased baking pan. Sprinkle the parsley, green onions, and mushrooms over the ham. Add the pheasant. Heat the brandy and chicken broth over high heat until bubbly, pour over all. Add the sprigs of thyme and season to taste with salt and pepper.

4. Cut puff pastry to fit over the top of the baking dish. Cut 2 slits on the top. Bake for 20 minutes, then lower heat to 350°F and bake another 15 to 20 minutes, until pastry is nicely browned. If pastry begins to brown too quickly, cover with parchment paper.

Toppings for Pot Pies
The traditional pot pie is topped with pie pastry crust. A shepherd's pie usually has a mashed potato crust. Pastries like phyllo and puff pastry bake quickly and are flaky golden brown and pretty. Dough can be dolloped on the hot mixture, too. Try the Buttermilk Biscuits (page 260) or Dropped Herbed Rolls (page 260) for a delicious topping, too.

Baked Partridge Bourbonaisse

This is a rich dish that is laced with bourbon. Other liquors could be substituted, like brandy, vermouth, sherry, Marsala, or white wine. Or leave the liquor out completely—it will still shine (without the moon).

Serves 6

2 partridge, approximately
    2½ pounds each
1 cup flour
½ teaspoon salt
2 teaspoons freshly ground
    black pepper
1 teaspoon dried thyme
1 teaspoon dried tarragon
¼ cup vegetable oil
2–3 tablespoons butter
2 cups heavy cream
1 cup chicken stock
¼ cup bourbon

1. Preheat oven to 325°F. Cut partridge into serving pieces, as you would chicken. Rinse thoroughly and pat dry.

2. Mix flour, salt, pepper, thyme, and tarragon in a large resealable plastic bag. Place several partridge pieces at a time in the flour mixture and shake to coat with seasoned flour. Save the flour mixture.

3. In a large, heavy skillet, heat oil and butter to medium high. Brown partridge pieces approximately 5 to 6 minutes per side. Place the drumsticks, thighs, and wings into a large Dutch oven. Place the breasts on top of the dark meat.

4. Add ¼ cup of the dredging flour to the remaining oil in the skillet. Cook over medium heat for 2 minutes. Slowly add the cream, chicken stock, and bourbon and cook for about 8 to 10 minutes or until it begins to bubble and thicken. Pour the cream sauce over the partridge. Bake the partridge in the oven for 2 to 2½ hours or until meat is tender when pierced with a fork. (Longer baking time will be required for older birds.) Remove partridge pieces to warmed platter and serve.

Serves 6

2 ptarmigan, cut into pieces
1 cup seasoned flour
3–4 tablespoons oil
2 onions, sliced
1 cup chicken stock
1½ cups half-and-half
½ cup sherry
Kosher salt and freshly
    ground black pepper
    to taste

Sherried Ptarmigan

Sherry adds a richness to this gravy. Serve with crusty bread, rice, egg noodles, or mashed potatoes on the side to sop up the gravy.

1. Dredge meat in seasoned flour, reserving 2 tablespoons flour.

2. Heat oil in a large skillet and brown the ptarmigan pieces in batches for 3 or 4 minutes per side until nicely browned. Remove the ptarmigan and set aside.

3. Sauté onions for 4 or 5 minutes. Add 2 tablespoons of the seasoned flour and cook for 2 or 3 minutes. Add chicken stock and whisk to blend. Whisk in the half-and-half and the sherry and bring to a boil.

4. Add the ptarmigan, reduce to a simmer, and cover tightly. Cook until meat is tender and beginning to fall off the bone. Season to taste with salt and pepper.

Cooking with Sherry
The amount of sherry used in most of the game recipes isn't very much. Use dry or cream sherry as you prefer. The dry sherry is more like a dry white wine, and the cream sherry is sweeter and similar to a sweet Italian wine like Marsala or Madeira. Do not use cooking sherry, as it is very unpleasant tasting.

Mustard Crumbed Ptarmigan

The essence of rosemary is light and fragrant in this dish,
so serve Rosemary Roasted Potatoes and Butternut Squash (page 267)
with this. It will be just the right touch.

Serves 4

4 boneless, skinless
    ptarmigan breast halves
4 tablespoons Dijon mustard
1 cup fresh bread crumbs
½ cup dry vermouth or white
    wine
½ cup heavy cream
2 tablespoons olive oil
1 teaspoon fresh rosemary,
    finely chopped
Kosher salt and freshly
    ground black pepper
    to taste

1. Preheat oven to 350°F. Grease a baking dish.

2. Coat breasts with mustard and roll in fresh bread crumbs to cover. Place in baking dish. Pour in vermouth and cream. Drizzle olive oil lightly over meat. Sprinkle with rosemary and season to taste with salt and pepper.

3. Place in the oven and bake for about 45 to 60 minutes, until sauce is bubbly and internal temperature of meat registers 160°F.

Mustard
Recipes often call for Dijon mustard or Dijon-style mustard (for example, Grey Poupon). German-style mustards can often be interchanged with Dijon. They are all robust. Grainy mustards are wonderful to cook with, too.

Goat Cheese Stuffed Ptarmigan Breast
with Wild Rice

Serves 4

1 (6-ounce) box wild rice mix
2 tablespoons unsalted butter
2 tablespoons all-purpose
    flour
½ cup milk
1½ cups chicken broth
½ cup almonds, sliced and
    toasted
4 boneless, skinless
    ptarmigan breast halves
4 ounces goat cheese
2 tablespoons olive oil
½ cup toasted bread crumbs

Think chicken and rice with the sophistication of goat cheese and the nutty richness of wild rice paired with the full flavor of wild ptarmigan. Yummy!

1. Preheat oven to 350°F. Grease a baking dish.

2. Prepare rice according to package instructions. Pour cooked rice into baking dish.

3. Melt butter in a saucepan. Add flour to form a roux and cook for about 3 or 4 minutes. Whisk in milk over medium-high heat. Add chicken broth and stir until slightly thickened, about 5 minutes. Pour sauce over rice and sprinkle with the toasted almonds.

4. Cut a slit to form a pocket in each breast. Stuff with 1 ounce of goat cheese and secure with a toothpick if necessary. Lightly coat with olive oil and roll in bread crumbs. Make 4 slight indentations in the rice and set each of the breasts in an indentation.

5. Bake for 45 to 60 minutes or until internal temperature of breast meat is 160°F to 165°F. Serve hot or warm.

Partridge and Rice
with Ginger Cream Sauce

This is a lovely and fragrant sauce. The cognac can be adjusted up or down to suit your taste. Also, brandy or sherry can be substituted for the cognac.

~

1. Cut breast meat from the bone and cube. Sprinkle with salt and pepper and set aside.

2. Heat cream and gingerroot to a boil. Lower heat and simmer until cream is reduced to about 1½ cups. Set aside.

3. In a sauté pan, heat oil and butter. Dredge breast meat in seasoned flour to lightly coat. Place meat in sauté pan and lightly brown over medium-high heat for about 2 minutes. Stand back, pour 3 tablespoons cognac into pan, and let flame. Turn off heat. When flame subsides, add cream and stir to blend. Reheat if necessary. Season to taste with salt and pepper. Serve over rice. Garnish with parsley.

Serves 4

2 whole partridge breasts
Kosher salt and freshly ground pepper to taste
2 cups cream
2 tablespoons gingerroot, freshly grated
2 tablespoons oil
2 tablespoons unsalted butter
1 cup seasoned flour
3 tablespoons cognac
3 cups cooked white rice
¼ cup parsley, finely chopped

Upland Game Bird Wild Rice Soup

This is a thick, hearty soup that can serve a crowd. It is delicious and meaty enough to serve as a main course. The great thing about soup is that by adding more liquid, it can stretch to feed a few more unexpected guests.

~

1. In a large soup pot, cook onion and celery in butter until tender. Add flour and stir to form a roux. Cook for 5 minutes. Slowly stir in the consommé and water. Cook for 30 minutes over medium heat, stirring until thickened.

2. Add remaining ingredients and cook for another 30 minutes, stirring frequently. Serve hot.

Serves 8 to 12

½ cup onion, chopped
½ cup celery, chopped
½ cup butter
¾ cup flour
4 cups chicken consommé
1 cup water, or more as needed to thin soup
1 cup carrots, finely chopped
3 cups cooked wild rice
¼ teaspoon kosher salt
1 teaspoon white pepper
1 teaspoon curry powder
½ cup Cheddar cheese, shredded
1 cup heavy cream
⅓ cup sherry
2–3 cups cooked game bird meat, chopped

Serves 8

1 pound bacon

8 boneless, skinless game bird
    breasts

1½ cups seasoned flour

2 onions, chopped

3 cloves garlic, minced

3 (10-ounce) cans Ro-Tel
    Original Diced Tomatoes
    and Green Chilies

2 (8-ounce) cans whole
    button mushrooms,
    drained

½ cup parsley, chopped

Zest of 1 lemon

Game Bird Breasts Marengo

A sinfully rich and delicious entree that is perfect for a celebration, sure to garner oohs and ahs. It can be made and assembled up to a day ahead. Serve with a green salad and garlic-buttered bread. Make this with the game bird breasts of your choice, such as pheasant, partridge, prairie chicken, ptarmigan, and grouse.

1. Preheat oven to 350°F. Lightly grease a large, deep baking dish and set aside.

2. In a large sauté pan, fry bacon until crisp. Remove bacon to drain on paper towels; crumble when cool and set aside. Keep bacon grease in pan.

3. Dredge game bird breasts in flour; save remaining flour. Brown breasts in bacon grease, cooking about 3 or 4 minutes on each side. Place breasts in baking dish.

4. Pour off half of the remaining bacon grease. Sauté chopped onions and garlic in grease until soft. Add ¼ cup seasoned flour and stir to form a roux. Add Ro-Tel, mushrooms, half the parsley, lemon zest, and half the bacon. Heat to boiling, stirring constantly. If tomato gravy is too thick, thin with water.

5. Pour gravy over breasts and top with remaining bacon. Bake for approximately 1 hour. Sprinkle remaining parsley over game birds and serve.

Canned Tomatoes

Ever wonder whether fresh tomatoes are better than canned tomatoes? Just let taste be your guide. Fresh summer garden tomatoes are the best, but their season is not long. The rest of the year, use canned tomatoes, but not just any canned tomatoes. Premium brands like S&W and Muir Glen offer canned Roma tomatoes with basil or fire-roasted tomatoes with bits of the charred skin still on the fruit. These are delicious. Buy an assortment of cans, including whole, chopped, and crushed tomatoes, so you will be ready for whatever your recipe calls for.

Chapter 9

Grouse, Sage Hen, Woodcock, Snipe, Rail, Pigeons, & Dove

Serves 6

1 cup (2 sticks) unsalted
     butter
4 tablespoons chives, snipped
6 (12-ounce) ruffed grouse,
     split
Kosher salt and freshly
     ground black pepper to
     taste

Grilled Grouse with Chive Butter

*You can replace the chives in the butter with any other herb,
such as rosemary, tarragon, parsley, oregano, et cetera.*

1. Prepare a medium-hot fire in a grill.

2. Melt butter in a large saucepan and stir in the snipped chives.

3. Dip grouse into the butter mixture and place on the grill. Grill for about 3 to 4 minutes per side, basting with additional butter. If not quite tender, stack grouse on top of each other on the indirect-heat side of the grill and cover. Let cook for another 5 to 10 minutes. Internal temperature should register about 150°F.

4. Season to taste with salt and pepper and serve hot.

A Grouse of a Different Color

There are several kinds of grouse and they are distinctively different from one another. Ruffed grouse and spruce grouse are tasty birds similar to quail. The ruffed has whitish meat, the spruce has darkish meat, and both weigh in around 12 to 16 ounces dressed. The sharptail grouse is next in size, at 1 to 1¼ pounds, with darkish meat. The blue grouse is a mountain bird with whitish meat, and it tips the scales at 1 to 2 pounds dressed. Then comes the big boomer, the sage grouse. They weigh 2 to 4 pounds and have dark meat with an extremely strong sage flavor.

Charcoal-Grilled Grouse
with Mandarin Orange Relish

This is the kind of recipe that builds on itself. The grilled grouse basted with lime butter is great on its own. Place it over greens and drizzle it with Mustard Vinaigrette for another version. Then add the color of the orange relish for the ultimate dish.

Serves 4

Mustard Vinaigrette (page 80)
Mandarin Orange Relish (page 17)
½ cup (1 stick) unsalted butter
Zest and juice of 1 lime
4 (6- to 8-ounce) sharptail grouse breast halves
Kosher salt and freshly ground black pepper to taste
4 cups salad greens

1. Prepare a hot fire in the grill. Melt the butter and add the lime zest and juice.

2. Pound grouse breasts to ¾ inch even thickness. Baste with the lime butter and season with salt and pepper. Grill over a hot fire for about 4 minutes per side, basting with additional lime butter.

3. Divide greens on four plates. Spoon the Mandarin Orange Relish over the lettuce. Place a grilled grouse breast on each salad. Spoon Mustard Vinaigrette over each salad and serve the extra on the side.

Serves 2 to 4

2 sage hens, cut into pieces
3–4 cups milk, for soaking
2 eggs, beaten
¾ cup all-purpose flour
½ cup saltines, finely crushed
1 teaspoon freshly ground
    black pepper
4 tablespoons vegetable oil
2–3 cups half-and-half

Crispy Bake-Fried Sage Hen

*This recipe can be reversed in that the bird can be dredged in flour
and dipped in egg, lightly browned, and finished in the oven.
The outside coating is not as crisp, but it is very good.*

1. Soak sage hens in milk for several hours or overnight.

2. Preheat oven to 325°F.

3. Place eggs in a shallow bowl. Combine flour, crackers, and pepper and place in a bowl. Dip meat in egg, then dredge in flour mixture.

4. Sauté meat in hot oil until golden brown. Place in a baking dish.

5. Pour 2 cups half-and-half over the meat and bake, covered, for 1 to 1½ hours or until meat is tender and falling off the bone. Add more cream halfway through baking if needed.

Smothered Birds
Tender game birds need to be sautéed, fried, or broiled quickly. If they are baked or braised, more cooking time is needed. Smothering birds in liquid, especially cream, is always a winner.

Woodcock and Morels
over Lemon Tarragon Wild Rice

Make an easy meal of this by preparing the Layered Spinach Salad (page 246) a day ahead.

Serves 6

6 woodcock
1 cup seasoned flour, 1
    tablespoon reserved
4–6 tablespoons butter
6 to 8 fresh morel
    mushrooms, halved
1 cup white wine
4 tablespoons lemon juice
1 cup hot water
Lemon Tarragon Wild Rice
    (page 252)

1. Dredge birds in flour and sauté in melted butter until nice and brown. Set aside.

2. Sauté morels in butter for about 5 minutes (add extra butter if needed). Set aside.

3. Add 1 tablespoon seasoned flour to pan to make a roux. Add wine and lemon juice and cook until bubbling. Stir in hot water. Add birds, cover, and simmer for about 1 to 1½ hours, until meat is fork tender. Add mushrooms and heat through.

4. Serve over Lemon Tarragon Wild Rice.

Serves 4

8 woodcock breasts
½ cup dry red wine
5 tablespoons hoisin sauce,
    divided
1 cup seedless raspberry
    preserves
1 teaspoon Dijon mustard
Zest and juice of 1 lime
Kosher salt and freshly
    ground black pepper
    to taste
2–3 tablespoons butter

Woodcock Frambois

Woodcock are delicious dark-meat birds. Cook them like duck.

1. Place woodcock in a bowl and pour the red wine and 4 tablespoons of the hoisin sauce over. Cover and refrigerate for 2 to 3 hours.

2. In a small saucepan, heat the raspberry preserves until melted. Add the mustard and lime zest and juice. Stir in the additional tablespoon of hoisin sauce. Keep warm.

3. Remove the woodcock from the marinade and pat dry. Sauté in melted butter for about 1 to 2 minutes per side over medium-high heat.

4. Remove the woodcock and pour the raspberry sauce into the pan with the drippings. Season to taste with salt and pepper. Heat until bubbly. Serve spooned over the woodcock breasts.

Frambois

Frambois is "raspberry" in French. Frambois sauces can be made with red or black raspberries. The sauce is simple to assemble with the shortcut method of using a jar of preserves. The raspberries have already been cooked down in a sugar-water base. Other liquids to add to thin down the preserves include wine, liqueur, chicken broth, and even water. Herbs and seasonings finish it off.

Woodcock in Cognac Cream Sauce

Serve this luscious, creamy, cognac-laced dish with Basic Wild Rice (page 251)
and Sherried Whole Tomatoes (page 250).

Serves 4

8 woodcock breast halves
½ cup seasoned flour
2 tablespoons olive oil
2 tablespoons unsalted butter
Cognac Cream Sauce (page 13)

1. Lightly dredge meat in seasoned flour.

2. Heat oil and butter in a skillet. Sauté woodcock over medium-high to high heat until lightly browned. Remove from pan.

3. Prepare the Cognac Cream Sauce in the skillet. Before it is reduced, add the woodcock and cook for another 5 minutes. Serve hot with the sauce.

Herbes de Provence Broiled Snipe or Doves

Snipe are a bit smaller than woodcock. Soak the birds in
salted water, refrigerated, for several hours if you wish.

Serves 4

2 tablespoons olive oil
8 whole snipe, flattened
2 tablespoons Herbes de Provence

1. Lightly oil the birds and sprinkle with Herbes de Provence.

2. Broil on medium-high about 3 to 4 inches from the broiler for 3 to 4 minutes per side or until done. Legs should be tender and pull away from the bone. Serve hot.

Herbes de Provence
This is a fragrant mixture of herbs including lavender, thyme, oregano, basil, and marjoram.

8 marsh hens
2 tablespoons salt
¼ cup Citrus Rub (page 23)
2–3 tablespoons unsalted
    butter
1 onion, finely chopped
8 ounces porcini mushrooms,
    sliced (or baby bellas)
2 tablespoons all-purpose
    flour
⅔ cup chicken broth
⅔ cup heavy cream
½ teaspoon kosher salt
½ teaspoon lemon pepper

Fricassee of Marsh Hens or Rails

*An ever-popular dish, serve fricassee over rice, noodles, buttered toast,
or biscuits. Rails are marsh hens and vice versa.*

1. Place birds in a stainless steel bowl and cover with water. Add 2 table-spoons salt and ¼ cup Citrus Rub. Marinate overnight in the refrigerator.

2. Pour liquid and birds into a pot and bring to a boil. Reduce heat and simmer until tender and meat pulls off the bone, about 30 minutes. Let cool.

3. Pull meat off the bones and chop the breast meat. Set aside.

4. Melt butter in a large skillet. Sauté onion and mushrooms for about 5 minutes. Sprinkle in flour and stir to combine. Add chicken broth, heavy cream, salt, pepper, and meat. Heat until bubbly and serve.

Pigeon Phyllo Strudel

This is a company dish that needs to partially cook a day ahead. Or make it, bake it, and freeze it. Then it's ready to pop in a hot oven and reheat when guests are coming. Any game bird can be substituted for the pigeon.

~

Serves 4

1½ pounds pigeon breast
½ pound porcini mushrooms
1 bunch green onions
¼ cup unsalted butter
2 tablespoons flour
2 cups heavy cream
4 ounces Boursin cheese
Kosher salt and seasoned
    pepper to taste
1 roll phyllo dough (4 sheets)
½ cup unsalted butter, melted

1. Chop the breast meat, mushrooms, and green onions. Melt ¼ cup butter in a pan. Sauté the chopped mixture over medium-high heat for several minutes until meat is cooked. Stir in the flour and cook for 2 minutes. Add cream and cheese and blend well. Season with salt and pepper to taste. Let cool and refrigerate for 4 hours or overnight.

2. Lay out 4 sheets of phyllo on a damp cloth and cover with another damp cloth.

3. Preheat oven to 425°F.

4. Place one sheet of phyllo on a work surface and brush with 1 tablespoon of melted butter. Place one-fourth of the chilled meat mixture on the upper center of the dough. Fold over the sides and roll. Butter outside of dough heavily. Repeat three times to make remaining strudels.

5. Bake for 20 minutes until golden brown and serve hot.

Working with Phyllo
The trick to working with phyllo is to not let it dry out. Once that happens, it becomes brittle and breaks apart. Butter should be quickly and lightly brushed on each layer. It's important that the butter be completely melted and still warm. Once it starts to congeal, it will tear the dough. For savory dishes, olive oil dispensed from a spray bottle or canister works nicely, too.

Serves 4

4 thin slices of prosciutto
4 pigeon breast halves
1 tablespoon olive oil
3 tart apples, cored, sliced and peeled
¼ cup golden raisins
5 tablespoons unsalted butter, divided
3 tablespoons dark brown sugar, packed
1 tablespoon all-purpose flour
½ cup Marsala

Drunken Pigeon Breasts
with Sautéed Apples

*This is a good-looking dish and very tasty, too.
Serve it for family and for company.*

1. Preheat oven to 450°F.

2. Wrap prosciutto around each pigeon breast. Lightly coat with oil. Place on a baking sheet and cook for 12 to 15 minutes. Remove and keep warm.

3. In a skillet, sauté apples and raisins in 3 tablespoons butter for about 2 or 3 minutes. Sprinkle with brown sugar to glaze. Divide buttered apples and raisins among four plates and set pigeon breasts on apples.

4. Melt 2 tablespoons butter in skillet. Stir in flour to make a roux. Add Marsala and stir until bubbly. Pour over pigeon and serve.

Deep-Fried Pigeon or Squab

Serve these fried birds Southern-style, with mashed potatoes and gravy.

Serves 4

Peanut oil for deep fryer
4 small pigeon
2 eggs
¼ cup heavy cream
1 cup seasoned flour

1. Prepare a deep fryer by heating peanut oil to 375°F.

2. In a medium bowl, beat eggs and cream together. Dip the pigeon into the egg mixture, then dredge in the flour.

3. Using lifting forks, carefully lower 1 bird at a time into the oil, being careful not to splash any of the hot oil. Fry birds for about 3 to 4 minutes per pound. Remove the birds. Legs should wiggle and meat should be fork tender.

4. Let birds cool for about 10 to 15 minutes before serving.

Squab

Squab is a young domesticated pigeon, usually just 4 weeks old. It has light-colored dark meat that is tender and tasty. It is considered a delicacy. So though not wild, a recipe is justified, just in case a smallish pigeon is bagged and brought home.

2 tablespoons olive oil
4 whole squab
Kosher salt and freshly
    ground black pepper to
    taste
2½ cups cooked wild rice
½ cup pecans, coarsely
    chopped
½ cup onion, chopped
2 garlic cloves, minced
¼ cup dried apricots,
    chopped
1 ½ tablespoons fresh parsley,
    chopped
8 strips bacon, cut in half

Wild Rice Stuffed Squab

Follow the recipe for Basic Wild Rice (page 251) to make the cooked rice.

1. Preheat oven to 350°F. Lightly oil squab and sprinkle with salt and pepper inside and out.

2. Combine rice, pecans, onion, garlic, apricots, and herbs. Stuff each bird loosely with rice mixture. Set in a roasting pan. Lay strips of bacon over the breasts.

3. Bake, uncovered, for 30 minutes. Then cover and roast for another 30 minutes or until legs wiggle and meat is tender.

4. Remove the stuffing. Either cut the breast meat off the bone or split the birds in half to serve with the stuffing on the side.

Sautéed Dove Breasts
in Bacon Drippings Gravy

Dove season comes in late summer to early fall. Dove cooked properly is a welcome treat that begins the rest of the bird-hunting season.

Serves 4

6 strips bacon
16 dove breast halves
1 cup seasoned flour, 3
    tablespoons reserved
1½ cups heavy cream
1 tablespoon Italian parsley,
    chopped

1. Fry bacon in a heavy skillet until crisp. Remove bacon and set aside. Keep bacon fat hot over medium-high heat.

2. Dredge dove breasts in seasoned flour and brown in the bacon fat for about 1 minute per side. Reduce heat and continue to cook until tender, for about 8 to 10 minutes. Set aside and cover with foil to keep warm.

3. Discard all but 3 tablespoons of the bacon drippings. Add 3 tablespoons of the seasoned flour and stir to combine over medium heat.

4. Slowly stir in the cream and continue to cook over medium heat until smooth and thick. Add the dove breasts to warm again. Serve 4 breasts per plate and garnish with chopped parsley.

Pigeon Lofts

In France and England, pigeons have long been considered delicacies. Many wealthy landowners of yore erected pigeon lofts above the castles or on their roofs for breeding purposes. The meat of the pigeon and the dove are similarly rich and dark.

Hickory-Smoked Bacon-Wrapped Dove Breast

These tasty morsels are perfect for serving as an appetizer.

Serves 6 to 8

24 dove breast halves
Smoked hickory salt, to taste
8 strips bacon, cut in thirds
½ cup (1 stick) unsalted butter
2 tablespoons soy sauce

1. Prepare a 225°F indirect fire in a smoker or grill. Add 3 to 4 water-soaked chunks of hickory wood to the fire.

2. Sprinkle the dove breasts with smoked hickory salt. Wrap each breast half with ⅓ strip of bacon. Secure with a toothpick.

3. Melt butter in a saucepan and stir in soy sauce. Brush mixture over dove breasts and place in the smoker. Smoke for about 1 to 2 hours, basting with butter mixture every 30 minutes.

Deviled Smothered Birds

Serve these spicy birds with tart cranberry relish.

Serves 4

4 game birds (pigeon, grouse, or woodcock)
1 cup seasoned flour
2–3 tablespoons unsalted butter
2–3 tablespoons olive oil
2 cups heavy cream
2 teaspoons dried tarragon
½ teaspoon red pepper flakes

1. Dredge birds in flour and sauté in melted butter and oil over medium-high heat until golden brown.

2. Add cream, crushed dried tarragon, and pepper flakes. Reduce heat to a simmer, cover, and cook for 1 to 1½ hours or until meat is fork tender.

Broiled Dove with Spiced Pear Salad

Substitute pheasant or quail for the dove if preferred.

~

1. Preheat oven to 350°F.

2. Place doves on a rack and set on a baking sheet. Melt 4 tablespoons butter and crush Italian herbs into the butter. Brush mixture on both sides of doves. Bake for about 15 to 20 minutes, until meat is tender and begins to pull away from the bone. Keep warm.

3. Arrange 1 cup of greens on each of four salad plates.

4. Melt 2 tablespoons butter and add the pears. Sprinkle pumpkin pie spice and brown sugar over pears and sauté about 4 minutes. Spoon ¼ of the pears over each plate of salad greens. Set 2 dove halves on each salad. Add ¼ of the cured olives and dried cranberries to each plate.

5. Add cider vinegar to sauté pan. Stir in mustard and olive oil and bring to a boil. Spoon over each salad and serve warm.

Serves 4

4 doves, split in half
4 tablespoons unsalted butter
1 teaspoon dried Italian herbs
4 cups mixed greens
2 tablespoons butter
4 ripe pears, peeled, cored, and sliced
1 tablespoon pumpkin pie spice
2 tablespoons dark brown sugar
¼ cup halved cured olives
2 tablespoons dried cranberries
4 tablespoons cider vinegar
1 tablespoon Dijon mustard
3 tablespoons olive oil

Chapter 10

Wild Ducks

1 duck, cleaned and rinsed
1 tablespoon olive oil
1 teaspoon poultry seasoning
Kosher salt and freshly
    ground pepper to taste
1 bunch parsley
3 cups chicken stock

Slow Cooker Duck

It doesn't get much easier than this. Simple ingredients and slow cooking make this a great beginner's recipe for cooking duck.

1. Pat duck dry. Lightly rub outside of duck with olive oil. Then sprinkle inside and out with poultry seasoning, salt and pepper.

2. Rinse the parsley and stuff inside the cavity of the duck.

3. Place duck in a slow cooker (like a Crock-Pot). Cover and cook on high for 45 minutes. Then turn to low heat, add the chicken stock, and cook for about 8 hours until duck is tender.

Cleaning Wild Ducks

Properly cleaned ducks are the difference between inedible and divine. When the fresh catch arrives, take the time to go over each bird, fine cleaning the inside cavity and picking any stray pin feathers that didn't get cleaned the first go-around. Some of the fine hairs can be singed off with a lighter flame, too. Soak the birds in a big bowl of water and rinse. Do this several times until the water is clear. Then place in a bowl of salted water, about 2 or 3 tablespoons salt per gallon of water, for about 30 minutes. Now they are ready to cook or freeze.

Fall-off-the-Bone Duck

*Every shred of meat can be eaten on Fall-off-the-Bone Duck.
The bones pick clean. Use the bits of meat for any of the soup or salad recipes
that follow toward the end of this chapter. Thus, this recipe calls for 6 or 7
pounds of duck to be cooked. It will either serve 6 to 8 people for a dinner
or you'll have scrumptious leftovers for another meal.*

Serves 6 to 8

3 mallard ducks, or the
equivalent of 6 to 7
pounds of duck
3 tablespoons salt, plus
kosher salt and freshly
ground black pepper to
taste
2 apples, quartered
1 orange, quartered
1 cup orange juice
¼ cup dark honey
¼ cup sherry
1 tablespoon Maggi or
Worcestershire sauce
2 tablespoons butter
2 tablespoons flour

1. Place ducks in a stock pot and cover with water. Add 3 tablespoons salt, apples, and orange, and bring to a boil. Cook for 45 minutes. Remove from water and place ducks in a pan.

2. Preheat the oven to 375°F. Combine orange juice, honey, sherry, and Maggi. Baste duck with sauce and place in oven for 30 minutes, uncovered.

3. Liberally baste again and add water to pan to prevent duck from sticking. Cover the pan tightly with a lid or cover tightly with heavy-duty foil.

4. Lower heat to 275°F degrees. Roast for 2½ to 3 hours more, depending on size of ducks, basting every 30 minutes. Add water to bottom of pan if dry. Ducks are done when leg joint falls apart.

5. To make gravy, add 2 tablespoons butter and 2 tablespoons flour to pan juices and cook until slightly thickened.

Freezing Ducks

Vacuum-seal freezer machines and bags cost a little over $100 and are the best for maintaining game in the freezer. Less costly, but also effective, is to wrap each duck in a 12" × 18" piece of plastic-coated freezer paper. Label dates on packages with a felt tip pen. Place 1 or 2 wrapped ducks in a resealable plastic freezer bag with as little air as possible. They will keep, frozen, for almost a year. Hopefully you'll have cooked all of the year's game prior to the next hunt. If not, remove the previous year's game from the freezer and discard to make way for the new.

Serves 4

2 (2-pound) mallard ducks or
    any other game duck
1 tablespoon olive oil
Kosher salt and freshly
    ground pepper to taste
2 tablespoons Herbes de
    Provence or a mixture
    of rosemary, basil, and
    oregano
2 onions, sliced thick
2 cups chicken stock or duck
    stock if you have it
1 cup red wine

Melt-in-Your-Mouth Mallard

This is another simple recipe that is easily embellished by adding more goodies to the pot. In addition to the layer of onions, add roughly chopped carrots. If you have a bunch of celery, chop the leafy tops and throw those into the pot, too. Like roasted red pepper? Then add some of those and a cup or two of chopped tomatoes, fresh or from the can. Allow for at least 3½ hours of cooking, which is the only time-consuming part of the recipe.

1. Preheat the oven to 450°F.

2. Lightly rub ducks with olive oil and season with salt, pepper, and herbs.

3. Place the slices of onion on the bottom of a Dutch oven or other heavy roasting pan. Set the ducks on top. Roast in hot oven for about 30 to 45 minutes.

4. Pour chicken stock and red wine over ducks and cover with a tight-fitting lid or heavy-duty foil. Lower heat to 350°F and bake for an hour. Lower heat to 275°F and bake for another 2 hours, until tender and falling off the bone.

The Size of Different Ducks

Large ducks like canvasbacks, mallards, and black ducks weigh in dressed at about 1½ to 2 pounds. Next come the medium ducks like redhead, goldeneye, and pintail, weighing a little over a pound. Wigeon, gadwall, lesser scaup, and ring-necked ducks weigh just under a pound. Wood ducks, buffleheads, and teal weigh less than ¾ pound, with teal coming in as the smallest, at 5 to 8 ounces each.

Tangerine-Glazed Teal

Teal are a small bird and perfect for serving a whole duck to each diner. These are so delicious that a ravenous duck eater may be obliged to pig out—so cook a couple more teal for backup.

Serves 4

4 teal
Kosher salt to taste
3 seedless tangerines
3 tablespoons red onion, chopped
2 tablespoons sugar
2 tablespoons white wine vinegar
2 tablespoons olive oil
1 tablespoon Dijon mustard

1. Preheat the oven to 450°F.

2. Sprinkle cavity and outside of ducks with salt to taste. Place in a roasting pan and cook for 15 minutes, uncovered, in the hot oven.

3. In a blender or food processor, chop the whole tangerines. Add the onion, sugar, vinegar, oil, and mustard and process to blend. Pour equally into 2 small bowls, one for basting and the other for serving as a sauce on the side.

4. Baste the duck with the tangerine mixture and place a heavy lid or heavy-duty foil over the pan. Reduce the heat to 350°F.

5. Cook teal for about 75 to 85 minutes for well-done, basting every 15 to 20 minutes. Serve the reserved tangerine glaze on the side.

Tangerines

Tangerines are actually a variety of mandarin orange. Others in this family include clementines, dancy, and satsuma. The clementines are usually seedless and would also work well with this recipe. Their season is from November to June. So substitute canned mandarin oranges, drained, in the off-season, and add some orange zest for the extra zing.

Serves 4

2 ducks
Kosher salt to taste
1 onion, quartered
1 apple, quartered
¼ cup butter, melted
¼ cup orange juice
¼ cup orange marmalade
2 tablespoons honey
2 tablespoons lemon juice
2 tablespoons dry sherry

Rare Roasted Winter Duck

Pink duck may not be everyone's cup of tea. But for rare-meat carnivores, this preparation style can't be beat. The only disappointment comes with tough little legs that need slow cooking to be tender. Some cooks save the legs and carcass and throw them back in the oven to slow cook until tender. The legs can be served as part of a salad. The roasted carcasses can be used to make duck stock (see "Duck Stock" sidebar, page 203).

1. Preheat the oven to 450°F.

2. Sprinkle cavity of ducks with salt and stuff with onion and apple quarters. Place in a roasting pan.

3. Combine the butter and orange juice and liberally baste the ducks. Roast 1-pound ducks for 20 to 30 minutes, 1½-pound ducks for 30 to 40 minutes, and 2-pound ducks for 40 to 50 minutes, basting every 10 minutes. Rare duck's temperature should be about 130°F to 135°F.

4. In a small saucepan, combine the marmalade, honey, lemon juice, and sherry. Season to taste with salt. Serve warm on the side with the rare sliced duck.

Brined Spit-Roasted Duck
with Apricot Brandy Glaze

Any of the brines listed in Chapter 2 would be great to use for this recipe. They add juiciness to the meat. The duck cooks uniformly on the spit, and the glaze is applied the last 20 to 30 minutes of cooking. If you don't have a rotisserie, try placing each duck over a can of beer. Open each can of beer and place duck above the can. Lower duck cavity over the can, keeping can upright. Carefully place duck and can of beer over low fire and follow steps 3 through 5. The beer is great for keeping the duck moist. Apply the baste as described below.

Serves 4

1 gallon brine
2 (2-pound) ducks
⅓ cup dry wood pellets or
    1 cup water-soaked wood
    chips (pecan, apple,
    peach, or oak)
8 ounces dried apricots,
    chopped
1 cup brandy
1 cup water

1. Brine the ducks in a large container in the refrigerator overnight. Remove from brine, rinse well, and pat dry.

2. Follow the manufacturers directions for setting up your rotisserie. Place a drip pan filled with 3 or 4 cups of water over a medium-hot fire. Attach the ducks to the rotisserie. Secure the clamps and place over the grill. Have the ducks over the water pan. Turn on the spit.

3. Pierce a foil packet of the dry wood pellets or the water-soaked wood chips with a fork to make about 8 or 10 holes. Place foil packet directly over the fire. Close the lid.

4. To make the glaze: Place the apricots and brandy in a small saucepan and cook until apricots are soft, about 15 minutes. Then add the water and heat to a boil, lower heat, and simmer for about 10 minutes or until mixture is thick. Thin with additional water if necessary.

5. Cook ducks for about 1 to 1½ hours, until a meat thermometer inserted into the thigh meat registers about 175°F. Baste with the glaze the last 20 to 30 minutes of cooking.

Serves 4

2 (2-pound) ducks
2 teaspoons olive oil
2 tablespoons Citrus Rub
    (page 23)
1 teaspoon kosher salt
1 teaspoon freshly ground
    black pepper
¼ cup maple syrup
¼ cup spicy barbecue sauce

Smoked Whole Duck

*A favorite way to serve smoked duck is in a soup, casserole, or salad.
The legs will probably be too tough to eat, but the breast meat will have a
wonderful smokiness. The smoking process can dry out a duck that isn't very
fatty. So if this is a concern, cut 2 or 3 pieces of bacon in half and drape over
the breasts of the bird to retain moisture. Baste on top of the bacon.
Then discard the bacon prior to serving if you wish.*

1. Place ducks on a shallow aluminum pan and rub with olive oil. Sprinkle Citrus Rub, salt, and pepper all over each duck, including the inside cavity.

2. Prepare a smoker for an indirect fire, including a water pan filled with hot water. Add 3 or 4 chunks of water-soaked wood to the fire. Smoke at 225°F for about 20 to 30 minutes per pound.

3. Combine the maple syrup and barbecue sauce. Baste with the sauce 2 or 3 times during cooking. Two ducks weighing 4 pounds total will take about 1½ to 2 hours. Internal temperature should register 160°F to 170°F.

4. If using a grill, prepare a low fire on one side of the grill, placing a water pan above the fire. Place the ducks on the indirect-heat side of the grill. Maintain the temperature and cooking times as described in steps 2 and 3.

Relishes to Serve with Duck

Favorite flavors to pair with duck include just about anything fruity: cranberries, applesauce, pears, cherries, blackberries, oranges, apricots, and on. Fresh fruits can be chopped and paired with minced garlic and chopped fresh herbs, making a sweet and savory relish. Gourmet shops and grocery stores offer a huge selection of bottled relishes to choose from.

Duck Pieces Braised in Pale Ale

*This is a lovely winter stew of sorts. Other beers can be substituted
for the pale ale. If you like dark beer, give it a try.*

1. Dredge duck pieces in the seasoned flour mixture. Set on a plate.

2. Heat the butter and oil in a large skillet with a cover. When hot and
   bubbling, add a few duck pieces at a time and brown well on all sides
   for about 10 to 15 minutes. Sauté in batches to avoid overcrowding the
   skillet. Add onion and sauté for about 5 minutes. Then add beer, stock,
   garlic, bay leaf, parsley, and lemon zest.

3. Cover and simmer gently about 60 to 90 minutes or until duck is tender.

4. Remove vegetables, bay leaf, parsley, and lemon zest with a slotted
   spoon. Skim fat from gravy. Stir in flour mixed with water and simmer
   for about 15 minutes to slightly thicken. Stir in Worcestershire sauce
   and check seasoning. Place duck pieces in a deep serving dish and
   pour gravy over them.

Seasoned Flour

*This can be as simple as 2 cups flour, 2 teaspoons kosher salt, and
2 teaspoons black pepper. Or make it a bit snazzier by adding 2 or
3 tablespoons of Herb Rub for Birds (page 22) to 2 cups flour. Use a
large bowl when dredging pieces of meat in seasoned flour. Afterward,
discard the remaining flour mixture. Seasoned flour may also be used to
thicken stew.*

Serves 6

2–3 ducks (about 5 pounds),
   cut into pieces
2 cups seasoned flour
2 tablespoons butter
2–3 tablespoons vegetable oil
1 small onion, chopped
1 cup pale ale or darker beer
   if you wish
1 cup chicken or duck stock
2 cloves garlic, minced
1 bay leaf
5–6 sprigs flat-leaf parsley
Zest of 1 lemon
3 tablespoons seasoned flour
   mixed with 4 tablespoons
   water
1 tablespoon Worcestershire
   sauce

Serves 8 to 10

3 ducks (about 6 pounds)
2 onions, peeled and
    quartered
4 stalks celery, roughly
    chopped
1 inch of fresh ginger, sliced
¾ cup sugar
¾ cup teriyaki sauce
½ cup dry vermouth or white
    wine
¼ cup plum sauce
1 pound orzo
1 bunch flat-leaf parsley

Asian Marinated Duck with Orzo

Although this recipe takes 2 days, don't pass it up. The beauty of it is the work is done the day before, and it is easy to assemble the next day for a large gathering. Also, it is good to make this recipe and freeze the broth to serve later on. Even the cooked duck can be picked from the bone and packaged for the freezer. It's best to use the frozen duck in 2 or 3 weeks. (See recipe for Ginger Duck Soup on page 205.)

1. Stuff ducks with onions and celery. Place in a pot and cover with water. Bring to a boil, cover, and reduce heat to a simmer. Cook for 1 hour.

2. Add ginger, sugar, and teriyaki to pot. Continue to simmer for another 1 to 2 hours, until duck is tender and almost falling apart. Let cool. Carefully lift ducks from pot and place in a casserole. Cover and refrigerate overnight. Also, cover and refrigerate the duck broth overnight.

3. Skim the congealed fat from the top of the duck broth. Then package the broth in containers to freeze for later use, reserving 2 cups of the broth to use now.

4. Remove ducks in casserole from the refrigerator. In a small bowl, combine the 2 cups duck broth with the vermouth and plum sauce. Pour over the ducks and place casserole in the oven. Turn oven to 350°F. Heat ducks for about 30 to 45 minutes, until hot. Baste with pan juices while warming.

5. While ducks are warming, cook the orzo according to package directions. Place hot orzo on a large platter. Set hot ducks on top of the orzo. Spoon the broth over all. Garnish with parsley.

Noodling Around

A bed of noodles makes for a great platter presentation. In the above recipe, egg noodles, fettuccini, small penne, or small shells could easily be substituted for the orzo. Even rice or couscous would make a good bed. The pasta and grains soak up all the good duck broth, making them delicious.

Duck Confit

Most recipes for duck confit use just the legs and thighs of domesticated duck. Since the wild birds are much smaller, the whole duck is used for this recipe. Just make sure not to overcook the breast meat.

Serves 4 to 6

2 ducks (about 4 pounds), preferably fatty
1 cup coarse kosher salt
1 tablespoon freshly ground black pepper
4 sprigs fresh thyme
4 bay leaves
2 cups peanut oil

1. Cut the duck into pieces, retaining as much skin as possible. Sprinkle all over with the salt and place in a large baking dish. Sprinkle the duck with the pepper and any remaining salt, then add the thyme and bay leaves. Cover the dish with plastic wrap and refrigerate for 24 hours, turning the duck pieces several times.

2. Remove the duck from the refrigerator and wipe off all the salt and juice with paper towels. Place the duck pieces skin-side down in a large nonstick skillet and brown over low heat until fat begins to ooze out of the meat, about 15 minutes. Reserve the fat and transfer duck to a slow cooker or a covered casserole. Pour the fat over the duck and add enough peanut oil to just cover the pieces. Cover the dish or slow cooker and bake or cook at 300°F for about 2 hours, until meat is falling-off-the-bone tender.

3. At this point, the duck can be placed in storage containers, completely covered with the cooking oil. Store in the refrigerator for 1 week to bring the flavor to its height. It will keep for at least one month refrigerated and may also be frozen for up to a year.

4. When ready to serve, simply wipe the duck clean of any excess fat. Then brown the pieces of duck in a skillet until the skin is crisp and the meat is warmed through.

Serves 4

4 duck breast halves with
   skin on
1 tablespoon dark brown
   sugar
½ cup soy
1 teaspoon toasted sesame
   oil
½ cup seedless raspberry jam
   or preserves
½ cup (1 stick) unsalted
   butter, room temperature
1 tablespoon Dijon mustard
1 teaspoon fresh thyme,
   chopped

Broiled Duck Breast
with Raspberry Thyme Butter

*Duck breasts are best when cooked to a perfect medium-rare. The tempera-
ture should be about 145°F in the thickest part of the meat. When overcooked,
the meat gets tough because it doesn't have very much fat or marbling.*

1. Place duck breasts in a shallow glass pan. Prick the skin with a fork.
   Sprinkle with the brown sugar and drizzle with the soy and sesame oil.
   Refrigerate for 30 to 60 minutes.

2. Combine raspberry jam, butter, Dijon, and thyme in a small bowl. Set
   aside.

3. Preheat the broiler. Cook under the broiler, skin-side up, until golden
   brown, about 5 minutes. Turn the breasts and cook the other side for
   about 3 minutes. Remove from the oven and let rest for 5 minutes.

4. Slice the duck breast on the diagonal into ¼-inch-thick slices and serve
   with a dollop of the butter on each breast.

Sautéed Duck Paillards
with Red Wine Demi-Glace

Deglazing a skillet with wine and then adding butter couldn't be simpler. The flavor is luscious and intense, so you don't need very much. It's not like a gravy, which might be served in spoonfuls. It is just a little bit, but oh so good. A cranberry relish served on the side is the ticket here.

Serves 4

4 duck breast halves, ½ inch thick
½ cup seasoned flour
4 tablespoons vegetable oil
½ cup dry red wine
2–3 tablespoons unsalted butter
Kosher salt and freshly ground pepper to taste

1. Dredge duck breasts in the seasoned flour.

2. Heat oil in a large skillet over high heat. When the oil is sizzling, place the duck breasts in the skillet. Sauté duck breasts for 2 minutes on one side, then turn and brown an additional 2 minutes. Place duck breasts on a dish and keep warm.

3. Drain the oil from the skillet and discard. While skillet is still very hot, carefully add wine. If it flames, don't panic. It will die out quickly. Let wine reduce by half. Then add 2 or 3 tablespoons of butter and stir to blend. Taste and then season with salt and pepper.

4. Place duck breasts on four plates and spoon the wine sauce evenly over each breast.

How Much Does a Duck Breast Weigh?
More importantly, let's talk about how much to serve. If dinner is planned with lots of hearty side dishes, a small duck breast that weighs in at 4 to 5 ounces would be perfect. For big meat eaters, plan on 6 to 8 ounces of meat. Small ducks like teal have 3- to 4-ounce breasts.

Serves 4

4 skinless, boneless duck
  breast halves
¼ cup seasoned flour
3 tablespoons olive oil
2 cloves garlic, minced
⅓ cup dry white wine
2 tablespoons German-style
  grainy mustard

Seared Duck Breast
with Garlic Mustard Sauce

*A quick pan sauté is the way to go when time is running short.
Using condiments like grainy German-style mustard adds lots of flavor easily
and quickly. If you prefer not to use wine, substitute chicken or duck stock.
Add steamed asparagus on the side and serve with roasted garlic couscous
that comes from a box and takes only 5 minutes to prepare.*

1. Dredge duck breasts in the seasoned flour.

2. Heat olive oil in a large skillet over high heat. When the oil is sizzling, place the duck breasts in the skillet. Sauté duck breasts for 2 to 3 minutes on one side, then turn and brown an additional 2 to 3 minutes. Place duck breasts on a dish and keep warm.

3. Quickly add garlic and sauté for about 30 seconds. Add wine and bring to a boil. Then add mustard and whisk to blend. Remove from heat.

4. Place 1 duck breast on each serving plate, spoon sauce over each breast, and serve.

Grilled Duck Breast
with Blackberry Sauce

Whether you grill over gas or charcoal, you need a hot fire. Here's how to tell if your fire is ready: hold your hand about 5 inches above the heat source; if you can count only two seconds before you must pull your hand away, it's hot.

Serves 4

4 boneless, skinless mallard
   duck breasts
1 tablespoon olive oil
2 tablespoons Coarse Kosher
   Salt And Freshly Cracked
   Pepper Rub (page 21)
2 tablespoons butter
2 tablespoons red wine
   vinegar
1 tablespoon sugar
2 tablespoons chives, snipped
1 cup blackberry jam
¼ cup chicken stock, or duck
   stock if you have it

1. Flatten duck breasts using the rim of a saucer. Pound the breast, starting in the middle and working your way out to the sides, until the meat is an even ¾ inch thick. Lightly coat with olive oil and season with the rub.

2. Prepare a hot fire in the grill.

3. For the sauce: in a small saucepan, melt the butter. Add the vinegar and sugar and reduce by half. Add the chives, jam, and stock and simmer until thick.

4. Place duck breasts on the grill directly over the hot fire. Grill for about 2 minutes on each side for medium-rare, 140°F to 145°F.

5. Serve the sauce spooned over the grilled duck breasts.

Duck Sandwiches

This is an excellent reason to grill extra duck. Cold grilled duck sandwiches the next day are perfect for lunch or supper. Or you can serve them hot. Buy some good-quality hoagie rolls. Split the rolls and butter each side. On the bottom half, place a duck breast, thinly sliced red onion, and crumbles of either feta or blue. Top with the other half of the roll. Place in foil and wrap securely. Heat in the oven at 350°F for about 10 to 15 minutes. Enjoy!

Serves 4

4 ripe pears, cut in half and
   cored
4 ounces blue cheese
   crumbles
4 duck breast halves,
   butterflied
½ cup seasoned flour
4 tablespoons vegetable oil
1 bunch watercress, rinsed
   and dried, for garnish
½ cup Vinaigrette Marinade
   (page 26), or store-
   bought vinaigrette of
   your choice

Butterflied Duck Medallions
with Baked Blue Cheese Stuffed Pear

*It is easiest to butterfly a duck breast when it is partially frozen.
Begin cutting in half through the thickest side of the breast. Stop before it's
sliced all the way through. The meat will open like a book. This is the same
concept as pounding the duck breast until it is an even thickness. This way,
the breast cooks more evenly all the way through. To make smaller
medallions, cut the duck meat in half, all the way through.*

1. Preheat oven to 350°F.

2. Place pears on a baking sheet and spoon crumbled blue cheese into
   the hollow. Bake in the oven for about 10 to 12 minutes, just to heat
   through.

3. Dredge duck breasts in the seasoned flour.

4. Heat oil in a large skillet over high heat. When the oil is sizzling, place
   the duck breasts in the skillet. Sauté duck breasts for 2 minutes on one
   side, then turn and brown an additional 2 minutes.

5. Place duck breasts on four dinner plates. Remove pears from oven and
   place 2 halves on each plate along with several sprigs of the watercress.
   Drizzle all with vinaigrette.

Mandarin Duck Salad
with Orange Vinaigrette

The vinaigrette makes twice as much as you'll use for this recipe. But it is delicious and will keep refrigerated for a couple of weeks. For a spectacular presentation serve the salad with a freshly grilled or pan-sautéed duck breast that is sliced and fanned over the top instead of the shredded duck meat.

Serves 4

6 cups assorted leafy greens
2 cups duck meat, cooked
    and shredded
1 orange, peeled and
    segmented
½ cup blue cheese, crumbled
2 tablespoons red onion,
    chopped
Zest and juice of 1 orange
⅓ cup white vinegar
⅔ cup vegetable oil
1 teaspoon kosher salt
4 teaspoons sugar

1. Place greens, duck meat, orange segments, blue cheese, and onion in a large salad bowl.

2. In a small bowl, add the zest and juice of 1 orange, vinegar, oil, salt, and sugar. Whisk to blend.

3. Dress the salad with about ½ cup of the dressing.

Duck Salad Sandwiches

All the little bits of meat that pick off the bone or leftovers that are rough chopped or sliced make for wonderful sandwiches. Combine 1 cup of chopped or shredded meat with 2 or 3 tablespoons of good-quality mayonnaise for the simplest sandwich spread. Jazz it up a bit with 2 tablespoons of any of the following: tapenade, diced sun-dried tomatoes, diced pimiento, artichoke relish, or finely chopped red onion. Be sure and serve the sandwich on rustic bread from the bakery.

4 cooked duck breasts, grilled
    or sautéed (See recipes for
    Seared Duck Breast with
    Garlic Mustard Sauce, on
    page 198, or Grilled Duck
    Breast with Blackberry
    Sauce, on page 199)
4 cups Napa cabbage, finely
    shredded
4 cups mixed greens
4 tablespoons dark brown
    sugar
1 teaspoon ground cinnamon
2 apples, cored and sliced
4 ounces semisoft goat
    cheese
½ cup Blackberry Jam
    Vinaigrette (page 28)
½ cup pecans, toasted

Autumn Duck, Baked Apple, and Goat Cheese Salad

Make this a main-course salad and serve with rosemary garlic bread. Be sure to make the vinaigrette first so it is ready to go.

1. Preheat the oven to 350°F. Prepare duck breasts, or if using leftovers, bring to room temperature.

2. Place cabbage and greens in a large bowl and set aside.

3. Combine brown sugar and cinnamon in a shallow bowl. Toss and coat apple slices and set on a baking sheet. Make four 1-ounce patties of the goat cheese and roll in the sugar mixture. Set on the baking sheet beside the apples. Place in the oven and bake for 10 to 15 minutes.

4. Lightly toss the greens with about ¼ cup of the vinaigrette. Arrange an equal amount of greens on each of four plates.

5. Fan one-fourth of the warm apple slices on a portion of the plate. Set the goat cheese on the apples. Place the duck breast on the other side. Sprinkle with pecans and drizzle with the remaining vinaigrette.

Wild Duck and Tortellini Pot de Bouillon

The Monterey Pasta Company makes some wonderful and unusual pastas. Two favorites for this soup are the Roasted Duck Borsellini, which is a veil-thin pasta purse, or the veal variety. If you can't locate these, then buy a good-quality tortellini, preferably from an upscale Italian grocer.

Serves 12

2 ounces dried wild
    mushrooms, like morels
    or porcini
16 cups beef consommé
1 pound tortellini
2–3 cups duck meat,
    shredded and cooked
2 cups chopped fire-roasted
    red pepper (optional)
½ cup brandy or cognac
Juice of 1 lemon, or 2
    tablespoons
1 teaspoon ground white
    pepper

1. In a large pot, bring the mushrooms and beef consommé to a boil. Reduce the heat and simmer for 20 to 30 minutes. Remove the mushrooms with a slotted spoon and discard.

2. Bring back to a boil and add the tortellini, cooking according to package instructions. When just cooked, add the rest of the ingredients. Serve in mugs or bowls.

Duck Stock

Commercially made duck stock may be purchased at some gourmet shops. It has a richness like veal and beef stock. To make your own, place several duck carcasses in a large stockpot. Add several cups of vegetables chunks, such as carrots, onions, and celery. Add the equivalent of 3 to 4 tablespoons of herbs, such as thyme, oregano, peppercorns, and bay leaves. Cover with water and place over high heat. Bring just to a boil. Then reduce to a medium-gentle simmer and do not stir. Simmer for 8 hours. Let cool and refrigerate overnight. Remove the fat that has congealed at the top of the pot and discard the vegetables, herbs, and bones. Strain through a couple of layers of cheesecloth to remove any other impurities. Freeze in small batches to use for soups or sauces.

Serves 4 to 6

1 onion, chopped

2 carrots, chopped

2 stalks of celery, chopped

4 tablespoons butter

4 tablespoons flour

2 (10-ounce) cans beef
    consommé

1 cup half-and-half

4 cups cooked wild rice

2 cups duck meat, or more,
    chopped and cooked

1 cup sharp Cheddar cheese,
    shredded

Kosher salt and freshly
    ground pepper to taste

Duck and Wild Rice Soup

*A hearty soup with wild rice and rich duck meat is a perfect
challenge to a chilly night. Use baked, grilled, or smoked duck
in this soup. If you want this to be the main dish, add more duck
meat and serve with crusty bread and a nice red wine.*

1. In a large Dutch oven, sauté onion, carrots, and celery in butter over medium-high heat. Cook for about 5 minutes.

2. Turn the heat to medium-low and add flour, stirring to make a roux. Add beef consommé and half-and-half and stir over medium heat until thickened, about 10 to 15 minutes.

3. Add the rice and duck meat and warm all the way through. Turn the heat to low, then add cheese and stir to melt. If soup is too thick, add more beef consommé or water to thin it down. Season to taste with salt and pepper.

Ginger Duck Soup

"Oh my," is what you'll say when you taste this sublime soup. There's a catch. You'll have to make the Asian Marinated Duck with Orzo recipe on page 194, then use the leftover meat and broth to make this. Serve with a good red wine and crusty bread for dunking.

Serves 10 to 12

4 tablespoons butter
1 medium onion, chopped
4 tablespoons flour
4 cups ginger duck broth
2 (10-ounce) cans beef
    consommé
2 cups carrots, finely chopped
1 cup celery, finely sliced
1 cup roasted red peppers,
    finely chopped
2 cups cooked orzo or rice
2–3 cups duck meat, cooked
    and shredded
½ cup dry sherry
Kosher salt and freshly
    ground pepper to taste

1. In a large pot, melt the butter and sauté the onion for about 3 to 4 minutes over medium-high heat. Lower the heat and add the flour to make a roux. Over medium heat, slowly add the duck broth and beef consommé while stirring. Bring to a boil and add the carrots, celery, and roasted red peppers. Lower heat and simmer for 30 minutes.

2. When vegetables are tender, add the orzo or rice, the cooked duck meat, and the sherry. Taste and season. If soup is too thick, add 1 or 2 cups of water to thin. Then taste again and readjust the seasonings.

Fresh Gingerroot
When buying fresh gingerroot, just break off the amount that you need. For flavoring broth and soup, there is no need to peel gingerroot since it will be discarded after use.

Chapter 11

Wild Goose

Vegetable oil for deep-frying
¼ cup seasoned flour
4 hard-boiled goose eggs
1 pound ground sausage
1 goose egg, beaten
1 cup white bread crumbs

Scotch Goose Eggs

*The Scotch egg can be served with a salad for a complete
meal or quartered and served as an appetizer.*

1. Heat the oil in a deep fryer to 350°F.

2. Place flour in a bowl and lightly roll each hard-boiled egg in the flour.

3. Divide the meat into fourths and flatten out into patties. Place each hard-boiled egg on a patty and carefully mold the meat around the egg, making sure there are no cracks.

4. Place beaten egg in a shallow bowl and bread crumbs in a shallow bowl. Roll meat-covered egg in the beaten egg and then in the bread crumbs until well covered.

5. Lower eggs into the hot oil and cook for about 5 to 6 minutes, until golden. Remove and set on a paper towel to drain. Cut into halves or quarters and serve.

The Golden Goose Egg

Let's begin this chapter with the goose who laid the golden egg. In early times, chicken eggs were very expensive in the New World. So eggs of geese, pigeon, quail, and pheasant were gathered or foraged when found. The goose egg is double the size or more of a chicken egg.

Teriyaki Goose and Pineapple Appetizers

Similar to rumaki, this is an excellent way to prepare goose breast for party fare.

Yields 2 dozen

1 boneless, skinless goose
     breast half
¼ cup teriyaki sauce
¼ cup hoisin sauce
1 tablespoon toasted sesame
     oil
12 bacon strips, halved
24 small pineapple chunks

1. Preheat oven to 500°F.

2. Cut breast meat into 1-inch cubes. Place in a bowl. Stir in teriyaki sauce, hoisin sauce, and sesame oil. Marinate, refrigerated, for 1 hour.

3. Lay bacon strip halves flat. Place a piece of goose and a pineapple chunk on one end of bacon and roll up. Secure with a toothpick.

4. Bake in the hot oven for about 15 minutes, until bacon is crisp and goose is done.

Bacon-Wrapped Soy and Honey Goose Bites

Another variation of rumaki, this is a tasty appetizer that people eat up. Good with other game birds such as duck, pheasant, partridge, and turkey.

Makes about 48 bites

1 whole goose breast (2
     halves)
1 pound bacon (not thick cut)
¾ cup soy sauce
⅓ cup honey
2 cloves garlic, minced
1 teaspoon fresh gingerroot,
     grated

1. Cut goose meat into 1-inch cubes. Cut bacon into thirds. Wrap a piece of bacon around a piece of goose and secure with a toothpick. Place in a container.

2. Combine the soy sauce, honey, garlic, and gingerroot and pour over the goose. Cover and refrigerate for 4 or 5 hours.

3. Preheat oven to 375°F.

4. Place a rack on top of the baking pan. Lay bacon-wrapped goose bites on a rack. Bake in the oven for about 20 to 25 minutes, until bacon is crisp. (If bacon is not getting crisp enough, turn on the broiler and broil for several minutes, turning to cook evenly.) Serve hot.

Serves 4

3 tablespoons butter

2 cups corn kernels (about 2–3 ears)

1 cup onion, chopped

2 tablespoons all-purpose flour

1½ cups half-and-half

2 cups cooked goose, chopped

1 cup grape tomatoes, halved (or chopped canned tomatoes)

1 tablespoon tarragon, freshly chopped (or 1 teaspoon dried tarragon)

Kosher salt and freshly ground pepper to taste

4 cups chicken stock

½ teaspoon kosher salt

1 cup cornmeal

½ cup Romano cheese, grated

6 slices crisp cooked bacon, crumbled

¼ cup parsley, finely chopped

Cooked Creamed Goose
over Crumbled Bacon Polenta

A creamy sauce is a great way to use leftover goose meat. If you want the mixture to be meatier, just add more meat. Don't like tomatoes and would rather add mushrooms? Please do so.

1. Melt butter in a large skillet and sauté corn and onion for about 4 to 5 minutes. Stir in flour and heat 4 to 5 minutes, until bubbly. Slowly pour in half-and-half, whisking to blend. Cook until thickened and bubbly. Add goose, tomatoes, and tarragon and season to taste with salt and pepper. Simmer over low heat to keep warm.

2. To make the polenta, cook chicken stock over high heat to a boil. Sprinkle in ½ teaspoon salt. Slowly sprinkle in the cornmeal, stirring to blend. Lower heat and cook until thickened. Remove from heat. Stir in cheese and bacon.

3. Spoon polenta into a shallow bowl and top with the creamy goose mixture. Garnish with chopped parsley.

Polenta

Made from cornmeal, it's polenta in Italy and grits in America. Cooked until it's a mush, it can be served with just a bit of butter, salt, and pepper for breakfast. Add Parmesan or Gorgonzola and let it sit to harden, and it becomes perfect to slice into squares or wedges and either fry or grill.

Golden Christmas Goose

The delicious sauce ingredients simmer while the goose is roasting, sending heavenly aromas throughout the kitchen and house. The savory fragrance will welcome the hungry for an exquisite holiday dinner.

～

Serves 8 to 10

1 (8- to 10-pound) goose
Kosher salt and freshly
    ground black pepper to
    taste
2 onions, 1 sliced and 1
    chopped
2 strips bacon
4 carrots, chopped
2 cloves garlic, minced
2 teaspoons dried thyme
2 teaspoons dried tarragon
6 tablespoons butter
1¼ cups flour
3 (14.5-ounce) cans beef
    broth
1 (14.5-ounce) can tomatoes,
    chopped
1–2 cups dry white wine

1. Preheat oven to 400°F. Rinse goose well and dry. Sprinkle salt and pepper inside and out. Place slices of onion on the bottom of a roasting pan, then set the goose on the onions. Set aside.

2. In a large Dutch oven or pot, fry the bacon until crisp. Remove the bacon to drain. Add the chopped onion and carrots and sauté for about 5 minutes. Add the garlic, thyme, and tarragon and sauté for another 2 or 3 minutes. Add the butter and melt. Slowly stir in the flour to form a roux. Slowly add the beef broth, whisking to avoid any lumps. Add the tomatoes and the white wine. Crumble the bacon and add. Bring to a boil and reduce to a simmer. Season to taste with salt and pepper. Continue to simmer the wine sauce while the goose cooks. Add the extra cup of white wine if sauce gets too thick.

3. Place goose in the hot oven and roast, uncovered, for 20 to 30 minutes. Reduce heat to 325°F. Pour 2 cups of the wine sauce over the goose. Cover tightly and roast for about 3 hours or more. Baste every 30 minutes, adding additional wine sauce if needed. Uncover last 15 to 30 minutes for goose to brown.

4. Goose is done when legs move easily when wiggled. Serve with the warm wine sauce on the side.

Roast Goose
with Sun-Dried Tomato Sauce

*This is an intensely flavored tomato sauce. Serve simply
prepared rice or noodles on the side.*

1. Preheat oven to 450°F. Rinse goose well and dry. Lightly coat with olive oil and sprinkle salt and pepper inside and out. Place in a roasting pan. Lay strips of bacon over goose breast. Set aside.

2. In a saucepan, combine the sun-dried tomatoes with 2 cups of water. Bring to a boil, then lower to a simmer. Cook for about 15 minutes, until tomatoes are soft. Drain and squeeze excess water from tomatoes. Place tomatoes, garlic, parsley, brown sugar, and lemon zest and juice in a food processor. Blend until coarsely chopped, then slowly add ½ cup oil or more until thinner than a paste. Season to taste with salt and pepper and process again.

3. Place goose in the hot oven and roast, uncovered, for 20 to 30 minutes. Reduce heat to 325°F. Pour 1 cup of the sun-dried tomato sauce over the goose. Pour the chicken broth into the pan. Cover tightly and roast for about 2 hours. Baste every 30 minutes, adding sauce if needed. Uncover last 15 to 30 minutes for goose to brown.

4. Goose is done when legs move easily when wiggled. Add any remaining sauce to the pan drippings and warm. Serve on the side.

Roast Goose
with Orange Marmalade Sauce

Other preserves, such as gooseberry, lingonberry, cherry, or apricot, can be substituted for the marmalade with good results.

Serves 4 to 6

1 (4- to 6-pound) goose
½ cup (1 stick) butter, melted
1 (12-ounce) jar orange
    marmalade
Kosher salt and seasoned
    pepper to taste
3 bacon strips
1 cup chicken broth

1. Preheat oven to 450°F. Rinse goose well and dry. Set in a roasting pan.

2. In a small saucepan, melt the butter and add the marmalade and stir until melted. Lightly brush goose with melted butter and marmalade. Sprinkle salt and pepper inside and out. Lay strips of bacon over goose breast. Set aside.

3. Place goose in the hot oven and roast, uncovered, for 20 to 30 minutes. Reduce heat to 325°F. Pour 1 cup chicken broth into the pan. Cover tightly and roast for about 2 hours. Baste every 30 minutes, adding sauce if needed. Uncover last 15 to 30 minutes for goose to brown.

4. Goose is done when legs move easily when wiggled. Add any remaining marmalade sauce to the pan drippings and warm. Serve on the side.

Goose Gravy

An easy way to make goose gravy is to add 1 or 2 cups of chicken broth to the roasting pan while the bird is cooking. After the bird is removed from the pan, place the pan on the stove. In a glass jar, combine 2 tablespoons flour with 4 tablespoons cold water. Close the lid and shake vigorously to combine, or use a whisk to make a smooth paste. Heat the pan juices to boiling. Slowly stir in the flour-and-water mixture. Season to taste with salt and pepper. Thin with additional chicken broth, as needed.

½ cup (1 stick) butter
1 cup celery, leaves and
    stems, chopped
1 onion, chopped
1 cup pitted dates, chopped
3 cups chicken broth
4 cups corn bread, crumbled
2 cups dried cubed French
    bread
1 tablespoon fresh parsley,
    chopped
Kosher salt and freshly
    ground black pepper to
    taste
2 eggs, beaten
1 (10- to 12-pound) goose
Kosher salt and freshly
    ground black pepper to
    taste
2 strips bacon
2 cups chicken bouillon

Roast Goose
with Date and Cornbread Stuffing

Serve the goose and stuffing with a cranberry relish or an apple dish.

1. Melt the butter in a large skillet and sauté the celery and onion until soft. Add dates and chicken broth and heat until warm.

2. Place the corn bread, French bread, and parsley in a large bowl. Add the chicken broth mixture and mix well. Taste and then season with salt and pepper. Add the eggs and mix well again.

3. Sprinkle goose inside and out with salt and pepper. Loosely stuff the goose with the cornbread and date stuffing. Any extra stuffing can be baked in a baking dish at 350°F for 30 to 40 minutes.

4. Place goose in a roasting pan and drape bacon over breast meat. Roast, uncovered, for 20 to 30 minutes. Reduce heat to 325°F. Pour chicken bouillon over the goose. Cover tightly and roast for about 3 to 4 hours. Baste every 30 minutes, adding additional chicken bouillon if needed. Uncover last 15 to 30 minutes for goose to brown.

5. Goose is done when legs move easily when wiggled. Remove the stuffing, slice the goose, and serve.

Smoked Roasted Goose

Smoke roasting is a technique that gives a kiss of smoke to the food. The food must be uncovered to infuse with the smoke for at least 1 hour. Food is finished in a 350°F oven. Fatty foods can roast uncovered. Leaner foods that might dry out are covered tightly and baked until done.

~

Serves 4 to 6

1 (4- to 6-pound) goose
1 cup red wine
¼ cup red wine vinegar
¼ cup Tandoori Rub (page 21)
3 bacon strips

1. Place the goose in a large resealable plastic bag. Combine the red wine, vinegar, and ¼ cup Tandoori Rub and pour into the bag. Carefully seal the bag, removing most of the air. Refrigerate for about 2 or 3 hours.

2. Build an indirect fire in a kettle grill or water smoker and add 3 or 4 water-soaked wood chunks (apple, oak, pecan, or other fruit wood) to the fire.

3. Remove the goose from the marinade and place on the indirect-heat side of the grill or smoker. Lay bacon strips over breasts. Slow smoke at 225°F for about 1 hour.

4. Preheat oven to 350°F. After goose has smoked for over an hour, cover tightly and roast in the oven for 1 to 1½ hours more or until a thermometer inserted into the thickest portion of the thigh meat registers 170°F to 180°F for well-done. Slice and serve.

Smoked Goose Sandwiches

The smokiness of the goose meat makes for great sandwiches. Use good-quality French, Italian, or sourdough bread. Slather with Dijon and mayonnaise. Add thin slices of meat, 2 or 3 crisp-cooked strips of bacon, thin slices of red onion, and a dollop of Fresh Cranberry-Orange Relish (page 18) or Quick Apricot Chutney (page 18).

2 (4-pound) geese
1½ cups brandy, divided
Coarse kosher salt and
cracked black pepper
to taste
1 cup (2 sticks) unsalted
butter
2 teaspoons thyme
4–6 strips bacon (optional)

Rotisserie Goose
with Buttered Brandy Sauce

Succulent and sweet, serve these geese in the summer with buttered corn and a fresh tomato salad. In the winter, serve geese with Sherried Whole Tomatoes (page 250) and Fresh Corn Pudding (page 265).

1. Lightly coat geese with ½ to ¾ cup of brandy. Sprinkle inside and out with salt and pepper.

2. Follow manufacturer's rotisserie directions: secure clamp and fork at one end of rotisserie rod, slide rod through center of meat (attaching some of the skin from the front and back of the geese). Attach the other fork and secure clamp. Make sure geese are balanced. Tie up loose wings and legs with string. Rotisserie cook at 300°F over pans of water with the lid closed.

3. Melt butter and add remaining brandy and thyme. Baste geese every 15 to 20 minutes, especially breast meat. If breast meat is getting too cooked, place 2 or 3 slices of bacon over the breast and secure with toothpicks.

4. Geese are done when leg joints begin to move easily and fall apart. Internal temperature in thigh will be about 170°F to 180°F. Let rest for 10 to 15 minutes and carve.

Throw Another Bird on the Spit
Rotisserie cooking is slow, requiring attention and basting every 20 minutes or so. So for all the effort, why not spit two birds at a time instead of just one? Invite some friends over and enjoy!

Pan-Seared Goose Breast Cutlets
with Blackberry Cream Sauce

The English would call this brambleberry cream sauce. It is delightful and rich. Experiment with other jams or preserves such as cranberry, raspberry, marmalade, and such. Serve this with Mandarin Orange and Blue Cheese Salad (page 245) and warm crusty bread and butter.

Serves 6

2 (about 18 ounces each) large goose breast halves
½ cup seasoned flour
6 tablespoons unsalted butter
4 tablespoons blackberry jam
½ cup heavy cream

1. While goose breast is slightly frozen, carefully slice each breast horizontally into 3 cutlets. Dredge in flour.

2. Melt butter in a skillet and sauté goose cutlets for about 3 minutes per side. Set on a plate.

3. Add the blackberry jam to the skillet and melt, stirring. Add heavy cream and stir until beginning to bubble. Add cutlets back to pan to warm. Then serve each cutlet with one-sixth of the cream sauce spooned over the top.

Versatile Goose Breasts

For many a goose hunter, space in the freezer is a concern. So along with freezing whole birds, some birds are breasted out. Freeze breasts separately so that 1 or 2 or so can be used as needed. The breast meat is great for bite-size appetizers. It is an elegant dish when pan seared and served with a sauce. Be sure to save the legs, too. These can be used to make the Goose Confit (page 220).

Baked Prosciutto-Wrapped Goose Breast

Wrapping the breast meat ensures a moist and juicy result.

Serves 4 to 6

2 (12- to 16-ounce each)
  goose breast halves
2 ounces goat cheese
4 basil leaves
6 pieces prosciutto
2 tablespoons olive oil

1. Preheat oven to 350°F.

2. Slit a pocket in each goose breast. Place 1 ounce goat cheese and 2 basil leaves in each slit. Wrap each breast with 3 pieces of prosciutto. Coat with olive oil.

3. Place goose breasts in a baking dish. Bake for about 30 to 40 minutes or until internal temperature is 160°F to 165°F. Let rest for about 5 minutes. Slice on the diagonal and serve.

Leaf-Wrapped Smoked Goose Breast
Stuffed With Feta and Dates

This is a sweet and savory smoked dish that is sure to win raves.

Serves 4 to 6

2 (12- to 16-ounce each)
  goose breast halves
3 ounces feta cheese
6 dates, pitted
4–6 grape leaves
2 tablespoons olive oil

1. Prepare a 225°F indirect fire in a grill or in a smoker, following manufacturer's directions. Place a water pan above the fire. When ready to smoke, add 3 or 4 water-soaked chunks of wood (apple, cherry, pecan, oak, or mesquite).

2. Slit a pocket in each goose breast. Slice feta into 6 slices. Cut each date almost in half and place a slice of feta in the date. Place 3 dates in each goose breast. Any extra feta can be stuffed in breasts too. Wrap each breast with 2 or 3 grape leaves. Coat with olive oil.

3. Place wrapped goose breasts directly on the grill grates, on the indirect-heat side, away from the fire. Smoke for about 60 to 70 minutes or until internal temperature is 160°F to 165°F. Let rest for about 5 minutes. Slice on the diagonal and serve.

Goose Liver Pâté

Serve pâté in a porcelain or pottery crock with buttered toast points, melba or rye crackers or flatbread, pepperoncini peppers, dates, and figs.

~

Serves 6 to 8

1 pound goose livers
1 cup chicken broth
1 small onion, sliced
1 sprig fresh rosemary
8 cooked bacon strips,
    crumbled
½ cup (1 stick) unsalted
    butter, softened
2 tablespoons brandy or
    cognac
1 tablespoon Dijon mustard
Kosher salt and freshly
    cracked black pepper to
    taste

1. Cut goose livers in half and simmer in chicken broth with onion and rosemary for about 15 minutes, until tender. Let cool. Reserve onion and ¼ cup of the broth. Remove leaves from the sprig of rosemary and chop fine.

2. In a food processor, combine liver, onion, ¼ cup broth, chopped rosemary, crumbled bacon, butter, cognac, and mustard. Process until smooth. Season to taste with salt and pepper.

3. Spoon pâté into a covered container. Refrigerate overnight so flavors will blend. Will keep 3 or 4 days in the refrigerator.

Stuffed Figs
Fresh California figs are a great accompaniment to game meat and pâté. This is a simple dish. Gently simmer 4 tablespoons orange juice, 3 tablespoons sherry, ⅓ cup chopped dried apricots, and ⅓ cup chopped dried apples in a small saucepan for 10 to 15 minutes until soft. Add 1½ teaspoons lemon zest and 1 tablespoon chopped black walnuts. Simmer longer if sauce needs to thicken. Slice 8 figs almost in half and stuff with the dried fruit mixture.

1 goose, preferably fatty
1 cup coarse kosher salt
4 cloves garlic, halved
8 whole cloves
12 whole peppercorns
2 cups peanut oil, if needed

Goose Confit

Confit is a way to preserve goose or duck by salting,
slow cooking, and immersing in fat.

1. Cut the goose into 6 pieces. Sprinkle all over with the salt and place in a large baking dish. Cover the dish with plastic wrap and refrigerate for 24 hours, turning the goose pieces several times.

2. Remove the goose from the refrigerator and wipe off all the salt and juice with paper towels. Cut any fat off the goose and place in a pot with the garlic, cloves, and peppercorns. Add 2 tablespoons water and heat until goose fat is almost melted. Place goose pieces in the pot and add peanut oil to barely cover the meat, if needed. Cover and cook over medium heat for about 1 hour or until juice runs clear from goose when pierced with a knife into a leg joint and the meat is fork tender. Remove meat from pot, cool, and debone.

3. Place the meat in a glass or earthenware container and cover completely with the strained fat and cooking oil. Store in the refrigerator for 1 week to bring the flavor to its height. It will keep for at least 1 month refrigerated and may also be frozen for up to a year.

4. When ready to serve, simply wipe the goose meat clean of any excess fat. The meat can be served as is or browned in a skillet and warmed through.

Chapter 12

Wild Turkey

1 (about 14 pounds) wild
    turkey
½ cup (1 stick) unsalted
    butter, softened
2 tablespoons fresh thyme,
    chopped
1 clove garlic, minced
Zest of 1 lemon, fruit reserved
Kosher salt and freshly
    ground pepper to taste
8 bacon strips
Cheesecloth
¼ cup olive oil

Thanksgiving Roast Wild Turkey

*Wild turkey is a lean bird and tends to dry out rather quickly.
This method of larding with an herbed compound butter in between the
skin and meat, covering with bacon, then covering with oiled or buttered
cheesecloth is a triple precaution to help produce a moist, juicy bird.*

1. Preheat oven to 325°F.

2. Rinse turkey and pat dry.

3. Combine butter, thyme, garlic, lemon zest, and salt and pepper to taste.
   Carefully spread the butter mixture between the skin and meat of the
   turkey, trying not to tear the skin. Sprinkle the cavity with salt and pepper and cut the lemon in half and place in the cavity. Truss the legs and
   place the turkey in a roasting pan. Lay bacon strips over turkey.

4. Soak a 15-inch length of cheesecloth in olive oil and place on top of the
   turkey. Bake turkey for about 10 to 12 minutes per pound. Baste with
   pan juices every 20 to 30 minutes. Remove cheesecloth and bacon for
   the last 10 to 15 minutes of cooking to allow bird to brown. Cook until
   the internal temperature is about 170°F when thermometer is inserted
   into the meaty part of the breast. Remove from oven. Rest for 15 minutes before carving. Internal temperature will continue to rise another
   5 degrees while resting.

Thanksgiving Groaning Board

*Aptly named for the vast amount of food that is served on Thanksgiving.
Here are several accompaniments to consider for a Thanksgiving
groaning board: Rosemary, Apple, and Golden Raisin Salsa (page
244); Mushroom, Water Chestnut, and Wild Rice Casserole (page 252);
Creamed Spinach (page 264); Scalloped Onions and Apples (page
266); and Smoked Acorn Squash with Spicy Butter (page 268). Don't
forget dessert: Hazelnut Crusted Cinnamon Apple Cheesecake (page
274), Missouri Pecan–Crusted Pumpkin Pie (page 277), and/or Spice
Cake with Homemade Caramel Sauce (page 285).*

Brined and Bagged Wild Turkey

Brine can be a simple mixture of salt and water. The meat is then placed in the brine for 4 to 12 hours, refrigerated. Most hunters find a cooler to be the easiest way to brine. Ice can be added to the cooler or to the brine to keep it cool enough during the brining process. It is important to thoroughly rinse the turkey after it is brined so that the saltiness doesn't overpower the meat.

Serves 6 to 8

1 (10- to 12-pound) whole wild turkey
Lemon Brine for Big Game (page 24)
Corn Bread and Italian Sausage Stuffing (page 256)
4 tablespoons olive oil
1 large stuffing bag
1 large oven roasting bag

1. Place 2 or 3 buckets of ice in the bottom of a large cooler. Place turkey in a large plastic bag (like a garbage sack) and set on top of the ice. Pour the brine into the bag and close with a twist tie. Add more ice as needed to keep cool, and brine for 8 to 12 hours.

2. Preheat oven to 350°F. Place the stuffing loosely in a large stuffing bag.

3. Remove turkey from the brine; rinse thoroughly with cold water and pat dry. Lightly coat turkey with olive oil. Place the stuffing bag in the cavity of the turkey. Any additional stuffing that doesn't fit can be baked in a casserole dish as per the stuffing recipe.

4. Follow the directions on a large roasting bag and place stuffed turkey in the floured bag. Place bagged turkey in a roasting pan and secure the tie. Cut six ½-inch slits in the top of the bag. Place in the oven and cook for 2½ hours.

5. Remove from oven and slit open roasting bag then pull stuffing bag out of the turkey. Let turkey rest for 15 to 20 minutes before carving.

Stuffing Bags
Stuffing bags are available at gourmet shops and some grocery stores. They are practical and neat. The bag is made of cheesecloth. It comes with directions. Place the stuffing mixture into the bag. Push the bag into the cavity of the turkey. Make sure it is not too tight because this is where the spread of bacteria is a problem. If it is loose, it will cook more evenly. Pull the bag out when the turkey is done. Turn the bag inside out and the stuffing goes right into the serving bowl.

Deep-Fried Wild Turkey

Serves about 8 to 12, depending on the size of the turkey

½ cup Herb Rub for Birds (page 22)
1 whole wild turkey
4 gallons or more peanut oil

A deep fryer or a turkey fryer is needed for this recipe. Make sure the unit is sturdy and big enough to hold a whole wild turkey. A wild turkey is a longer, narrower bird than a store-bought turkey. Follow the manufacturer's directions and use a turkey lifter to lower and raise the turkey in and out of the hot oil. Protect forearms from any oil that might splatter by wearing a long-sleeved shirt and long heavy-duty mitts.

1. Sprinkle rub on the turkey and inside the cavity. Let sit while oil is heating.

2. Prepare a deep fryer by heating peanut oil to 375°F.

3. Using a turkey lifter, slowly lower the turkey into the hot oil, being careful not to splash any of the oil.

4. Deep-fry the turkey for 3 to 4 minutes per pound. Carefully lift turkey out of the fryer. Let rest for 10 to 15 minutes. Then slice and serve.

5. Peanut oil may be cooled and refrigerated to use again. Follow manufacturer's directions.

Deep Fryer Safety
The most important feature of a turkey fryer is its frame. Make sure the legs are sturdy, and place the fryer on a flat surface that is flame retardant. A brick or stone patio is ideal. Read the manufacturer's directions thoroughly before using.

Apple-Smoked Turkey Breast

The texture and flavor of a smoked wild bird are superb.
Serve this with the Rosemary, Apple, and Golden Raisin Salsa (page 244)
or slice the meat for sandwiches with all the fixings.

Serves 8

½ cup balsamic vinegar
2 tablespoons water
1 tablespoon paprika
1 tablespoon kosher salt
1 tablespoon lemon pepper
¼ teaspoon marjoram
2 (1½- to 2-pound) wild
    turkey breast halves

1. Combine the vinegar, water, paprika, salt, pepper, and marjoram in a glass jar and shake to blend.

2. Place the turkey breasts in a large resealable plastic bag. Pour the marinade into the bag and carefully seal the bag, removing most of the air. Refrigerate for about 1 to 2 hours.

3. Build an indirect fire in a kettle grill or water smoker and add 3 or 4 water-soaked apple wood chunks to the fire.

4. Remove the turkey breasts from the marinade and place on the indirect-heat side of the grill or smoker. Slow smoke at 225°F for about 1½ to 2 hours or until a thermometer inserted into the thickest portion of the breast meat registers 165°F to 170°F for well-done.

5. The turkey will have a slightly pink color from the slow smoking and the wood. Slice and serve.

Serves 4 to 6

2 (1½- to 2-pound) turkey
    breast halves
½ cup crumbled Saga blue
    cheese, plus more for
    garnish
2 tablespoons golden raisins,
    plus more for garnish
2 tablespoons Italian parsley,
    chopped, plus more for
    garnish
2 tablespoons olive oil
2 tablespoons Dijon mustard
2 tablespoons lemon juice

Grilled Saga Blue Stuffed Turkey Breast

*Saga blue cheese is creamy, pungent, and perfect for this recipe,
but really any good blue cheese will do, like Stilton from England,
Roquefort from France, Gorgonzola from Italy, or Maytag from Iowa.*

1. Slice a pocket in each turkey breast and stuff with the blue cheese, raisins, and parsley. Set meat in a shallow dish.

2. In a small bowl, whisk together the olive oil, Dijon mustard, and lemon juice. Pour over the turkey breasts. Cover with plastic wrap and marinate in the refrigerator for about 2 to 4 hours, turning 2 or 3 times.

3. When ready to grill, prepare a hot fire.

4. Remove turkey from marinade and sear over the hot fire for about 5 minutes on each side. Move turkey to indirect-heat side of the grill and cover with the lid. Continue to cook for another 20 minutes or until the turkey breast meat registers 170°F when inserted in the thickest part of the breast meat for well-done. (The meat will continue to rise another 5 degrees or more while resting.)

5. Let rest for about 5 minutes. Then slice on the diagonal. Present on a platter with a garnish of parsley, crumbled blue cheese, and golden raisins.

Meat Temperatures on the Rise

Remember that meat cooked in the oven, on the grill, or in a sauté pan continues to rise another 5-plus degrees after it is removed from the heat source. So if overcooking has been a problem, take your meat off the heat sooner, or 5 degrees short of the doneness temperature desired.

Monterey Jack Cheese, Bacon, and Green Chile Stuffed Turkey Breasts

Delicious stuffed turkey breasts are also very pretty when sliced. Create a signature stuffing by thinking of flavor and color. Try Brie with sun-dried tomatoes and fresh basil leaves, or white Cheddar cheese with apricot preserves and chopped fresh rosemary.

Serves 4 to 6

2 (1½- to 2-pound) turkey breast halves
4 whole mild green chilies (canned)
6 ounces Monterey Jack cheese, sliced
4 bacon strips, cooked crisp
4–5 tablespoons olive oil
Kosher salt and freshly ground black pepper to taste

1. Preheat oven to 350°F.

2. Slice a pocket in each turkey breast. Slit open each green chili and place 1 or 2 slices of the cheese and a piece of crisp bacon inside. Insert 2 chilies in each turkey breast. Slit the breast open a little more if needed, but do not cut all the way through. Close turkey breasts and secure with toothpicks.

3. Place turkey breasts in a baking dish. Lightly coat with olive oil. Season to taste with salt and pepper. Bake, covered, for ½ hour or until meat registers 155°F to 160°F. Then uncover, drizzle with a bit more olive oil, and broil for about 5 minutes to brown. Let rest for about 5 minutes. Then slice on the diagonal and serve.

6 thin slices of sourdough
    bread
Dijon mustard, grainy
    mustard, and lemon
    mayonnaise (2
    tablespoons mayonnaise
    mixed with ½ teaspoon
    lemon zest)
6–8 thin slices cooked turkey
    breast
4 tablespoons cranberry
    relish or cranberry
    conserve
8 slices bacon, crisply cooked
2 thin slices red onion
2 leaves butter lettuce
1 bunch fresh cilantro
    (optional)
Kosher salt and freshly
    ground pepper to taste

After Thanksgiving Cranberries and Turkey Club

*Don't like cranberries? Substitute peach jam, strawberry
preserves, or chutney for the cranberries.*

1. Lay out 6 slices of bread. Slather 2 slices with Dijon, 2 slices with grainy mustard, and 2 slices with lemon mayonnaise.

2. Lay 1 or 2 slices of turkey on the Dijon-slathered bread and spread 1 tablespoon of cranberry on the turkey; add 2 slices of bacon and a slice of onion. Cover with the grainy mustard–slathered bread. Slather the bread with 1 tablespoon of the cranberries, then top with 1 or 2 slices of turkey, 2 slices of bacon, and a lettuce leaf. Add several sprigs of fresh cilantro to one or each layer for a Southwest flavor (optional). Sprinkle salt and pepper to taste on the lemon mayonnaise–slathered bread. Place on top of the sandwich.

3. Repeat the process for the second sandwich. Cut sandwiches into diagonal halves and chow down.

Club Sandwiches

The classic club consists of 3 slices of bread or toast slathered with mayonnaise and filled with layers of sliced chicken or turkey, bacon, lettuce, and tomato. Let the sandwich maker add whatever else sounds good to create a masterpiece. Try apricot preserves, Dijon or German-style mustards, jalapeno pepper slices, sliced red onion.

Turkey Burgers

Ground turkey is as versatile as ground beef or ground venison and can be substituted in recipes for meatballs, meat sauce, sloppy joes, tacos, enchiladas, moussaka, and more. The easiest way to grind turkey meat is to partly freeze it before chopping it in a food processor. An old-fashioned hand-cranked meat grinder with a medium blade works well, too.

Serves 4

1 pound ground turkey
1 tablespoon German-style grainy mustard
1 tablespoon horseradish
1 tablespoon Maggi
Kosher salt and freshly ground white pepper to taste
4 good-quality hamburger buns
Garnishes like lettuce leaves, red onion slices, and sliced tomatoes
Mustard, mayonnaise, or chutney for bread spreads

1. In a large bowl, combine the turkey, mustard, horseradish, and Maggi. Season to taste with salt and pepper. Form into 4 patties about ¾ inch thick.

2. To cook in a nonstick skillet, heat skillet over medium-high heat. Cook turkey patties for about 3 or 4 minutes per side, until golden brown and done in the middle. To grill outside, preheat a hot fire in the grill. Place an oiled grill rack over the hot fire until it is hot. Place patties on the grill rack and grill for about 3 minutes per side, turning once. The meat may be somewhat loose, so using a grill rack will keep the meat from falling apart and dropping between the grill grates.

3. Serve on buns with garnishes and bread spreads.

4 turkey tenderloins
6 tablespoons unsalted butter
Zest and juice of 1 lemon
½ teaspoon freshly ground
*   black pepper*
½ teaspoon hot sauce
Kosher or sea salt to taste

Grilled Turkey Tenders with Citrus Butter

If getting kids or the uninitiated game eater to try something
they will love, this is it. Similar to grilled chicken fingers but with much
more flavor, guests will find them delightful. This recipe also works well
by cutting turkey breast meat into 1-inch-thick strips.

1. Prepare a hot fire in a grill. Rinse and dry turkey tenderloins. Place on a plate and set aside.

2. In a small saucepan, melt the butter and add the lemon, pepper, hot sauce, and salt to taste. Brush butter mixture on both sides of turkey strips.

3. Place turkey tenderloins over the hot fire and grill for about 3 minutes on each side, brushing with additional Citrus Butter as needed. Turkey tenderloins should register 170°F for well-done.

Wild Turkey Tenderloins

Wild turkey is delicious. Its meat is sweet and more textured than farm-raised varieties. The tenderloin is the small strip of turkey breast meat closest to the bone. It is the most sweet and tender piece of meat on the whole turkey.

Turkey Jerky

The trick to cooking jerky in a relatively shorter amount of time has to do with how thin the meat is cut. Cut the strips very thin the first time this recipe is prepared. It will cook in less than a day. You can make thicker jerky; it will just take longer to cook.

Yields 8 to 10 dozen strips

1 whole turkey breast, cut into very thin strips
4 tablespoons sugar
3 tablespoons seasoned salt
3 tablespoons seasoned pepper, divided
1 tablespoon garlic salt
1 teaspoon red pepper flakes
2 tablespoons liquid smoke, hickory flavored
2 tablespoons Worcestershire sauce
1 cup water

1. Place turkey strips in a plastic container with a tight-fitting lid.

2. Combine the sugar, salt, 1½ tablespoons seasoned pepper, garlic salt, red pepper flakes, liquid smoke, Worcestershire sauce, and water. Pour over turkey. Cover and refrigerate a day and a half (about 36 hours). Turn the container to mix the marinade several times.

3. When ready to cook, preheat oven to 150°F.

4. Remove turkey from marinade (discard marinade) and pat dry. Place on parchment-paper-lined baking trays and sprinkle with the remaining 1½ tablespoons seasoned pepper. Loosely crumple some aluminum foil and place on oven racks. Set baking trays on foil. Bake for 10 to 20 hours or more, rotating baking trays every 6 hours.

Jerky

There are myriad ways to prepare jerky, from baking in the sun or oven to smoking it hot or cold. The trick is to get the moisture out of the meat so that it stores at room temperature in plastic bags or glass jars for many months. Jerky is lightweight and high in protein and was popular with the early settlers. Today it's popular with hikers and backpackers.

Oregon Trail Soup
with Turkey Jerky

A hearty bean soup that is made with homemade turkey broth and garnished with homemade Turkey Jerky. To make it an authentic settlers' soup, look for heirloom beans, available at gourmet markets and health food stores.

Serves 6 to 8

1-pound bag assorted beans
2 tablespoons olive oil
1 onion, chopped
6 ribs celery, chopped
6 carrots, chopped
4 cloves garlic, minced
2 bay leaves
7 cups Turkey Broth (page 234) or chicken stock
Kosher salt and freshly ground black pepper to taste
2 tablespoons Italian parsley, chopped
24 strips of Turkey Jerky (page 231) or commercially made jerky

1. Place the beans in a large pot and cover with boiling water. Let soak overnight.

2. Drain beans in a colander and set aside. Heat the oil in the pot and sauté the onion, celery, carrots, and garlic for 6 or 7 minutes. Add the beans, bay leaves, and Turkey Broth. Bring to a boil, then cover. Lower heat to a simmer and cook for 2 or 3 hours or until beans are tender. Season with salt and pepper to taste.

3. When ready to serve, remove bay leaves. Ladle soup into individual bowls and garnish with chopped parsley and 3 or 4 strips of Turkey Jerky.

Wild Turkey Game Management
Through proper game management and good conservation practices, wild turkey abound where they were once dangerously low in numbers. The wily bird's keen senses of sight and hearing have made many hunters come home empty-handed, which adds to their increased population.

Wild Turkey Hash

Turkey hash is a great way to use up the last bits of a bird, with some stuffing or potatoes or a combination of both. Try a different cheese like white Cheddar or Parmesan for an entirely different flavor. The hash can be served with poached eggs, vegetables, or salad on the side and cranberry relish.

~

1. In a large bowl, combine the turkey and stuffing or potatoes and set aside.

2. Melt butter in a skillet. Add onion and celery and sauté for about 5 minutes. Add to the turkey mixture along with the chilies, cheese, and beaten eggs. Mix together and season to taste with salt and pepper. Form into patties.

3. In the same skillet, sauté the patties over high heat for about 3 or 4 minutes each, until cooked through and golden brown. Serve hot.

Hash

A hash is a combination of finely chopped meat, potatoes, and seasonings, usually fried crisp. The most commonly known hash is corned beef hash. Other ingredients added to hash include green pepper, onion, and cheese. There are even sophisticated hashes such as lobster hash in champagne sauce or salmon hash with mornay sauce and lemon drizzle.

Serves 4

2 cups chopped cooked turkey meat
2 cups leftover stuffing or mashed potatoes
¼ cup butter
1 onion, chopped
2 stalks celery, including the leafy tops, chopped
1 (4-ounce) can green chilies, chopped
1 cup pepper jack cheese, shredded
2 eggs, beaten
Kosher salt and freshly ground black pepper to taste

1 meaty turkey carcass
4 tablespoons butter
4 tablespoons flour
12 green onions, chopped
    green and white parts
1 jalapeno pepper, seeded
    and finely chopped
3 cups bread crumbs, divided
5 eggs, divided
Kosher salt and freshly
    ground black pepper to
    taste
4 tablespoons vegetable oil or
    more for frying

Turkey Broth and Turkey Croquettes

Here's a recipe for using a meaty carcass after the white meat has been breasted out. The end result is lots of tender cooked turkey meat to make the lovely croquettes or other casseroles in this chapter. The bonus is turkey broth to use for any soups that call for chicken broth. Freeze it in 2-cup freezer bags. Don't forget to label and date. Use within 6 months.

1. Cut turkey carcass into pieces, place in a large pot, and just cover with water. Bring to a boil, then lower the heat to a simmer and cover. Cook for about 30 minutes or until the meat is tender and begins to fall off the bone. Remove the bones and let cool. Pick off the meat and reserve. Put bones back in the pot of water and bring to a boil again. Reduce heat to medium so that it barely boils. Cook for 1 or 2 hours, uncovered, to cook the liquid down, which intensifies the flavor of the broth. Do not stir. Remove and discard the bones. Pour the broth through a strainer lined with cheesecloth into a large jar or bowl. Hand-chop the cooked turkey meat and set aside.

2. Melt butter in a skillet and stir in the flour to make a roux. Slowly add 1 cup of the turkey broth and stir to blend, cooking over medium heat for about 5 minutes to thicken. Remove from the heat and add the chopped turkey, green onions, jalapeno pepper, and 1 cup of the bread crumbs. Beat 2 eggs in a small bowl and add to the turkey mixture, mixing well. Season to taste with salt and pepper.

3. Place the remaining 2 cups of bread crumbs in a shallow bowl. In another shallow bowl, beat the remaining 3 eggs for dipping the croquettes in.

4. Shape the turkey mixture into oval croquettes. Roll each croquette in the bread crumbs and then in the egg and roll again in the bread crumbs until well coated.

5. Heat the vegetable oil in a skillet. Sauté the croquettes over medium-high heat until golden brown and cooked through, about 2 to 3 minutes per side.

Turkey Hot Dish

Creamed turkey mixtures can easily be turned into chowders or soups. Simply add turkey or chicken broth to thin. For a richer soup add cream, too.

⟋

1. Preheat oven to 350°F. Lightly grease a large baking dish.

2. Chop the turkey and set aside.

3. Melt butter in a large skillet. Add onion and mushrooms and sauté for about 5 minutes. Add water chestnuts, red pepper, celery soup, cream, and turkey. Stir to blend and cook over medium heat for another 5 to 7 minutes. Pour mixture into the baking dish.

4. In a small bowl, combine the crushed cornflakes and cheese. Sprinkle evenly over the turkey mixture. Bake for 1 hour or until mixture is bubbling hot and cheese has melted and browned on top.

Minnesota Hot Dish

Known as casseroles in other parts of the country, these all-in-one dishes are the cornerstone of family cooking in Minnesota. Whether the base is meat and potatoes, noodles and tuna fish, or ham and eggs, hot dishes with a topping of something crunchy, like cornflakes mixed with a sharp cheese, are ever popular.

Serves 8

4 cups cooked wild turkey
4 tablespoons butter
1 onion, chopped
2 cups mushrooms, sliced
1 cup water chestnuts, sliced
1 cup roasted red pepper, chopped
1 (10-ounce) can cream of celery soup
1 cup heavy cream
2 cups cornflakes, crushed
1 cup Romano cheese, grated

Serves 8 to 10

2 pounds ground wild turkey
½ cup soft bread crumbs
4 cloves garlic, minced
1 tablespoon Italian
    seasoning
1 tablespoon fennel seeds,
    crushed
1 egg, beaten
6 cups spaghetti sauce
1 teaspoon salt
1 pound thin spaghetti

Fowl Balls and Spaghetti

*Serve fowl balls with spaghetti sauce in a chafing dish
for an appetizer or make a hoagie for lunch.*

1. In a large bowl, combine turkey, bread crumbs, garlic, Italian seasoning, crushed fennel seeds, and beaten egg. Mix well with hands. Form
   into meatballs, and place on a baking sheet. Refrigerate 30 minutes.

2. Preheat the oven to 350°F. Place baking tray of chilled meatballs in the
   oven and bake for about 20 to 30 minutes.

3. Pour the spaghetti sauce into a large pot and heat over medium-high
   heat. Add the number of meatballs you wish. (Any extra meatballs
   can be wrapped and frozen for up to 6 weeks.) When sauce begins to
   bubble, lower the heat and simmer for 30 to 60 minutes.

4. Heat another large pot with water and bring to a boil. Add salt and
   then add the spaghetti and cook until al dente, about 8 to 10 minutes
   or according to manufacturer's directions.

5. Place hot cooked pasta on each plate and top with the sauce and several meatballs.

Turkey Tetrazzini

Make this a day or two ahead and refrigerate. Invite a crowd over and pop it in the oven. It may also be prepared ahead and frozen for 1 month, thawed, and cooked. Serve with the Mandarin Orange and Blue Cheese Salad (page 245) and a crusty rustic bread.

———

Serves 10 to 12

1 (10¾-ounce) can cream of celery soup
1 (10¾-ounce) can chicken broth
2 cups half-and-half
¼ cup sherry
1 teaspoon celery salt
½ teaspoon red pepper flakes
½ teaspoon marjoram
4 cups chopped cooked wild turkey
1 (8-ounce) can mushrooms, sliced
1 roasted red pepper, chopped
1 cup onion, chopped
1 cup frozen green peas
1 pound thin spaghetti, cooked al dente
2 cups sharp Cheddar cheese, shredded
½ cup seasoned bread crumbs
1 cup Parmesan cheese, grated

1. Preheat oven to 400°F. Lightly grease a large, deep baking dish and set aside.

2. In a large bowl, combine the celery soup, chicken broth, half-and-half, sherry, celery salt, red pepper flakes, and marjoram. Add the turkey, mushrooms, red pepper, onion, and peas, mixing thoroughly.

3. In layers, spread one-third of the spaghetti over the bottom of the baking dish, half of the chicken mixture, 1 cup of the Cheddar cheese; repeat, ending with layer of spaghetti. Sprinkle the bread crumbs and Parmesan cheese over the top.

4. Bake for 30 to 40 minutes or until hot and bubbly. Let set 10 minutes before serving.

Chicken Tetrazzini
Classic Chicken Tetrazzini is a dish said to be named after opera singer Luisa Tetrazzini. It is a combination of spaghetti and cooked pieces of chicken laced with a sherry-Parmesan cream sauce. It is topped with bread crumbs and/or more Parmesan cheese and cooked until bubbly and browned.

1 pound raw wild turkey
    breast
4–5 cups chicken bouillon
1 cup yellow onion, chopped
1 cup carrots, chopped
1 cup celery, chopped
1 (12-ounce) package frozen
    egg noodles, homestyle
    or thick cut
4 tablespoons Italian parsley,
    chopped
1 tablespoon lemon juice
Kosher salt and freshly
    ground pepper to taste

Homestyle Turkey and Noodles

After a busy chilly winter day, when an evening by a warm fire sounds heavenly, a simple meal of turkey and noodles is the ticket. Add a salad or relish on the side. The dish can be prepared a couple of days ahead and kept in the refrigerator until ready to reheat and serve. If using leftover turkey, add 2 to 3 cups cubed meat to the pot for the last 10 minutes of cooking to warm it through.

1. In a large Dutch oven or stockpot, combine the turkey, bouillon, onion, carrots, and celery. Bring to a boil, then turn down heat to medium-low and simmer the turkey for 30 minutes.

2. When turkey is done, remove to a platter to cool, then cut into cubes.

3. Bring liquid back to a boil and add noodles, 2 tablespoons parsley, and lemon juice and season to taste. Cook noodles for about 20 minutes. Add turkey to reheat another 10 minutes. Add additional liquid to the pot if mixture is too thick, either chicken bouillon or water.

4. Serve hot with additional fresh parsley sprinkled on top.

5. If reserving to serve later in the week, pour mixture into a large casserole dish. Let cool. Then cover with foil or plastic wrap and refrigerate for 2 or 3 days. Reheat in a 325°F oven for 45 to 60 minutes. Add more liquid to thin down if necessary.

Tough Old Toms

The longer the beard, the older the bird, and unfortunately, the tougher the old Tom turkey. Any of the braising dishes or dishes with sauce help to moisten the tough, dry meat. Why not give it a try in a Crock-Pot? Layer some slices of carrots, onions, and celery in the bottom of a Crock-Pot. Then place the cut-up legs, thighs, and breasts of the turkey in next. Season with salt and pepper. Add a couple of cups of liquid like turkey or chicken broth and white wine or beer. Cook on low for 8 to 10 hours or until the meat begins to fall off the bone.

White Turkey Chili

This has a Southwest flair that's mighty tasty. There's a bit of heat from the onion, garlic, and jalapeno. The chopped fresh cilantro adds the finishing touch. Serve it with Jalapeno Cheddar Beer Bread (page 259). Make some flavored butter to spread on the bread by combining a stick of softened butter and 3 tablespoons finely chopped jalapeno, cilantro, garlic, and onion.

~

1. In a large pot, brown the ground turkey, keeping the meat in small clumps rather than breaking it into fine pieces. Add the onions and garlic, cooking until soft. Add the oregano and cumin and mix well to blend. Then add the tomatoes, beans, and chicken broth. Simmer for about 1 hour.

2. When ready to serve, set up a garnishing station with a bowl of cheese, a bowl of green onion, a bowl of jalapeno, and a bowl of cilantro. Spoon up the bowls of chili and let everyone garnish to their liking.

Serves 8 to 12

2 pounds ground wild turkey
2 onions, chopped
4 cloves garlic, minced
2 teaspoons oregano
2 teaspoons cumin
2 (10-ounce) cans Ro-Tel Original Diced Tomatoes and Green Chilies
3 (15-ounce) cans cannellini beans
6 cups chicken broth
2–3 cups sharp Cheddar cheese, shredded
1 cup green onion, chopped
1 cup jalapeno, seeded and chopped
1 cup fresh cilantro, chopped

Serves 10 to 12

4 tablespoons butter
1 onion, chopped
2 stalks celery, chopped
4 tablespoons all-purpose
flour
5 cups turkey or chicken broth
2–3 potatoes, scrubbed clean
and diced
3–4 cups chopped cooked
turkey
2 (10-ounce) cans creamed
corn
1 cup heavy cream
2 tablespoons tarragon,
chopped or 1 tablespoon
dried tarragon
2 tablespoons parsley,
chopped or 1 tablespoon
dried parsley
Kosher salt and freshly
ground pepper to taste

Creamed Corn and Turkey Chowder

This is a wonderful homey soup. Serve it with corn bread and honeyed butter.

1. Melt butter in a large pot. Add onion and celery and sauté for about 5 minutes over medium heat. Stir in the flour and cook for about 5 minutes. Slowly add the broth and whisk to blend.

2. Turn up heat and bring to a boil. Add the potatoes and lower heat to medium; cook, covered, for about 15 minutes.

3. Add the turkey, corn, cream, tarragon, and parsley. Season to taste with salt and pepper. Heat to desired warmth and serve.

Chowders or Soups

A chowder is a kind of soup, but a soup is not necessarily a chowder. Soups can be thick or thin, hot or cold. Thick chunky soups made with seafood, fish, or vegetables are known as chowders. Clam chowder and corn chowder are the most famous.

Chapter 13

All the Trimmings

Serves 6 to 8

4 cups applesauce
¼ cup dark brown sugar
1 tablespoon cinnamon
¼–½ cup miniature
   marshmallows

Baked Applesauce

*This is simple comfort food at its best, and it all begins
with store-bought applesauce. Serve this from autumn to spring
with the game of your choice. Kids will love it, too.*

1. Preheat the oven to 350°F. Lightly butter a shallow 1-quart baking dish.

2. Combine room-temperature applesauce with brown sugar and cinnamon. Pour into prepared baking dish. Sprinkle the marshmallows in the center of the applesauce. Bake for about 20 to 30 minutes, until warmed through and marshmallows melt and begin to brown.

Homemade Applesauce
Great homemade applesauce is easy to make. Peel, core, and slice 6 tart apples like Jonathan, Braeburn, or Granny Smith. Place apple pieces in a stainless steel pot. Add 2 tablespoons water and cover. Simmer over low heat for about 1 hour. Add from ½ to 1 cup sugar to taste. Add 1 to 3 teaspoons cinnamon, if you like. Continue to cook until apples become mushy. Stir several times during the cooking process. Mash with a potato masher or run through a food mill. Keep in a covered container or glass jar(s) in the refrigerator for a couple of weeks.

Red Hot Cinnamon Apples

Serves 8

2 cups water
1½ cups sugar
¾ cup Red Hots
8 apples

These apples keep for a couple of weeks refrigerated, if they last that long. The amount of sugar and Red Hots can be adjusted to suit your own taste. The apples can be sliced into rings, halved, or quartered. They are a beautiful ruby red addition to a holiday table. Serve with roasted or smoked wild turkey or the game of your choice.

1. In a large pot, heat water and sugar to boiling, then add Red Hots, stirring until dissolved.

2. Peel, core, and halve the apples. Place in the syrup and cook over medium heat until just tender, about 10 minutes.

3. Serve warm or refrigerate to chill and serve cold.

Sautéed Cinnamon Apples

This version is without the Red Hots. In a sauté pan, melt 4 tablespoons butter. Peel, core, and thickly slice 2 firm apples and add to the butter. Cook over medium heat for 3 or 4 minutes. Combine 3 tablespoons sugar with 1 tablespoon ground cinnamon. Sprinkle over the apples and cook for a minute. Serve warm as a side dish or as a dessert, with honeyed whipped cream.

1 tart green apple, cored and
    chopped
1 tart red apple, cored and
    chopped
1 yellow bell pepper, seeded
    and chopped
10 green onions, chopped
⅓ cup golden raisins
⅓ cup dried apricots,
    chopped
2 teaspoons fresh rosemary,
    finely chopped
¼ cup lemon juice
½ cup olive oil
½ teaspoon kosher salt
½ teaspoon freshly ground
    black pepper

Rosemary, Apple, and Golden Raisin Salsa

A modern twist on fruit salad, serve this from late spring to early fall with grilled and smoked wild game. It is especially nice with smoked turkey.

1. Combine all of the ingredients in a large bowl. Toss to mix well.

2. Cover with plastic wrap and refrigerate for 1 to 2 hours. Serve slightly chilled.

Colorful Vegetable and Fruit Dishes

Eye appeal can be as important as the flavor of a dish. In fact, the look of a dish is often enhanced by adding colorful ingredients. A dish with red, green, and yellow peppers looks great and has a dimension of sweetness with the variety of peppers, each with it's own subtle differences. The same goes with apples—an array of colors looks great, and each variety of apple has a different texture as well as taste.

Mandarin Orange and Blue Cheese Salad

Think of this recipe as a blueprint and customize it with what you have on hand or prefer. No oranges? Try strawberries and raspberries. Don't like blue cheese? Try crumbled feta. Extras or alternatives to try include dried cranberries, toasted nuts, crumbled bacon, hearts of palm, artichoke hearts, red onion, pickled baby beets, olives, et cetera. Serve this salad year-round with the game of your choice.

Serves 4

2 heads butter lettuce
1 (4-ounce) can mandarin oranges, drained
4 ounces blue cheese crumbles
¼ cup toasted pecans
¼ cup white vinegar
⅓ cup vegetable oil
1 tablespoon sugar
½ teaspoon kosher salt
1 clove garlic, minced

1. Rinse and tear off tough outer leaves of butter lettuce. Core, tear into bite-sized pieces, and dry. Place leaves in a large salad bowl. Add the orange segments, crumbled blue cheese, and toasted pecans.

2. Combine the vinegar, oil, sugar, salt, and garlic. Shake to blend and pour desired amount over the salad. Toss and serve.

Salad Bar Salads

So many grocery stores have wonderful salad bars. Take advantage of them and customize your mealtime salads. Buy the greens in a separate container. Buy the goodies in one or two additional containers. The greens will last longer without the goodies wilting them. Everyone is happy because each gets to add just what he or she wants to his or her salad. Serve with homemade or store-bought salad dressings.

Serves 8 to 10

3 cups baby spinach leaves
¼ teaspoon seasoned ground
    black pepper
1 teaspoon sugar
1 pound bacon, fried crisp
6 hard-boiled eggs, sliced
3 cups red lettuce, torn
1 cup water chestnuts, sliced
¼ teaspoon seasoned ground
    black pepper
1 teaspoon sugar
1 (10-ounce) package frozen
    peas, not thawed
1 cup green onion, sliced
1 package dry Caesar salad
    dressing
1½ cups light sour cream
1 cup mayonnaise
1½ cups freshly grated
    Romano cheese

Layered Spinach Salad

Prepare this salad in a big glass bowl to show off all the pretty layers.
It is perfect for a game buffet and can be made the day ahead.

1. In a large 3-quart salad bowl, spread baby spinach leaves. Sprinkle pepper and sugar over spinach. Layer, beginning with crumbled bacon, then sliced eggs, lettuce, water chestnuts, seasoned pepper, sugar, peas, and green onion.

2. In a small bowl, combine the dry Caesar salad dressing, sour cream, and mayonnaise. Spread over the top of the salad to seal. Sprinkle the cheese on last.

3. Refrigerate overnight, covered tightly with plastic wrap. Toss just before serving.

Layered Salads

These make-a-day-ahead layered salads came onto the American culinary scene in the mid-1900s. Their ingredients vary, and a popular version uses iceberg lettuce with all of the above crunchy vegetables, topped with buttermilk dressing and Cheddar cheese. Be creative and layer with your own favorites—sliced black olives, artichoke hearts, roasted red pepper strips, et cetera.

White Cheddar Coleslaw

This is such a simple salad and so refreshing to serve with grilled or smoked game. Add your favorite herbs, such as parsley, cilantro, lovage, or dill, for an extra touch.

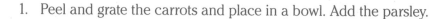

1. Place slaw mix in a bowl.

2. Combine oil, vinegar, dry mustard, celery seed, sugar, garlic salt, and white pepper in a small bowl and whisk to blend. Pour over cabbage and toss. Sprinkle cheese over top and serve.

Serves 6 to 8

1 (16-ounce package) slaw mix
½ cup oil
¼ cup cider vinegar
¼ teaspoon dry mustard
1 teaspoon celery seed
2 tablespoons sugar
½ teaspoon garlic salt
½ teaspoon white pepper
1 cup white Cheddar cheese, shredded or crumbled feta or blue cheese

Freshly Grated Carrot Salad

Delightful and delicious uncooked vegetable salads are very European. So why not serve this root vegetable uncooked for a winter repast and bring a bit of brightness to the table?

1. Peel and grate the carrots and place in a bowl. Add the parsley.

2. Combine the lemon, mustard, garlic, and oil in a glass jar with a tight-fitting lid. Shake to blend. Pour over salad and toss to coat well. Add salt and pepper to taste.

Serves 4 to 6

2 pounds carrots
½ cup Italian parsley, chopped
Zest and juice of 1 lemon
1 teaspoon Dijon mustard
1 large clove garlic, minced
¼ cup extra-virgin olive oil
Kosher salt and freshly cracked black pepper to taste

1 pound beefsteak tomatoes
1½ cups cherry or grape tomatoes, red or yellow
½ cup Kalamata olives, pitted
4 ounces feta cheese
⅔ cup extra-virgin olive oil
Zest of 1 lemon
Juice of 2 lemons (about 5–6 tablespoons)
2 tablespoons pesto
Kosher salt and freshly cracked black pepper to taste

Tomato Salad
with Pesto Vinaigrette

Fresh-picked garden tomatoes are one of summer's most popular bounties. Never refrigerate tomatoes, if possible. If they must be refrigerated because of over-ripeness, then use them in a baked casserole instead of serving them in a fresh salad like this.

1. Slice the beefsteak tomatoes and arrange on a platter. Slice some of the cherry or grape tomatoes in half and leave some of them whole and spread over the sliced beefsteaks. Scatter olives, then cheese over the tomatoes.

2. In a glass jar, combine the oil, lemon zest and juice, and the pesto. Cover with lid and shake to blend. Season with salt and pepper to taste. Drizzle over salad. Dressing will keep covered in the refrigerator for up to 1 week.

Herb Pesto
Pesto is an herb gardener's best friend. When you have too many chives or too much lemon balm, basil, thyme, oregano, or mint, make pesto. A classic pesto recipe is 2 cups fresh herbs, 2 cloves garlic, ¼ cup pine nuts, and ½ cup olive oil combined in a food processor. Salt and pepper to taste and stir in ½ cup freshly grated Parmesan or Romano cheese.

Bacon and Tomato Bake

When the garden is overflowing with cherry and grape tomatoes, try this casserole, which is lovely as a side dish at dinner or as a brunch dish. It goes with roasted, braised, baked, and grilled game of every kind. The addition of toasted bread in this mixture helps to absorb the juiciness of the tomatoes. If there is a bit of tomato liquid still, serve with rustic bread to sop up the tasty elixir.

~

1. Preheat oven to 350°F. Grease a baking dish and set aside.

2. Slice 3 cups of the tomatoes in half and leave the other 3 cups whole. Combine tomatoes, toast, goat cheese, cottage cheese, cream, eggs, salt, and pepper. Pour into prepared baking dish. Top with shredded Cheddar cheese and crumbled bacon.

3. Bake for about 35 to 40 minutes or until casserole is set and barely wiggles in the middle when gently shaken.

4. Remove from oven and let rest for about 5 minutes. Serve hot or warm.

5. Leftovers may be covered and refrigerated for 2 or 3 days. Reheat a serving at a time in the microwave for about 15 to 20 seconds on high.

Serves 6 to 8

6 cups cherry or grape tomatoes
2 pieces toasted bread, cut into ½-inch cubes
2 ounces goat cheese, cut into ½-inch pieces
2 cups cottage cheese
½ cup heavy cream
4 eggs, beaten
½ teaspoon kosher or sea salt
½ teaspoon freshly ground black pepper
8 ounces (2 cups) sharp Cheddar cheese, shredded
4 slices crisply cooked bacon

Serves 4

4 large tomatoes
4 tablespoons sherry
Freshly ground black pepper
    to taste
3 tablespoons mayonnaise
1 tablespoon Dijon mustard
4 tablespoons Romano
    cheese, finely grated

Sherried Whole Tomatoes

This dish is especially nice with late-harvest tomatoes that have lost that summer freshness. Medium-sized tomatoes are pretty, but smallish tomatoes work fine too. Just allow 2 or 3 small tomatoes per person. Red and yellow tomatoes make a pretty platter.

1. Preheat oven broiler to high.

2. Remove core from each tomato and slice off the top. Prick each tomato with a fork. Sprinkle each tomato with 1 tablespoon sherry and pepper to taste.

3. Combine mayonnaise and mustard. Spread 1 tablespoon over cut top of each tomato. Then sprinkle 1 tablespoon of cheese over top.

4. Place under the broiler for 2 to 3 minutes, until bubbly and golden brown. Serve immediately.

S'More for Tomato Lovers

Also known as the love apple, tomatoes are a versatile fruit. They are served fresh, grilled, broiled, stewed, sun-dried, and adorned with everything from anchovies to goat cheese. They are a welcome addition to the hunter's table.

Basic Wild Rice

Wild rice is a grain that grows in marshy bogs, lakes, and rivers. It is also grown in man-made paddies. Its nutty flavor pairs well with meats and wild game. It can be served warm with or without a sauce. Mixed with dried fruit and nuts, it becomes a pleasant chilled salad, too.

Serves 6 to 8

1 cup wild rice
1 teaspoon salt
4 cups water

1. Rinse wild rice in a strainer under cold water. Place rice, salt, and water in a large saucepan. Bring to a boil and cover. Lower heat to a simmer and cook for about 45 to 55 minutes. (Rice can also be simmered in chicken or beef broth. Check the salt content of the broth and lessen the amount of salt added.)

2. Rice is done when the dark kernels pop open and are tender but not mushy. Serve warm.

3. The cooked rice will keep refrigerated for 1 to 2 weeks. It may also be frozen in plastic freezer bags for up to 2 or 3 months.

Doctored-Up Wild Rice
To the cooked Basic Wild Rice recipe add any of the following combinations to create a delicious variation.

1. *Stir in ½ cup golden raisins, ¼ cup chopped dried apricots, ½ cup chopped green onion, and ½ cup chopped yellow pepper. Refrigerate and serve with dressing as a cold salad.*
2. *Sauté ½ cup chopped onion, 1 clove minced garlic, and ¼ cup chopped Italian parsley in 4 tablespoons of butter. Stir into the rice and serve warm.*
3. *Sauté 1 cup pecan halves in 6 tablespoons butter for about 5 minutes. Add to warm wild rice and serve.*
4. *Sauté 1 cup chopped celery and ½ cup sliced almonds in 6 tablespoons butter. Add to warm rice and serve.*

Mushroom, Water Chestnut, and Wild Rice Casserole

Any of the leftover wild rice concoctions with vegetables can be frozen for up to 2 months and used in any of the wild rice game soups in this book. See recipes on pages 167, 204, and 205.

1. Preheat oven to 350°F. Butter a 9" × 13" baking dish.

2. In a large bowl, combine rice, onion, water chestnuts, mushrooms, and broth and stir to blend. Pour mixture into the prepared baking dish. Place pats of butter on top of casserole and scatter the crumbled bacon.

3. Bake for 35 to 40 minutes or until liquid has been absorbed into rice. Serve warm.

Lemon Tarragon Wild Rice

Try this quick and easy stir-together recipe—it's short on preparation time and big on flavor.

1. Melt butter in a pot. Add chicken broth and lemon zest and juice and bring to a boil. Add the cooked rice and heat through, stirring until liquid is absorbed.

2. Add tarragon and season to taste with salt and pepper. Serve hot with tarragon sprigs for garnish.

Baked Risotto
with Sun-Dried Tomatoes

This is a luscious and rich rice dish. It's a perfect company dish that can be assembled earlier in the day, then baked prior to serving.

⟞⟜

1. Preheat oven to 350°F. Butter a baking dish and set aside.

2. Sauté onion in butter for 3 or 4 minutes. Add garlic and rice and cook for another 2 to 3 minutes, stirring until rice is slightly opaque but not brown. Add rosemary, sun-dried tomatoes, chicken broth, heavy cream, and seasonings, stirring to combine over medium-high heat for about 4 to 5 minutes. Pour into casserole and stir in cheese.

3. Cover tightly and bake for 1 hour. Check to see if most of the liquid has been absorbed. If not, bake a little longer. Serve hot or warm.

Arborio Rice
Arborio rice is a short, fat kernel of rice that is high in starch content. This extra starchiness is why it is the choice for making creamy rice dishes.

Serves 6

½ cup onion, chopped
3 tablespoons butter
2 cloves garlic, minced
1 cup arborio rice
1 teaspoon fresh rosemary, minced
½ cup sun-dried tomatoes packed in olive oil, chopped
2¼ cups chicken broth
1 cup heavy cream
Kosher or sea salt and freshly ground pepper to taste
1 cup Romano cheese, freshly grated

Serves 6 to 8

1 cup (8 ounces) orzo
1 cup reserved pasta water
1 bunch green onions,
    chopped
1 red bell pepper, seeded and
    chopped
½ cup fresh Italian parsley,
    chopped
8 ounces cured olives, pitted
8 ounces feta cheese,
    crumbled
⅓ cup olive oil
⅓ cup lemon juice
1 clove garlic, minced
Kosher salt and freshly
    ground black pepper
    to taste

Warm Orzo
with Feta and Cured Olives

Pasta salads are best when dressed while still warm.
The dressing is absorbed for maximum flavor.

1. Cook orzo according to manufacturer's directions until al dente. Drain water, reserving 1 cup for later use.

2. Place warm orzo in a big bowl. Add the green onions, bell pepper, parsley, olives, and cheese.

3. Combine the olive oil, lemon juice, and garlic in a glass jar with a lid and shake to blend. Pour over the pasta salad. Season to taste with salt and pepper.

4. If pasta is dry, add reserved pasta water a little at a time until moist. Serve warm. May be refrigerated for 2 days.

Pasta Shapes
Orzo is a small pasta shaped like a large grain of rice. It is smooth and creamy. Other pastas to substitute in this salad are gemelli, small shells, orecchiette, small macaroni, small penne, or even linguine.

Smoked Gouda Grits

Smoked Gouda adds a new twist to this classic Southern dish. Try using other cheeses for a different flavor, such as creamy Camembert, blue cheese, Gruyère, or Romano.

Serves 6

1 cup quick-cooking grits
½ cup (1 stick) butter
8 ounces smoked Gouda, shredded
2 cloves garlic, minced
2 eggs
¾ cup whole milk

1. Preheat oven to 350°F. Lightly grease a 2-quart baking dish and set aside.

2. In a large saucepan, cook grits according to manufacturer's directions. Remove from heat. Add butter and stir until melted. Add the cheese and garlic and stir.

3. In a 2-cup measuring cup, beat the 2 eggs and add milk to measure 1 cup. Add to cooled grits and stir to blend. Pour into greased casserole dish and bake for 40 to 45 minutes, until a knife inserted in the middle comes out clean. Serve hot.

Grits

Grits are ground hominy. For this recipe, grits ground fine or medium-fine work best. Regular grits may be used in this recipe, too, as opposed to the quick-cooking variety.

½ cup (1 stick) butter

1 cup celery, leaves and
    stalks, chopped

1 medium onion, chopped

1 jalapeno pepper, seeded
    and chopped (optional)

3 cups chicken broth

4 cups corn bread, crumbled

4 slices sourdough bread,
    toasted and cubed

½ pound Italian sausage,
    spicy or mild

Giblets from turkey, chopped
    (optional)

1 teaspoon dried sage (or
    substitute marjoram or
    rosemary)

Kosher salt and freshly
    ground pepper to taste

2 eggs, beaten

Corn Bread and Italian Sausage Stuffing

*Stuffing can be as creative as you want it to be. Think of how
many kinds of bread there are and then quadruple that (at least) to come up
with how many different recipes for stuffing there are. It is pretty difficult to
mess up stuffing. As you make it, you want it to be moist but not mushy.
Depending on the bread, you may need to alter the amount of liquid.
Make it with meat or seafood. Make it meatless. Add corn, fresh or canned.
Leave out the onions. It's all a personal taste thing.*

1. Melt the butter in a large skillet and sauté the celery, onion, and pepper for 5 minutes or until soft. Add the chicken broth and heat until warm.

2. Place the corn bread and toasted cubes in a large bowl. Add the chicken broth mixture and mix well.

3. In the same skillet, brown the Italian sausage. Add the chopped giblets and cook until done, about 5 to 7 minutes. Add the sage and stir to blend. Add sausage to the bread mixture and mix well. Taste and then season with salt and pepper. Add the eggs and mix well again.

4. Place the stuffing in a buttered casserole dish and bake at 325°F for about 45 to 50 minutes. Do not cover.

Herbed Cheese Soufflé

*This makes a fairly large amount of cheese soufflé. But that's okay.
It's a wonderful midnight snack, breakfast, or leftover side dish for
another meal later in the week, if it lasts that long. To reheat, spoon
a serving onto a plate and zap it in the microwave for 10 to 15
seconds. Serve this with simply prepared game meats.*

Serves 8 to 10

½ cup (1 stick) unsalted butter
½ cup all-purpose flour
2⅔ cups whole milk
½ teaspoon salt
½ teaspoon ground white
    pepper
6 large eggs
3 cups hard cheese
    (Parmesan, Romano, or
    Asiago), grated
¼ cup fresh mixed herbs,
    chopped (parsley, chive,
    tarragon, or thyme)

1. Preheat oven to 400°F. Butter a 2-quart baking dish and set aside.

2. Melt butter in a saucepan and whisk in flour to form a paste. Add ½
   cup of the milk and whisk to blend. Add the remaining milk and whisk
   while bringing to a boil. Season with salt and pepper and set aside to
   cool.

3. Beat eggs in a separate bowl and whisk in the grated cheese(s) and
   mixed herbs. Pour into the cooled milk mixture. Then pour into the
   buttered baking dish. Bake for 35 to 45 minutes or until the soufflé has
   puffed and is golden brown. Serve immediately.

Soufflés

*Many vegetable dishes can be turned into soufflés with the addition of
a white sauce (butter, flour, and milk) plus some eggs. Try adding 1 cup
of creamed spinach to this recipe for a spinach soufflé. Or serve this for
brunch and add some cubed ham or crumbled bacon.*

1 loaf flatbread
Olive oil for brushing
1 cup fresh cilantro, chopped
3 cloves garlic, minced
1 teaspoon caraway seeds
1 teaspoon cumin seeds
½ teaspoon cardamom seeds
1 red bell pepper, seeded and
    roughly chopped
1 jalapeno, seeded and
    roughly chopped
4 tablespoons olive oil
Kosher salt and freshly
    ground black pepper to
    taste

Grilled Flatbread
with Aromatic Cilantro Spice Sauce

While you're at the grill cooking duck breasts, elk or venison steaks, or other game, make this excellent bread and sauce to go with it.

1. Lightly brush flatbread with olive oil and set aside.

2. In a food processor, combine cilantro, garlic, caraway, cumin, and cardamom. Blend until smooth.

3. Add the red pepper, jalapeno, and olive oil. Pulse to coarsely chop the peppers, and season with the salt and pepper. Set aside.

4. Prepare a hot fire in a grill. Grill flatbread for about 2 or 3 minutes per side, until warmed and browned.

5. Serve flatbread with sauce and wild game of choice.

Jalapeno Cheddar Beer Bread

Serve bread hot, toasted, or at room temperature. Bread will keep, refrigerated, for a week, or wrap and freeze for up to 2 months.

Serves 6 to 8

3 cups self-rising flour
3 tablespoons sugar
¼ cup or more jalapeno peppers, sliced
¼ cup blue cheese crumbles
2 cups sharp Cheddar cheese, shredded
1 can beer, any kind
2 tablespoons butter, softened

1. Preheat oven to 350°F. Grease a 9" × 5" × 3" loaf pan.

2. In a large bowl, mix together the flour and sugar. Add the jalapeno peppers, blue cheese, and Cheddar cheese and mix well.

3. Make a well in the middle of the mixture and pour in the beer. Stir just until blended. If too dry, you may need to moisten with 2 or 3 more tablespoons of beer.

4. Pour batter into the prepared loaf pan and bake for 45 minutes. Brush the softened butter on the top of the bread and bake for another 15 minutes. Let cool on a rack for 10 to 15 minutes prior to slicing.

Variations of Beer Bread

The original beer bread recipe has three ingredients: 3 cups self-rising flour, 3 tablespoons sugar, and 1 can of beer. This little recipe can be twisted and turned to make bread with the goodies that you like best. So begin with the three ingredients and build on from there. For Parmesan Artichoke Bread, add 1 cup chopped artichokes and 1 cup grated Parmesan cheese; for Sun-Dried Tomato and Asiago Cheese Bread, add 1 cup chopped sun-dried tomatoes and 1 cup Asiago cheese; for Jalapeno Corn Bread, add ¼ cup chopped jalapenos, 1 cup canned Mexicorn, and 1 cup shredded Monterey jack cheese. If the batter is too dry because of all the extra added goodies, add some additional beer and drink the rest.

Serves 4 to 6

2 cups flour
3 teaspoons baking powder
1 teaspoon salt
4 tablespoons butter, cold
¾ cup buttermilk
½ teaspoon baking soda

Buttermilk Biscuits

Biscuits are so homey. Serve them for breakfast or dinner with jam and honey. If you have a game dish with gravy, make it biscuits and gravy with game. For herbed biscuits, add 2 or 3 tablespoons of chopped fresh herbs at the end of the blending.

1. Preheat oven to 425°F.

2. In a medium bowl, whisk together the flour, baking powder, and salt. With a pastry cutter, cut in the cold pats of butter.

3. Pour the buttermilk into a measuring cup and stir in the baking soda.

4. Make a hollow in the dry ingredients and pour in the buttermilk. Stir until just blended.

5. Place dough on a lightly floured board. Turn dough to lightly cover with flour. Pat dough to ½-inch thickness. Cut with biscuit cutters and place on a baking sheet. Bake for 12 to 15 minutes in the preheated oven. Remove from oven and lightly brush with softened butter.

Serves 6 to 8

1 cup (2 sticks) unsalted
    butter, softened
2 cups self-rising flour
1 tablespoon sugar
1 cup sour cream
4 tablespoons fresh herbs,
    chopped (chives, parsley,
    tarragon, or thyme)

Dropped Herbed Rolls

Dropped rolls are perfect for topping a meat pie or bird casserole.

1. Preheat oven to 350°F. Grease a baking sheet and set aside.

2. In a large bowl, cut butter into flour and sugar. Stir in the sour cream. Add the herbs last. Drop by rounded spoonfuls onto the prepared baking sheet. Bake for 20 minutes or until rolls are firm and slightly browned. Serve warm.

Grilled Asparagus

The easiest way to trim asparagus is simply to hold an end of each spear in your hand and snap. If the asparagus is a bit old, it's best to blanch the spears in boiling water for a minute. Remove from the water and drain on a towel. Then place in the glass dish to drizzle with oil and season with salt. A quick dipping sauce of half mayonnaise and half Dijon mustard turns this delectable vegetable into an appreciated low-cal appetizer.

Serves 6 to 8

2 pounds asparagus
2–3 tablespoons olive oil
Fine kosher or sea salt to taste

1. Prepare a hot fire in a grill.

2. Lay the asparagus spears in a deep glass casserole dish and drizzle with olive oil to lightly coat. Sprinkle with kosher salt.

3. Place the asparagus spears perpendicular to the grill grates so that they do not fall through the grates. Grill until crisp-tender and slightly charred. Serve at room temperature.

Asparagus

Springtime is asparagus-eating time. The elegant spears peek through sandy fields from April though June throughout the Midwest. Whether they are steamed, roasted, or grilled, be sure not to overcook them. They should still have a slight bite to them and should never be mushy. Steaming takes about 6 to 8 minutes. Roasting in a hot oven requires a drizzle of olive oil and about 6 to 8 minutes, too. Yes, they may be eaten with your fingers.

1 pound morel mushrooms
½ cup flour
1 cup fresh sourdough bread
   crumbs
½ teaspoon kosher salt
¼ teaspoon freshly ground
   black pepper
1 egg
½ cup whole milk
½ cup or more vegetable oil
½ cup (1 stick) or more butter

Pan-Fried Morels

*During the spring wild turkey season, many a hunter has come home
with a bag of wild morel mushrooms when the wily prey has outsmarted
him or her. Or perhaps that was the prey to be bagged all along.*

1. Slice morels in half and place in a big bowl of cold salted water. Let
   soak for 10 or 15 minutes, gently stirring them every now and then. Pour
   off the residue and water and repeat process until they are clean. Then
   drain the mushrooms and place on towels to absorb all of the liquid.

2. In a large bowl, combine the flour, bread crumbs, salt, and pepper.

3. In another bowl, combine the egg and milk and beat well.

4. Heat 4 tablespoons oil and 4 tablespoons butter in a large skillet.

5. Dip each piece of mushroom in the egg mixture, then in the flour mixture, and carefully place in the hot skillet. Cook for about 1 or 2 minutes
   on each side or until golden brown and crispy. Place on a serving platter. Do not crowd the skillet; cook in several batches. Add additional oil
   and butter to the skillet as needed. Serve with a green salad and crispy
   hot bread and butter.

Wild Mushroom Ragout

These mushrooms are a wonderful addition to serve on the side or to spoon on top of any red-meat game or poultry. Or serve them as an appetizer over any kind of rustic bread that has been toasted and buttered.

Serves 4 to 6

1 pound wild mushrooms (morels, shiitake, cremini, or oyster)
¼ cup butter
1 leek, cleaned and tender white part sliced
2 cloves garlic, minced
¼ cup dry white wine
½ cup heavy cream
Kosher salt and freshly ground white or black pepper to taste

1. Brush mushrooms clean and remove any tough stems. Slice larger mushrooms, halve medium-sized, and leave small ones whole. Set aside.

2. Melt butter in a large skillet over medium-high heat. Add sliced leek and sauté for a minute. Add garlic and cook for another minute. Then add mushrooms. Toss to coat and cook until tender and browned, about 3 to 4 minutes. Add wine and cook until reduced by half. Add cream and bring just to a boil. Season to taste with salt and pepper and serve hot.

Dried Mushrooms
Sometimes it is best to buy exotic or wild mushrooms dried. Reconstitute them in warm water for about an hour, until flexible. Discard the water.

Serves 4 to 6

2 (10-ounce) packages frozen
    spinach, chopped
½ cup (1 stick) unsalted butter
½ cup flour
1 cup half-and-half
Kosher salt and seasoned
    pepper to taste
2–4 tablespoons Romano
    cheese (optional)

Creamed Spinach

*The convenience of frozen chopped spinach makes this wintry
side dish ready to make when fresh spinach is not in season.*

1. Place frozen spinach in a large saucepan. Add 1 cup of water and bring to a boil. Cook until thawed. Drain in a colander (reserving ½ cup of the liquid) and set aside.

2. Melt butter in saucepan. Add flour to form a roux (a paste) and cook for about 3 or 4 minutes. Slowly add half-and-half and stir until thickened. Add the spinach and heat through. If too thick, add some of the cooking liquid from the spinach. Season to taste with salt and pepper. Add cheese if you like. Serve hot.

Cream of Spinach Soup

The easiest and quickest way to make cream of spinach soup is to use leftover creamed spinach. For rustic-style soup, simply warm the creamed spinach and add additional liquid (milk, cream, or chicken broth) to give it a soupy consistency. For a classic French-style soup, puree the spinach mixture, then add the liquid. A sprinkling of Parmigiano-Reggiano over the top is pretty and tasty, too.

Fresh Corn Pudding

Many people think of corn pudding as a Thanksgiving side dish, especially since it can be made with canned corn or frozen corn. This recipe is no exception, and canned or frozen corn can be substituted for the fresh stuff. But my, oh my, when corn is fresh picked and available at the farmer's market, this recipe is sublime. Serve in the summer with grilled or smoked game or in the winter with roasted game.

~

Serves 6 to 8

3 cups fresh corn kernels (about 4–5 large ears)
1 fire-roasted red pepper, chopped (from a jar is okay)
5–6 green onions, chopped
2 tablespoons flour
2 teaspoons sugar
½ teaspoon kosher salt
¼ teaspoon red pepper flakes
3 eggs
1½ cups heavy cream

1. Preheat oven to 350°F. Grease a 1½-quart casserole and set aside.

2. Combine corn, pepper, and onions in a large bowl.

3. Blend flour, sugar, salt, and red pepper flakes together and add to corn mixture.

4. Beat eggs and cream together and add to corn mixture, stirring well. Pour into the greased casserole. Place dish in a larger shallow pan filled with 1 inch of water. Bake in the oven for about 1 hour, or until a knife inserted in the middle comes out clean.

Adding Heat to a Dish

What to do? Spicy-hot recipes call for cayenne pepper, hot paprika, red pepper flakes, chipotle peppers, jalapenos, or even habaneros. Do all of these hot items need to be kept in a person's pantry? For most purposes, the cayenne pepper, hot paprika, or red pepper flakes will do the trick.

3 sweet onions
5 apples
Kosher salt and freshly
    ground black pepper to
    taste
½ cup beef consommé
6 bacon strips
1 cup bread crumbs

Scalloped Onions and Apples

This sweet and savory Southern side is a wonderful addition to a winter buffet. Pair it with the game of your choice and watch your guests' lips smack together and then curl upward in an approving smile.

1. Preheat oven to 350°F. Grease a large baking dish and set aside.

2. Peel onions and slice thinly. Peel, core, and thinly slice the apples. Arrange alternating layers of onions and apples in the baking dish. Lightly season with salt and pepper to taste. (Remember that the consommé and bacon are salty.) Pour the consommé over all.

3. Fry the bacon until crisp. Remove to paper towels and let cool. Keep 2 or 3 tablespoons of bacon grease in skillet and add the bread crumbs and brown. Crumble bacon over casserole, then sprinkle bread crumbs over the top. Bake, covered, for 30 minutes, then uncover and bake an additional 10 to 15 minutes more. Serve hot or warm.

Simple Baked Onions

For a quick-as-a-wink baked onion dish, try this. Slice 2 or 3 onions and place the layers in a casserole. Pour heavy cream over onions shy of covering, about 1 to 1½ cups. Sprinkle with Parmesan or Romano cheese and bake at 350°F for about 30 to 40 minutes, until bubbly and golden brown.

Herbed German-Style Potato Salad

Oftentimes a hot German potato salad includes bacon and bacon drippings. Not this recipe, and it does not lack for want of the traditional ingredients. Give it a try, it's tasty!

Serves 8 to 10

5 pounds red potatoes
1 large white onion, diced
3 large kosher dill pickles, diced
1 (8-ounce) jar fire-roasted red peppers, drained and diced
½ cup white vinegar
Kosher salt and freshly ground black pepper to taste

1. In a pot, bring potatoes to a boil and cook for 20 minutes or until just fork tender. Let cool.

2. Peel potatoes and cut into chunks. Place in a large bowl and add all of the ingredients. Mix well. Season with salt and pepper to taste. Serve hot, warm, or cold.

Rosemary Roasted Potatoes and Butternut Squash

Roasting with garlic and rosemary gives winter squash a savory alternative to the sweeter version with cinnamon, butter, and brown sugar.

Serves 6 to 8

1 cup all-purpose flour
1 tablespoon ground rosemary
3–4 large baking potatoes, cut into 1-inch chunks
1 large butternut squash, cut into 1-inch chunks
½ cup Romano cheese, finely grated
2 large cloves of garlic, finely chopped
4–5 tablespoons olive oil
Freshly ground black pepper to taste

1. Preheat oven to 400°F. Lightly grease a baking sheet.

2. In a large bowl, combine flour and rosemary. Toss potatoes and squash in the flour mixture and place on the baking sheet. Sprinkle with cheese and garlic. Drizzle with olive oil and sprinkle with pepper to taste.

3. Bake for 30 to 40 minutes. Serve hot or warm.

Serves 6

3 acorn squash, cut in half
    and seeded
3 teaspoons olive oil
6 tablespoons butter
2 teaspoons cinnamon
¼ cup brown sugar
1 teaspoon red pepper flakes
Fine kosher salt to taste

Smoked Acorn Squash
with Spicy Butter

*If smoking is not your thing, simply preheat an oven to 350°F.
Place acorn squash on a baking sheet and bake for about 45 minutes.
Then drizzle the goodies into each squash as directed below.*

1. Prepare a smoker or an indirect fire in a grill. Add 2 or 3 chunks of water-soaked wood of your choice, like apple or oak.

2. Brush the cut side of each squash half with the oil. Cover each squash half with foil. Poke holes in the foil to let the smoke through, and put the squash, cut-side down, in a 225°F smoker. Smoke for 2 hours, or until the squash is tender. Remove from smoker.

3. Melt butter in a saucepan and add the rest of the ingredients. To serve, spoon the spicy butter equally over each squash half and serve.

Winter Squash
Whether it's a butternut squash or a Hubbard, most recipes for cooking a certain kind of hard winter squash will adapt for the different varieties.

Texas-Style Baked Pinto Beans

*This is not a difficult recipe, it just takes time. The result is well worth it.
The dried beans have a great texture. The flavors of this dish
can be made more or less spicy by adding more or less hot stuff.
Serve this with grilled or smoked wild game.*

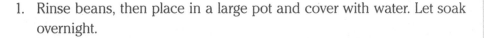

Serves 10 to 12

1 pound dry pinto beans
1 onion, chopped
3 jalapeno peppers, sliced
6 slices bacon, chopped
½ teaspoon cumin
½ teaspoon chili powder
½ teaspoon red pepper flakes
½ teaspoon garlic salt
*2 (10-ounce) cans Ro-Tel
    Original Diced Tomatoes
    and Green Chilies*

1. Rinse beans, then place in a large pot and cover with water. Let soak overnight.

2. Drain water from beans. Add all of the rest of the ingredients and enough water to just cover beans. Bring to a boil. Reduce heat to a simmer and cook slowly for 5 to 6 hours. Stir occasionally to keep beans from sticking to the bottom of the pot.

Dried Beans

Dried beans are nutritious and simple to use. They can be soaked overnight or simmered for 1 or 2 hours for the quicker cooking method. They are inexpensive and don't take up as much pantry space as canned beans do. The texture of dried beans is very nice, too. Give them a try.

Chapter 14

Delicious Desserts

1 cup unsalted butter

1 cup sugar

12 ounces semisweet
   chocolate chips

½ cup espresso or very strong
   coffee

4 eggs

1 cup heavy cream

2 tablespoons coffee-flavored
   liqueur

Decadent Flourless Chocolate Espresso Cake

A book with desserts cannot be complete without something chocolate. Since this is the single chocolate recipe, it is truly dense and rich with chocolate. For individual servings, pour into 8 to 10 small buttered porcelain baking cups. Bake about 15 to 20 minutes. These could be served warm or chilled with the whipped cream. Enjoy!

1. Preheat oven to 350°F. Butter a 9" springform pan. Line the pan with foil and butter the foil. Set aside.

2. Melt butter and sugar in a saucepan and bring just to a boil. Remove from heat. Add the chocolate chips and let sit for 5 minutes. Stir the chocolate until it is well blended. Stir in the espresso and let cool for 3 or 4 minutes.

3. Beat the eggs and whisk into the cooled chocolate mixture. Pour into the pan. Bake for 30 minutes only. Remove from oven and set out to cool. Refrigerate overnight.

4. When ready to serve, whip the cream and add the liqueur.

5. Peel the foil off of the cake and set on a platter. Spoon whipped cream over the top. Slice and serve.

Heirloom Apple Cake

*A versatile, simple cake that is as good for breakfast
as it is for dessert after an autumn game dinner.*

〜

Serves 8 to 10

*3 cups all-purpose flour
2 cups sugar
1 teaspoon baking soda
2 teaspoons pumpkin pie
   spice (or cinnamon)
1 teaspoon salt
1¼ cups vegetable oil
3 eggs, beaten
2 teaspoons vanilla extract
5–6 heirloom apples, peeled,
   cored, and chopped
1 cup nuts, chopped (pecans,
   black walnuts, or English
   walnuts)*

1. Preheat oven to 375°F.

2. Combine flour, sugar, baking soda, pumpkin pie spice or cinnamon, and salt. Stir to blend. Stir in oil, eggs, and vanilla extract (mixture will be dense). Stir in apples and nuts. Pour batter into a 9" springform pan and bake for about 75 minutes or until the top of the cake is crusty and dark brown.

3. Remove from oven and let cool for 15 minutes. Run a knife around the edges of the cake before releasing it from the springform pan. Will keep for several days at room temperature.

Heirloom Apples

Unique heirlooms are finding their way into orchards and farmers markets. Try a medley of heirlooms like Doctor Matthews, Holiday, Keepsake, Rome, or White Winter Pearmain. If none are available, substitute Jonathan or Red or Golden Delicious.

1½ cups all-purpose flour
½ cup (1 stick) unsalted
    butter, melted
1¼ cups sugar, divided
½ cup hazelnuts, chopped
2 (8-ounce) packages low-fat
    cream cheese, softened
2 eggs
2 teaspoons vanilla extract
2–3 crisp apples, peeled,
    cored, and sliced
2 teaspoons cinnamon

Hazelnut Crusted Cinnamon Apple Cheesecake

*A buttery rich hazelnut crust cradles the cheesecake topped
with cinnamon spiced apples. A rustic, pretty finish to any meal.
Serve it naked or with lightly whipped heavy cream.*

1. Preheat oven to 350°F.

2. Combine flour, butter, ½ cup sugar, and nuts, and pat into a 9" spring-form pan (bottom and sides). Bake for 12 minutes or until beginning to brown. Set aside to cool.

3. Increase oven temperature to 400°F.

4. Combine cream cheese, ½ cup sugar, eggs, and vanilla extract and pour into crust.

5. Toss apples with ¼ cup sugar and cinnamon. Arrange slices on the outer edge of cake, then arrange an inner circle of apple slices, too. Place 3 smaller slices in the middle. Bake for 25 minutes or until cream cheese has just begun to set. Let cool for 15 minutes and serve warm. Or cool and refrigerate and serve cold.

Cookie Crusts

Cookie crusts usually have a fair amount of sugar in them. They are easy to make and can be hand-patted into the cake or pie tin. Be creative and use different nuts in dessert crusts. Try native pecans or hand-cracked and picked black walnuts. Macadamia nuts or almonds can easily be exchanged for one another, too.

Rustic Apple Charlotte

Simply sublime.

Serves 6 to 8

¾ cup (1½ sticks) plus 1
    tablespoon unsalted
    butter
6–8 slices good-quality stale
    bread, crusts removed
1 tablespoon plus ¼–½ cup
    sugar, to taste
¼ cup water
1½ pounds Red or Golden
    Delicious apples
1 teaspoon instant tapioca
Cream or ice cream for
    serving

1. Melt the ¾ cup butter in a small saucepan. Line a sieve with dampened cheesecloth and pour the butter through. Discard the white solids that remain in the cheesecloth and save the clarified butter.

2. Cut the bread to fit the bottom, top, and sides of a charlotte mold, a 4-cup soufflé dish, or a mixing bowl. Set the bread pieces aside.

3. Using a pastry brush dipped in the clarified butter, coat the inside of the mold. Sprinkle 1 tablespoon of sugar into the mold and tip it all around so the sugar coats the inside. Dip the bread in clarified butter and line the bottom and sides of the mold. Set aside.

4. Melt the 1 tablespoon of butter in a large saucepan. Add the water. Peel, core, and slice the apples and add them plus the ¼ to ½ cup sugar to taste and the tapioca. Cover and cook over low heat for about 20 minutes, until apples are soft and pulpy. Remove the lid and cook until water is evaporated, about another 5 to 10 minutes. Let the apples cool.

5. Preheat oven to 400°F. Pour apples into the prepared mold. Dip the bread lid in clarified butter and place on top of mold. Bake for 20 minutes. Turn the temperature down to 375°F and bake for 20 minutes more or until the charlotte is browned and bubbling. Serve either warm with heavy cream or cold with ice cream.

Charlottes

Molded desserts lined with sponge cake, lady fingers, or buttered bread are charlottes. Classic fillings are custard and whipped creams, which are then refrigerated. The apple charlotte is the exception; it is filled with sautéed apples, then baked.

Serves 6 to 8

1 cup heavy cream
¾ cup sour cream
¼ cup amber-colored honey
6 tablespoons unsalted butter
6 tart apples, peeled, cored,
   and sliced
⅔ cup golden raisins
½ cup dried apples, roughly
   chopped
½ cup light brown sugar
1 teaspoon lemon zest
1 teaspoon ground cinnamon
¼ teaspoon nutmeg, freshly
   grated

Sautéed Apples
with Amber Honeyed Whipped Cream

*Think of this dessert as akin to apple strudel without the crust.
A lovely finish to a smothered quail dinner.*

1. In a small bowl, whip the cream and fold in the sour cream and honey. Set aside.

2. Melt the butter and add the apples, raisins, dried apples, brown sugar, lemon zest, cinnamon, and nutmeg. Sauté for about 10 to 15 minutes or until apples have softened but are not mushy.

3. Divide apples into pretty bowls and spoon over the honeyed whipped cream.

How to Whip Cream

Most Americans overwhip cream. Perhaps we get confused with the stiff peaks that need to be obtained for whipped egg whites. But overwhipping cream can turn it into butter. However, overwhipped cream can be saved by adding something like sour cream or yogurt or liquid. Liquid? Yes, try rum, whiskey, Grand Marnier, or a raspberry liqueur.

Missouri Pecan–Crusted Pumpkin Cream Pie

*This creamier version of pumpkin pie is complemented by the nutty crust.
A dollop of whipped cream laced with rum would be a nice topping. Whip
1 cup of heavy cream and add 2 or 3 tablespoons of rum, sugar is optional.*

1. Preheat oven to 450°F.

2. Cream the butter and sugar, then add the flour and nuts to make the crust. Pat into a 9" pie tin or springform pan (bottom and sides).

3. Combine pumpkin, cream cheese, heavy cream, sugar, eggs, vanilla, spice, and salt. Pour into crust. Bake for 10 minutes. Reduce heat to 375°F and bake for an additional 30 minutes or until a knife inserted in the middle of the pie comes out clean.

Native Missouri Pecans
Grown in the Ozarks, these pecans are a bit smaller than the typical store-bought pecans and have a more intense flavor, too.

Serves 8

½ cup (1 stick) unsalted butter, softened
⅓ cup sugar
1 cup all-purpose flour
½ cup Missouri pecans, chopped
1 (15-ounce) can pumpkin
1 (8-ounce) package low-fat cream cheese
½ cup heavy cream
½ cup sugar
2 eggs
2 teaspoons vanilla
2½ teaspoons pumpkin pie spice
½ teaspoon salt

¾ cup butter, softened
1½ cups sugar
3 cups sifted flour
3 teaspoons baking powder
¼ teaspoon salt
1 cup whole milk
1 teaspoon vanilla extract
3 egg whites, stiffly beaten
1 cup black walnuts, hickory
    nuts, hazelnuts, or
    pecans, chopped

Holiday Nut Cake
with Maple Syrup Frosting

This is a delightful layer cake that is as homespun as an old-fashioned Christmas. The frosting is soft and puddles a bit, so set the cake on a large enough plate to hold the loose icing. The frosting recipe follows on page 279.

1. Preheat oven to 350°F. Grease and flour two 8" cake pans and set aside.

2. Cream the butter and sugar in a large bowl.

3. Combine the flour, baking powder, and salt in a small bowl and whisk to blend. Add half of the flour mixture to the butter mixture and blend. Add half of the milk and blend. Repeat and then add the vanilla.

4. Fold in the egg whites and then the nuts.

5. Pour batter into prepared cake pans. Bake for about 30 minutes, until a toothpick inserted in the center of the cake comes out clean.

6. Let cake cool for about 20 to 30 minutes. Then frost.

Black Walnuts

Oftentimes people say that they do not care for black walnuts, citing too strong a flavor for their liking. Perhaps it is because they have eaten black walnuts that were past their prime. These walnuts have a high volume of fat, which, if the nuts are not properly stored, can cause them to turn rancid quicker than most other nuts. They are fuller flavored than English walnuts and their earthiness is well suited to desserts and cookies served after a wonderful game meal.

Maple Syrup Frosting

Please use real maple syrup. The consistency and flavor make a tremendous difference.

Frosts an 8"
double layer cake

1 cup maple syrup
2 egg whites
¼ teaspoon salt
1 cup black walnuts, hickory
    nuts, hazelnuts, or
    pecans, chopped

1. Heat maple syrup in a small saucepan until a candy thermometer inserted in the liquid registers 245°F.

2. Place egg whites in a large stainless steel bowl. Slowly add the hot maple syrup to the egg whites, whisking or mixing with a beater the whole time. Add the salt and continue to beat until thick.

3. Frost cake and sprinkle with the nuts.

Maple Syrup

Maple syrup is sap from the sugar maple tree that has been boiled down to make a thick syrup. It ranges in color from a light amber to a dark variety that looks and tastes like molasses. It is fairly expensive but worth it for the pure flavor. Inexpensive maple-flavored syrups are made with corn syrup or sweeteners and just a small amount of real maple syrup.

Serves 8 to 10

½ cup (1 stick) unsalted
   butter, softened
1¼ cups sugar, divided
¼ cup heavy cream
2 teaspoons vanilla extract
Zest of 1 lemon
3 large eggs
1½ cups all-purpose flour
1 teaspoon baking powder
¼ teaspoon salt
1½ pounds plums
1 teaspoon cinnamon

French Plum Cake

*Wild plums are found in plum thickets, appropriately named because
they are so dense you can barely walk through them. The smallish plums,
sometimes referred to as sand plums, are very hard and bitter, best used
for jams and jellies. For this recipe, use red or purple plums.*

1. Preheat the oven to 350°F. Butter and flour a 9" springform pan and set aside.

2. Cream the butter and 1 cup sugar together. Then add the heavy cream, vanilla extract, and lemon zest. Add one egg at a time, blending well.

3. Mix the flour, baking powder, and salt together. Add to the batter and combine until just blended. Pour into the prepared springform pan.

4. Pit and slice the plums and toss with the remaining ¼ cup sugar and 1 teaspoon ground cinnamon.

5. Lay the slices of plum slightly overlapping from the outside edge of the pan. Then turn the plum slices the opposite way and layer inward in a concentric circle. Repeat again with 2 or 3 slices mounded in the middle for a pretty finish. Bake for about 60 minutes or until cake holds firm when lightly shaken. Let cool. Run a knife around the pan edge. Release the springform and serve at room temperature.

Fresh Pears
with Crème Fraîche and Chokecherry Syrup

This is an elegant dessert that makes up quick if you buy the crème fraîche. One cup sour cream stirred smooth with 2 tablespoons of heavy cream can be a quick substitute, if you like. Chokecherry syrup can be purchased at gourmet shops. Otherwise, use the fruit syrup of your choice.

~

Serves 4 to 8

4 ripe pears, peeled, cored, and halved
1 teaspoon lemon juice
4 tablespoons sugar
1 cup crème fraîche
¾ cup chokecherry syrup (or raspberry syrup or sauce)

1. Place pear halves in a bowl and gently toss with lemon juice and sugar.

2. Place 2 pear halves on a plate for each serving (or 1 half pear per person).

3. Spoon crème fraîche over each pear half. Drizzle with chokecherry syrup and serve.

Crème Fraîche

Upscale gourmet grocers may have ready-made crème fraîche available for purchase, but it is easy to make. Pour 1 cup heavy cream into a glass container. Add 2 tablespoons cultured buttermilk. Cover with a tea towel or cloth and let stand at room temperature in a warm place for about 8 to 12 hours, until thick. Will keep refrigerated for up to a week.

2 tablespoons plus ½ cup
  (1 stick) unsalted butter
¾ cup brown sugar
2–3 ripe peaches, peeled,
  pitted, and sliced thick
½ cup sugar
⅓ cup heavy cream
2 large eggs
Zest and juice of 1 lemon
1 cup all-purpose flour
1 teaspoon baking powder
1 teaspoon ground cinnamon
¼ teaspoon salt

Peaches and Cream Upside-Down Skillet Cake

Luscious! Serve with heavy cream on the side.

1. Preheat oven to 375°F.

2. Melt 2 tablespoons butter in a 9" cast-iron skillet and remove from heat. Sprinkle evenly with brown sugar. Arrange peach slices overlapping around the outermost part of the skillet. Then arrange the inner slices overlapping in the opposite direction (concentric circles). Place 3 slices in the center, if there is room.

3. In a large bowl, cream together ½ cup butter and ½ cup sugar. Add heavy cream, eggs, and lemon zest and juice. Blend well.

4. In a separate bowl, sift together the flour, baking powder, cinnamon, and salt. Add to the creamed mixture to just blend. Pour batter over the peaches. Bake for about 45 minutes, until the top is brown and the cake has risen. Reduce heat to 350°F and bake another 10 to 15 minutes, until a knife inserted in the center of the cake comes out clean.

Persimmon Crumble Ice Cream

This is a simple ice cream that can be made at the last minute since the cream mixture is assembled cold. The crumble adds a nice crunch to the texture. Any buttery type of cookie, with or without nuts, can be used.

Makes about 1 quart

3 cups heavy cream
1 cup sugar
1 teaspoon vanilla extract
1 cup persimmon pulp, chilled
1 cup crumbled butter cookies or Brown Sugar Shortbread (page 296)

1. Combine cream, sugar, and vanilla extract and pour into ice cream maker and begin to freeze according to manufacturer's directions.

2. After 5 minutes, add the persimmon pulp. After another 5 minutes, add the crumbled butter cookies. Finish freezing the ice cream, then serve.

Persimmons

Wild persimmons are ready to eat after the first hard frost. Pick them when they are mushy. It is fairly easy to squeeze the seeds and the pulp apart. If using store-bought persimmons, hachiyas soften when they are ripe and are preferable to Fuyus, which are crunchy like an apple. The flavor and texture are somewhat similar to pumpkin's, so substitute canned pumpkin for dessert recipes, if you like.

Gingersnap Ice Cream

Makes about 1 quart

3 cups heavy cream
1 cup sugar
1 teaspoon vanilla extract
1½ cups gingersnap cookies,
crumbled

*Serve this spicy ice cream with Perfect Gingersnap Cookies (below)
or the Spice Cake with Homemade Caramel Sauce (page 285).
Use homemade or store-bought gingersnaps for the gingersnap
crumbs that add the terrific crunch to this ice cream.*

1. Combine cream, sugar, and vanilla extract and pour into ice cream maker and begin to freeze according to manufacturer's directions.

2. After 5 minutes, add the gingersnap crumbs. Finish freezing the ice cream, then serve.

Perfect Gingersnap Cookies

Makes 5 to 6 dozen

1½ cups (3 sticks) unsalted
butter
2 cups sugar, plus additional
for rolling cookies
2 eggs
½ cup molasses
4 cups all-purpose flour
2 teaspoons ground
cinnamon
2 teaspoons ground cloves
3 teaspoons ground ginger
2 teaspoons baking soda
½ teaspoon salt

*This recipe makes lots. You can fill a holiday tin for friends and still
have plenty for your own family. The cookies freeze well, too.*

1. Preheat oven to 350°F.

2. In a food processor, cream butter and sugar, then add eggs and molasses.

3. Sift together the remaining dry ingredients. Add in two or three batches to the creamed mixture, pulsing to blend. Dough will form a ball in the food processor.

4. Form dough into balls and roll in the additional sugar. Place on a cookie sheet and bake for 8 to 10 minutes (ball will flatten out and tops will crack during baking).

Spice Cake
with Homemade Caramel Sauce

*If you'd rather make a spice cake from a package mix, do so, but
add 1 tablespoon of ground cloves and cinnamon for spicier results.
Don't forgo this homemade caramel sauce. It is the pièce de résistance.*

~

Serves 10 to 12

3 cups sifted all-purpose flour
1 tablespoon ground allspice
*1 tablespoon ground
   cinnamon*
1 teaspoon baking soda
⅛ teaspoon salt
*1 cup seedless raisins or
   currants*
*1 cup (2 sticks) butter,
   softened*
2¼ cups sugar
5 eggs
1 cup buttermilk
1 cup sugar for caramel sauce
¼ cup water
¾ cup heavy cream

1. Preheat oven to 350°F. Lightly grease a Bundt pan and set aside.

2. Sift together flour, spices, baking soda, and salt. Mix raisins or currants with ¼ cup of the flour mixture and set aside.

3. In a large bowl, cream together the butter and sugar. Add the eggs, one at a time, and beat well. Alternately add the flour mixture and the buttermilk, ending with the flour. Beat only until blended. Stir in floured raisins or currants and pour batter into the Bundt pan. Bake for 60 to 65 minutes or until a toothpick inserted in the middle of the cake comes out clean. Cool on a wire rack for 20 minutes before turning out.

4. To make the caramel sauce, place 1 cup sugar and ¼ cup water in a heavy saucepan and bring to a boil, stirring. Reduce heat to simmer and swirl liquid in pan a couple of times (but do not stir) until it's a deep golden brown. Remove from the heat. Slowly whisk in the cream. Let sit for about 5 minutes, then drizzle half of the sauce over the cooled cake. Serve the rest of the sauce on the side.

3–4 cups cubed panettone,
    toasted
3 cups half-and-half
6 large eggs
4 large egg yolks
½ cup sugar
1 teaspoon vanilla or rum
    extract
1 cup heavy cream
2 tablespoons Marsala or
    orange liqueur

Panettone Bread Pudding

Some of the best desserts are those with humble ingredients. Bread pudding was created to use up leftover stale bread. So think creatively and use artisan breads studded with fruits and nuts. In this recipe, we use the Italian holiday bread, panettone, and toast it. The whipped cream is nice to serve with coffee, too.

1. Preheat oven to 325°F. Butter a 9" × 13" baking dish and lay the cubed panettone in the dish.

2. In a large saucepan, blend the half-and-half, eggs, yolks, sugar, and vanilla or rum extract. Whisk and cook over medium heat for about 10 to 15 minutes. Then pour over the bread. Bake in a water bath for about 50 to 60 minutes or until a knife inserted in the middle of the pudding comes out clean.

3. Whip the cream until it has very soft peaks. Stir in the liqueur and spoon over the individual servings of the bread pudding.

What's a Water Bath?

Known in France as a bain-marie, it is a large baking dish filled with about 1-inch of water into which is placed a smaller dish of food to bake. This is a gentler way of baking a custard that might get too hot and curdle.

Puff Pastry Raspberry Almond Tarts

*The puff pastry is baked separate from the raspberries in this recipe.
It keeps longer and doesn't get soggy with the berries
because it is assembled just prior to serving.*

Serves 6 to 8

1 (10" × 15") sheet of frozen
    puff pastry
½ cup sugar
½ cup almonds, sliced
2 pints fresh raspberries
Sugar to taste
1 cup heavy cream, whipped

1. Preheat oven to 400°F.

2. Cut semithawed puff pastry in half to make 2 tarts. Place each pastry on a baking sheet. Prick center of pastry with the tines of a fork. Sprinkle ¼ cup sugar on each pastry. Then press ¼ cup sliced almonds into each pastry, leaving a ½-inch border. Bake for about 15 minutes, until pastry has puffed and is golden brown. Remove from oven and lightly press center down.

3. Rinse and pick through raspberries when ready to serve. Pour 1 pint raspberries in each tart. Sprinkle with sugar to taste. Serve with whipped cream.

Frozen Puff Pastry

Often overlooked by the home cook, frozen puff pastry is so handy to have. Making puff pastry from scratch requires several days of preparation, so opt for the frozen. Simply take it out of the freezer and let it partially thaw. Assemble your dessert, bake, and voila! A dessert worthy of the King of France.

½ cup (1 stick) unsalted butter
1½ cups flour
1½ cups sugar
2 teaspoons baking powder
⅛ teaspoon salt
1 cup half-and-half
4 cups marionberries
½ cup brown sugar

Marionberry Cobbler

This is an easy cobbler. The dough cooks up around the berries. Of course, if marionberries aren't available, substitute or combine these berries for a mixed-berry cobbler: blackberries, raspberries, cloudberries, dewberries, wineberries, elderberries, or mulberries. Persimmon Crumble Ice Cream (page 283) would be delectable with this dessert.

1. Preheat oven to 350°F.

2. Melt the butter in a 9" × 13" baking dish.

3. Sift the flour, sugar, baking powder, and salt in a bowl. Add the half-and-half and stir together. Pour batter over the butter in the baking dish, but do not stir.

4. Combine berries and brown sugar and evenly distribute over the batter.

5. Bake for about 30 to 40 minutes or until a knife inserted into the center of the cake comes out clean.

Brown Sugar

Ever get confused or wonder why some recipes call for light brown sugar and others call for dark? It is merely a matter of taste. The lighter brown sugar gives a lighter molasses flavor, and the dark brown sugar has a more robust molasses flavor.

Huckleberry Buckle

Many berries may be interchanged in recipes. Try blueberries, marionberries, blackberries, cranberries, mulberries, or elderberries in this delicious buckle that does double duty as dessert or as a coffee cake.

⁓

1. Preheat the oven to 350°F. Butter a 9" × 13" baking pan and set aside.

2. In a small bowl, sift the flour, baking powder, salt, and baking soda together and set aside. In a medium bowl, cream together the butter, sugar, and vanilla extract. Beat in the eggs. Add the sifted dry ingredients, alternating with the sour cream, and blend well. Set aside.

3. In a small bowl, blend together the streusel topping ingredients with your fingers to make clumps.

4. Pour half the batter in the prepared baking pan. Sprinkle the huckleberries over the batter. Then top with the remaining batter and sprinkle with the streusel topping. Bake for 50 to 60 minutes or until a toothpick inserted in the center comes out clean.

Serves 10 to 12

3¼ cups all-purpose flour
3 teaspoons baking powder
1 teaspoon salt
1 teaspoon baking soda
1¼ cups (2½ sticks) unsalted butter, softened
1¼ cups sugar
2 teaspoons vanilla extract
3 eggs
1½ cups sour cream
3 cups frozen huckleberries

Streusel Topping

½ cup (1 stick) unsalted butter
½ cup all-purpose flour
2 teaspoons ground cinnamon
1⅓ cups light brown sugar, firmly packed
1⅓ cups pecans, chopped

2 cups rhubarb, chopped

2 peaches, peeled, pitted, and
   sliced

2 cups wild berries
   (blueberries,
   huckleberries, or
   blackberries)

1 cup sugar

Zest and juice of 1 lemon

½ cup (1 stick) unsalted
   butter, chilled

1 cup all-purpose flour

1 cup brown sugar

1 teaspoon ground cinnamon

Rhubarb, Peach, and Wild Berry Crisp

*A scoop of Gingersnap Ice Cream (page 284) begs to
dress the top of this fragrant fruity crisp.*

1. Preheat oven to 375°F.

2. Butter a large baking dish. Toss the rhubarb, peach slices, berries, sugar, and lemon zest and juice together in a bowl. Pour into the baking dish.

3. Cut the butter into 8 or 10 pats and combine in a bowl with the flour, brown sugar, and cinnamon. Crumble with your fingers until the mixture is coarse crumbs. Scatter the crumbs over the fruit and bake for about 30 to 40 minutes. Crumb top should be dark golden brown and fruit mixture should be bubbling. Let set for 10 minutes and serve warm.

Wild Berries

Foraging for berries has its just rewards—sweet sun-kissed berries gathered for breakfast or dessert, if you can keep from eating them all. Just make sure to watch out for bears! Every region has several berry varieties to call its own: strawberry, raspberry, marionberry, Saskatoon, blackberry, mulberry, blueberry, elderberry, cranberry, partridgeberry, foxberry, and gooseberry, to name a few. Oftentimes berries can be interchanged in recipes. Use common sense when doing so. For instance, the cranberry is very tart, so it will need more sugar than a blueberry. Also, certain berries such as cranberries may need to be cooked to be juicy, whereas others such as strawberries and raspberries are just fine served raw with or without sugar.

Wild Strawberry Fool

If lucky enough to have wild strawberries and willing enough to share them, this preparation is a way to stretch them to serve your lucky guests.

Serves 4

2 cups wild strawberries
2 tablespoons brown sugar or
    to taste
2 cups whipped cream
4 sprigs of mint and 4–8 wild
    strawberries for garnish

1. Place the berries in a bowl and lightly crush them with the brown sugar. Taste to adjust the amount of sugar.

2. Gently fold in the whipped cream, making sure that the mixture still has plenty of marbling and isn't completely blended.

3. Spoon into glass bowls or stemmed glasses and serve with a sprig of mint and 1 or 2 whole berries on the top.

Wild Strawberries

These delectable little berries can be found in the woodsy countryside and along fence rows and roadsides in springtime. They have such an amazing flavor that to cook them is a crime. They are best eaten off the vine or in a bowl with a dusting of sugar and a dash of champagne. A drizzle of rum or Chambord over the berries is nice, too. An early summer breakfast of wild strawberries and heavy cream with a Belgian waffle or a crispy English muffin . . . Oh my!

1½ cups all-purpose flour
½ cup butter, melted
1¼ cups sugar, divided
1 (8-ounce) package cream
cheese, softened
1 egg, beaten
1 teaspoon vanilla extract
5 cups blueberries, rinsed,
divided
⅓ cup water
1 teaspoon ground cinnamon

Warm Cinnamon Spiced Blueberry Cheesecake

The blueberry sauce is excellent served over pound cake or angel food cake and topped with vanilla ice cream.

1. Preheat oven to 350°F.

2. Combine flour, butter, and ½ cup sugar. Pat mixture into the bottom and up the sides of an 8" springform pan. Bake for 12 minutes, until lightly browned. Set aside to cool.

3. Combine cream cheese, ¼ cup sugar, egg, and vanilla. Pour into the crust. Bake at 400°F for 20 to 25 minutes. Remove from oven and cool.

4. Combine 3 cups of the blueberries, ⅓ cup water, and ½ cup sugar in a heavy saucepan. Bring to a boil, stirring constantly. Lower heat to a simmer and continue stirring until mixture thickens, about 15 minutes. Add remaining 2 cups of berries and the cinnamon. Spread over the cream cheese tart filling just before serving. If there is extra blueberry sauce, serve it on the side. It will keep refrigerated for 1 to 2 weeks.

Cranberry-Gooseberry Clafouti

Clafouti is a French dessert from the Limousin region. It is composed of a layer of fruit (traditionally black cherries) topped with a thin cake batter. Try this also with bing cherries, blueberries, blackberries, and even sliced pears, apples, apricots, tangerines, or peaches.

Serves 8

1 pound mixed cranberries
    and gooseberries
2 tablespoons sugar
1 cup all-purpose flour
½ teaspoon salt
1 cup heavy cream
1 cup whole milk
3 large eggs
½ cup sugar
2 teaspoons vanilla extract

1. Preheat oven to 450°F.

2. Butter a baking dish and layer the fruit over the bottom. Sprinkle with 2 tablespoons sugar.

3. In a large bowl, combine the flour and salt.

4. In a smaller bowl, combine the cream, milk, eggs, sugar, and vanilla extract. Whisk to blend. Pour half the liquid into the middle of the flour and whisk to just blend. Add the rest of the liquid to the batter and just blend. Let rest for about 5 minutes. Pour batter over the fruit and bake for about 25 to 30 minutes or until golden brown and puffed. Let cool before serving.

The Gooseberry

Found extensively in European countries, the gooseberry is a tart berry that grows wild on bushes in rocky areas throughout the Northern states and the Midwest. Similar in size to cranberries, gooseberries' tartness while underripe is preferable for cooking; they turn a darker color when they ripen.

Makes 12 dozen

1 cup dark brown sugar,
    firmly packed
1 cup sugar
½ cup (1 stick) unsalted butter
½ cup (1 stick) margarine
2 eggs
2 teaspoons vanilla extract
4 cups all-purpose flour
1 teaspoon cream of tartar
1 teaspoon baking soda
½ teaspoon salt
2 cups Missouri pecans,
    chopped
Powdered sugar

Missouri Pecan Icebox Cookies

Yes, this makes lots of cookies. The beauty of the recipe is the dough can be refrigerated for a week or kept in the freezer for 1 or 2 months. Take the dough out when you want to bake a dozen fresh cookies (or more). Make two different kinds of cookies by dividing the dough in half prior to adding the nuts. Add 1 cup of nuts to each batch and choose from among hazelnuts, black walnuts, English walnuts, macadamia nuts, almonds, and pecans.

1. Cream together sugars, butter, and margarine. Then add eggs and vanilla and beat well.

2. Sift together flour, cream of tartar, baking soda, and salt. Add to the batter. Then fold in the nuts. Form dough into rolls about 1 to 1½ inches in diameter. Wrap in waxed paper or plastic wrap and place in resealable plastic bags. Refrigerate overnight.

3. Preheat oven to 350°F. Slice cookies ¼-inch thick. Place on an ungreased cookie sheet and bake for about 8 minutes (longer for browned and crispier cookies). Remove from baking sheet and sprinkle with powdered sugar.

Black Walnut Brickle

*This is similar to shortbread but is not as thick and is much crisper.
Make sure the butter is very soft. This makes it easier to spread
the dough thin and evenly over the baking sheet.*

Makes about 24 pieces

1 cup (2 sticks) unsalted
    butter, very soft but not
    melted
½ cup white sugar
½ cup brown sugar, packed
1 teaspoon salt
2 teaspoons vanilla butter
    and nut extract
2 cups flour
1 cup black walnuts or
    English walnuts or
    pecans, chopped

1. Preheat the oven to 350°F.

2. Mix together the butter, sugars, and salt until creamy. Add the vanilla butter and nut extract and mix again. Stir in the flour until just blended.

3. Press dough onto an ungreased 16" × 10" × 1" baking sheet. Spread with the heels of your hands to cover the sheet. It does not have to be perfect, as dough will spread when baking. Sprinkle with chopped nuts and lightly press into the dough.

4. Bake for about 20 minutes until light golden brown. Remove from oven and score pieces with a knife. Let cool for about 15 minutes and then slice and serve.

Vanilla Extracts
Southern grocery stores carry a vanilla butter and nut extract that is delicious in nutty desserts. If it is not available in your area, substitute vanilla extract and butter extract to equal the amount called for in the recipe.

½ cup (1 stick) unsalted
butter, softened
2 cups dark brown sugar,
firmly packed
3 eggs
1½ cups flour
1 teaspoon baking powder
¼ teaspoon salt
2 teaspoons vanilla extract
24 walnut halves, or pecan or
black walnut halves

Brown Sugar Shortbread

*Shortbread has been a staple served with afternoon tea for hundreds of years.
Taste this and join the crowd. Lighter brown sugar will yield a more buttery
and less molasses-flavored cookie, or biscuit, as the English would say.*

1. Preheat the oven to 350°F. Lightly grease a 9" × 13" baking pan and set
   aside.

2. Cream butter and sugar together in a large bowl. Add 1 egg at a time
   and continue to mix until light and fluffy.

3. Sift flour, baking powder, and salt together. Add to the creamed mixture and combine until smooth. Add the vanilla and stir once more.

4. Pour batter into prepared pan and spread evenly. Place 6 nut halves
   across the length of the pan, in four rows across the width of the
   pan. Lightly press into batter. Bake for about 30 minutes, until golden
   brown.

5. Let shortbread cool for about 15 minutes, then cut into squares.

Cookies That Travel Well

*Cookies or bars that are thick and fairly sturdy are the best bet for ship-
ping to friends and family. Bar cookies like shortbread travel well, as do
gingersnaps and walnut brickle. Make sure to pack the cookies fairly
tightly—loosely packaged cookies will move around and have a greater
chance of breaking. These are also great to send out into the field or into
the blind with your favorite hunter.*

Web Sites

There is an enormous amount of Web sites for hunters, fishermen, and wild game cooks. Use keywords like "wild fish and game recipes" or "rabbit and squirrel recipes" or "ducks unlimited recipes" or "wild game and conservation magazines" and the results are noteworthy. Included below are many Web sites that offer recipes and more. But they are just the tip of the iceberg!

Alaska Outdoor Journal
Great Web site for information about hunting and fishing in Alaska and more. "What's Cookin'? in Marylin's Kitchen" includes recipes for bear, moose, beaver, salmon, ptarmigan, and lots more.
www.alaskaoutdoorjournal.com

Ask the Meat Man
This site is filled with information and products for processing game meats at home. There are many recipes, too, including wild boar.
www.askthemeatman.com

Bear Hunting
This is the site for Bear Hunting magazine. Recipes are included in each issue.
www.bear-hunting.com

Big Game Hunt
Interesting site that says it is "for hunters and by hunters." There is a sign-up for an e-newsletter, a page for "tall stories," recipes, and more.
www.biggamehunt.net

Cook Wild Game
This is a good-looking collection of recipes for wild game. There are a few free recipes. There is a modest fee to become a member of the site, which includes access to all of the recipes as well as information on hunting and fishing in California.
www.cookwildgame.com

Deer & Deer Hunting
This is the site for *Deer & Deer Hunting* magazine. It includes recipes.
www.deeranddeerhunting.com

Ducks Unlimited

This is the Web site for *Ducks Unlimited*. They offer membership in their organization, which is a world leader in wetland conservation.
www.ducks.org

Field & Stream

This is the Web site for *Field & Stream*, a popular magazine on hunting and fishing.
www.fieldandstream.com

Fisherman's Express

Alaskan seafood online store offers wild fish for sale, plus many recipes for salmon, halibut, king crab, scallops, shrimp, clams, oysters, and squid.
www.fishermansexpress.com

Food Reference

An amazing site with all things food from cooking schools to food quotes and history, plus plenty of wild game recipes.
www.foodreference.com

Gray's Sporting Journal

The magazine site for Gray's Sporting Journal offers articulate writing, photography, and wildlife information.
www.grayssportingjournal.com

Gulf Coast Fisherman Magazine

www.gulffishing.com

Lake Cumberland Game Birds

This site includes luscious recipes. Just remember that they are for farm-raised birds, which are fattier than wild birds and therefore can stand a longer cooking time before drying out.
www.lakecumberlandgamebirds.com

Magazine Site for Missouri Conservationist

This site includes articles and information about wildlife in Missouri for hunters and nature lovers and foragers alike.
http://mdc.mo.gov/

An Online Mule Deer and Elk Hunting Magazine

The site has a cookbook section.
www.monstermuleys.com

National Wild Turkey Federation Site

www.nwtf.org

Outdoor Alabama

Hunting and fishing information, recreation and conservation articles, plus coastal information are here. Recipes for squirrel, too.
www.outdooralabama.com

Outdoor Life Magazine

An industry favorite.
www.outdoorlife.com

Pheasant Country

This Web site boasts that it is "where pheasant hunters come to roost." It's packed with recipes.
www.pheasantcountry.com

Quail Recipes

This site links to other sites that feature quail recipes and other wild game.
www.quailrecipes.com

Rabbit Hunting Online

Everything to do with hunting rabbits is here, from buying beagles to cooking the rabbit feast.
www.rabbithuntingonline.com

Treo Ranches

High-style recipes are offered on this site from Treo Ranches in Heppner, Oregon. They offer pheasant and chukar hunting and sporting clay packages, and their lodge is available for retreats, too. Their toll-free phone number is 888-276-6794.
www.treoranches.com

Pig Out Publications

This is a barbecue and grill cookbook Web site with a wild game cookbook category. The bulk of the recipes are for grilling and smoking.
www.pigoutpublications.com

Wild Fowling

This is an extensive e-magazine on all things duck and goose hunting in the United States and the United Kingdom.
www.wildfowling.co.uk

Index

Y

THE EVERYTHING SERIES!

BUSINESS & PERSONAL FINANCE

Everything® Accounting Book
Everything® Budgeting Book, 2nd Ed.
Everything® Business Planning Book
Everything® Coaching and Mentoring Book, 2nd Ed.
Everything® Fundraising Book
Everything® Get Out of Debt Book
Everything® Grant Writing Book, 2nd Ed.
Everything® Guide to Buying Foreclosures
Everything® Guide to Fundraising, $15.95
Everything® Guide to Mortgages
Everything® Guide to Personal Finance for Single Mothers
Everything® Home-Based Business Book, 2nd Ed.
Everything® Homebuying Book, 3rd Ed., $15.95
Everything® Homeselling Book, 2nd Ed.
Everything® Human Resource Management Book
Everything® Improve Your Credit Book
Everything® Investing Book, 2nd Ed.
Everything® Landlording Book
Everything® Leadership Book, 2nd Ed.
Everything® Managing People Book, 2nd Ed.
Everything® Negotiating Book
Everything® Online Auctions Book
Everything® Online Business Book
Everything® Personal Finance Book
Everything® Personal Finance in Your 20s & 30s Book, 2nd Ed.
Everything® Personal Finance in Your 40s & 50s Book, $15.95
Everything® Project Management Book, 2nd Ed.
Everything® Real Estate Investing Book
Everything® Retirement Planning Book
Everything® Robert's Rules Book, $7.95
Everything® Selling Book
Everything® Start Your Own Business Book, 2nd Ed.
Everything® Wills & Estate Planning Book

COOKING

Everything® Barbecue Cookbook
Everything® Bartender's Book, 2nd Ed., $9.95
Everything® Calorie Counting Cookbook
Everything® Cheese Book
Everything® Chinese Cookbook
Everything® Classic Recipes Book
Everything® Cocktail Parties & Drinks Book
Everything® College Cookbook
Everything® Cooking for Baby and Toddler Book
Everything® Diabetes Cookbook
Everything® Easy Gourmet Cookbook
Everything® Fondue Cookbook
Everything® Food Allergy Cookbook, $15.95
Everything® Fondue Party Book
Everything® Gluten-Free Cookbook
Everything® Glycemic Index Cookbook
Everything® Grilling Cookbook
Everything® Healthy Cooking for Parties Book, $15.95
Everything® Holiday Cookbook
Everything® Indian Cookbook
Everything® Lactose-Free Cookbook
Everything® Low-Cholesterol Cookbook

Everything® Low-Fat High-Flavor Cookbook, 2nd Ed., $15.95
Everything® Low-Salt Cookbook
Everything® Meals for a Month Cookbook
Everything® Meals on a Budget Cookbook
Everything® Mediterranean Cookbook
Everything® Mexican Cookbook
Everything® No Trans Fat Cookbook
Everything® One-Pot Cookbook, 2nd Ed., $15.95
Everything® Organic Cooking for Baby & Toddler Book, $15.95
Everything® Pizza Cookbook
Everything® Quick Meals Cookbook, 2nd Ed., $15.95
Everything® Slow Cooker Cookbook
Everything® Slow Cooking for a Crowd Cookbook
Everything® Soup Cookbook
Everything® Stir-Fry Cookbook
Everything® Sugar-Free Cookbook
Everything® Tapas and Small Plates Cookbook
Everything® Tex-Mex Cookbook
Everything® Thai Cookbook
Everything® Vegetarian Cookbook
Everything® Whole-Grain, High-Fiber Cookbook
Everything® Wild Game Cookbook
Everything® Wine Book, 2nd Ed.

GAMES

Everything® 15-Minute Sudoku Book, $9.95
Everything® 30-Minute Sudoku Book, $9.95
Everything® Bible Crosswords Book, $9.95
Everything® Blackjack Strategy Book
Everything® Brain Strain Book, $9.95
Everything® Bridge Book
Everything® Card Games Book
Everything® Card Tricks Book, $9.95
Everything® Casino Gambling Book, 2nd Ed.
Everything® Chess Basics Book
Everything® Christmas Crosswords Book, $9.95
Everything® Craps Strategy Book
Everything® Crossword and Puzzle Book
Everything® Crosswords and Puzzles for Quote Lovers Book, $9.95
Everything® Crossword Challenge Book
Everything® Crosswords for the Beach Book, $9.95
Everything® Cryptic Crosswords Book, $9.95
Everything® Cryptograms Book, $9.95
Everything® Easy Crosswords Book
Everything® Easy Kakuro Book, $9.95
Everything® Easy Large-Print Crosswords Book
Everything® Games Book, 2nd Ed.
Everything® Giant Book of Crosswords
Everything® Giant Sudoku Book, $9.95
Everything® Giant Word Search Book
Everything® Kakuro Challenge Book, $9.95
Everything® Large-Print Crossword Challenge Book
Everything® Large-Print Crosswords Book
Everything® Large-Print Travel Crosswords Book
Everything® Lateral Thinking Puzzles Book, $9.95
Everything® Literary Crosswords Book, $9.95
Everything® Mazes Book
Everything® Memory Booster Puzzles Book, $9.95

Everything® Movie Crosswords Book, $9.95
Everything® Music Crosswords Book, $9.95
Everything® Online Poker Book
Everything® Pencil Puzzles Book, $9.95
Everything® Poker Strategy Book
Everything® Pool & Billiards Book
Everything® Puzzles for Commuters Book, $9.95
Everything® Puzzles for Dog Lovers Book, $9.95
Everything® Sports Crosswords Book, $9.95
Everything® Test Your IQ Book, $9.95
Everything® Texas Hold 'Em Book, $9.95
Everything® Travel Crosswords Book, $9.95
Everything® Travel Mazes Book, $9.95
Everything® Travel Word Search Book, $9.95
Everything® TV Crosswords Book, $9.95
Everything® Word Games Challenge Book
Everything® Word Scramble Book
Everything® Word Search Book

HEALTH

Everything® Alzheimer's Book
Everything® Diabetes Book
Everything® First Aid Book, $9.95
Everything® Green Living Book
Everything® Health Guide to Addiction and Recovery
Everything® Health Guide to Adult Bipolar Disorder
Everything® Health Guide to Arthritis
Everything® Health Guide to Controlling Anxiety
Everything® Health Guide to Depression
Everything® Health Guide to Diabetes, 2nd Ed.
Everything® Health Guide to Fibromyalgia
Everything® Health Guide to Menopause, 2nd Ed.
Everything® Health Guide to Migraines
Everything® Health Guide to Multiple Sclerosis
Everything® Health Guide to OCD
Everything® Health Guide to PMS
Everything® Health Guide to Postpartum Care
Everything® Health Guide to Thyroid Disease
Everything® Hypnosis Book
Everything® Low Cholesterol Book
Everything® Menopause Book
Everything® Nutrition Book
Everything® Reflexology Book
Everything® Stress Management Book
Everything® Superfoods Book, $15.95

HISTORY

Everything® American Government Book
Everything® American History Book, 2nd Ed.
Everything® American Revolution Book, $15.95
Everything® Civil War Book
Everything® Freemasons Book
Everything® Irish History & Heritage Book
Everything® World War II Book, 2nd Ed.

HOBBIES

Everything® Candlemaking Book
Everything® Cartooning Book
Everything® Coin Collecting Book
Everything® Digital Photography Book, 2nd Ed.

Everything® Drawing Book
Everything® Family Tree Book, 2nd Ed.
Everything® Guide to Online Genealogy, $15.95
Everything® Knitting Book
Everything® Knots Book
Everything® Photography Book
Everything® Quilting Book
Everything® Sewing Book
Everything® Soapmaking Book, 2nd Ed.
Everything® Woodworking Book

HOME IMPROVEMENT

Everything® Feng Shui Book
Everything® Feng Shui Decluttering Book, $9.95
Everything® Fix-It Book
Everything® Green Living Book
Everything® Home Decorating Book
Everything® Home Storage Solutions Book
Everything® Homebuilding Book
Everything® Organize Your Home Book, 2nd Ed.

KIDS' BOOKS

All titles are $7.95

Everything® Fairy Tales Book, $14.95
Everything® Kids' Animal Puzzle & Activity Book
Everything® Kids' Astronomy Book
Everything® Kids' Baseball Book, 5th Ed.
Everything® Kids' Bible Trivia Book
Everything® Kids' Bugs Book
Everything® Kids' Cars and Trucks Puzzle and Activity Book
Everything® Kids' Christmas Puzzle & Activity Book
Everything® Kids' Connect the Dots
     Puzzle and Activity Book
Everything® Kids' Cookbook, 2nd Ed.
Everything® Kids' Crazy Puzzles Book
Everything® Kids' Dinosaurs Book
Everything® Kids' Dragons Puzzle and Activity Book
Everything® Kids' Environment Book $7.95
Everything® Kids' Fairies Puzzle and Activity Book
Everything® Kids' First Spanish Puzzle and Activity Book
Everything® Kids' Football Book
Everything® Kids' Geography Book
Everything® Kids' Gross Cookbook
Everything® Kids' Gross Hidden Pictures Book
Everything® Kids' Gross Jokes Book
Everything® Kids' Gross Mazes Book
Everything® Kids' Gross Puzzle & Activity Book
Everything® Kids' Halloween Puzzle & Activity Book
Everything® Kids' Hanukkah Puzzle and Activity Book
Everything® Kids' Hidden Pictures Book
Everything® Kids' Horses Book
Everything® Kids' Joke Book
Everything® Kids' Knock Knock Book
Everything® Kids' Learning French Book
Everything® Kids' Learning Spanish Book
Everything® Kids' Magical Science Experiments Book
Everything® Kids' Math Puzzles Book
Everything® Kids' Mazes Book
Everything® Kids' Money Book, 2nd Ed.
Everything® Kids' Mummies, Pharaoh's, and Pyramids
     Puzzle and Activity Book
Everything® Kids' Nature Book
Everything® Kids' Pirates Puzzle and Activity Book
Everything® Kids' Presidents Book
Everything® Kids' Princess Puzzle and Activity Book
Everything® Kids' Puzzle Book

Everything® Kids' Racecars Puzzle and Activity Book
Everything® Kids' Riddles & Brain Teasers Book
Everything® Kids' Science Experiments Book
Everything® Kids' Sharks Book
Everything® Kids' Soccer Book
Everything® Kids' Spelling Book
Everything® Kids' Spies Puzzle and Activity Book
Everything® Kids' States Book
Everything® Kids' Travel Activity Book
Everything® Kids' Word Search Puzzle and Activity Book

LANGUAGE

Everything® Conversational Japanese Book with CD, $19.95
Everything® French Grammar Book
Everything® French Phrase Book, $9.95
Everything® French Verb Book, $9.95
Everything® German Phrase Book, $9.95
Everything® German Practice Book with CD, $19.95
Everything® Inglés Book
Everything® Intermediate Spanish Book with CD, $19.95
Everything® Italian Phrase Book, $9.95
Everything® Italian Practice Book with CD, $19.95
Everything® Learning Brazilian Portuguese Book with CD, $19.95
Everything® Learning French Book with CD, 2nd Ed., $19.95
Everything® Learning German Book
Everything® Learning Italian Book
Everything® Learning Latin Book
Everything® Learning Russian Book with CD, $19.95
Everything® Learning Spanish Book
Everything® Learning Spanish Book with CD, 2nd Ed., $19.95
Everything® Russian Practice Book with CD, $19.95
Everything® Sign Language Book, $15.95
Everything® Spanish Grammar Book
Everything® Spanish Phrase Book, $9.95
Everything® Spanish Practice Book with CD, $19.95
Everything® Spanish Verb Book, $9.95
Everything® Speaking Mandarin Chinese Book with CD, $19.95

MUSIC

Everything® Bass Guitar Book with CD, $19.95
Everything® Drums Book with CD, $19.95
Everything® Guitar Book with CD, 2nd Ed., $19.95
Everything® Guitar Chords Book with CD, $19.95
Everything® Guitar Scales Book with CD, $19.95
Everything® Harmonica Book with CD, $15.95
Everything® Home Recording Book
Everything® Music Theory Book with CD, $19.95
Everything® Reading Music Book with CD, $19.95
Everything® Rock & Blues Guitar Book with CD, $19.95
Everything® Rock & Blues Piano Book with CD, $19.95
Everything® Rock Drums Book with CD, $19.95
Everything® Singing Book with CD, $19.95
Everything® Songwriting Book

NEW AGE

Everything® Astrology Book, 2nd Ed.
Everything® Birthday Personology Book
Everything® Celtic Wisdom Book, $15.95
Everything® Dreams Book, 2nd Ed.
Everything® Law of Attraction Book, $15.95
Everything® Love Signs Book, $9.95
Everything® Love Spells Book, $9.95
Everything® Palmistry Book
Everything® Psychic Book
Everything® Reiki Book

Everything® Sex Signs Book, $9.95
Everything® Spells & Charms Book, 2nd Ed.
Everything® Tarot Book, 2nd Ed.
Everything® Toltec Wisdom Book
Everything® Wicca & Witchcraft Book, 2nd Ed.

PARENTING

Everything® Baby Names Book, 2nd Ed.
Everything® Baby Shower Book, 2nd Ed.
Everything® Baby Sign Language Book with DVD
Everything® Baby's First Year Book
Everything® Birthing Book
Everything® Breastfeeding Book
Everything® Father-to-Be Book
Everything® Father's First Year Book
Everything® Get Ready for Baby Book, 2nd Ed.
Everything® Get Your Baby to Sleep Book, $9.95
Everything® Getting Pregnant Book
Everything® Guide to Pregnancy Over 35
Everything® Guide to Raising a One-Year-Old
Everything® Guide to Raising a Two-Year-Old
Everything® Guide to Raising Adolescent Boys
Everything® Guide to Raising Adolescent Girls
Everything® Mother's First Year Book
Everything® Parent's Guide to Childhood Illnesses
Everything® Parent's Guide to Children and Divorce
Everything® Parent's Guide to Children with ADD/ADHD
Everything® Parent's Guide to Children with Asperger's
     Syndrome
Everything® Parent's Guide to Children with Anxiety
Everything® Parent's Guide to Children with Asthma
Everything® Parent's Guide to Children with Autism
Everything® Parent's Guide to Children with Bipolar Disorder
Everything® Parent's Guide to Children with Depression
Everything® Parent's Guide to Children with Dyslexia
Everything® Parent's Guide to Children with Juvenile Diabetes
Everything® Parent's Guide to Children with OCD
Everything® Parent's Guide to Positive Discipline
Everything® Parent's Guide to Raising Boys
Everything® Parent's Guide to Raising Girls
Everything® Parent's Guide to Raising Siblings
Everything® Parent's Guide to Raising Your
     Adopted Child
Everything® Parent's Guide to Sensory Integration Disorder
Everything® Parent's Guide to Tantrums
Everything® Parent's Guide to the Strong-Willed Child
Everything® Parenting a Teenager Book
Everything® Potty Training Book, $9.95
Everything® Pregnancy Book, 3rd Ed.
Everything® Pregnancy Fitness Book
Everything® Pregnancy Nutrition Book
Everything® Pregnancy Organizer, 2nd Ed., $16.95
Everything® Toddler Activities Book
Everything® Toddler Book
Everything® Tween Book
Everything® Twins, Triplets, and More Book

PETS

Everything® Aquarium Book
Everything® Boxer Book
Everything® Cat Book, 2nd Ed.
Everything® Chihuahua Book
Everything® Cooking for Dogs Book
Everything® Dachshund Book
Everything® Dog Book, 2nd Ed.
Everything® Dog Grooming Book

Everything® Dog Obedience Book
Everything® Dog Owner's Organizer, $16.95
Everything® Dog Training and Tricks Book
Everything® German Shepherd Book
Everything® Golden Retriever Book
Everything® Horse Book, 2nd Ed., $15.95
Everything® Horse Care Book
Everything® Horseback Riding Book
Everything® Labrador Retriever Book
Everything® Poodle Book
Everything® Pug Book
Everything® Puppy Book
Everything® Small Dogs Book
Everything® Tropical Fish Book
Everything® Yorkshire Terrier Book

REFERENCE

Everything® American Presidents Book
Everything® Blogging Book
Everything® Build Your Vocabulary Book, $9.95
Everything® Car Care Book
Everything® Classical Mythology Book
Everything® Da Vinci Book
Everything® Einstein Book
Everything® Enneagram Book
Everything® Etiquette Book, 2nd Ed.
Everything® Family Christmas Book, $15.95
Everything® Guide to C. S. Lewis & Narnia
Everything® Guide to Divorce, 2nd Ed., $15.95
Everything® Guide to Edgar Allan Poe
Everything® Guide to Understanding Philosophy
Everything® Inventions and Patents Book
Everything® Jacqueline Kennedy Onassis Book
Everything® John F. Kennedy Book
Everything® Mafia Book
Everything® Martin Luther King Jr. Book
Everything® Pirates Book
Everything® Private Investigation Book
Everything® Psychology Book
Everything® Public Speaking Book, $9.95
Everything® Shakespeare Book, 2nd Ed.

RELIGION

Everything® Angels Book
Everything® Bible Book
Everything® Bible Study Book with CD, $19.95
Everything® Buddhism Book
Everything® Catholicism Book
Everything® Christianity Book
Everything® Gnostic Gospels Book
Everything® Hinduism Book, $15.95
Everything® History of the Bible Book
Everything® Jesus Book
Everything® Jewish History & Heritage Book
Everything® Judaism Book
Everything® Kabbalah Book
Everything® Koran Book
Everything® Mary Book
Everything® Mary Magdalene Book
Everything® Prayer Book

Everything® Saints Book, 2nd Ed.
Everything® Torah Book
Everything® Understanding Islam Book
Everything® Women of the Bible Book
Everything® World's Religions Book

SCHOOL & CAREERS

Everything® Career Tests Book
Everything® College Major Test Book
Everything® College Survival Book, 2nd Ed.
Everything® Cover Letter Book, 2nd Ed.
Everything® Filmmaking Book
Everything® Get-a-Job Book, 2nd Ed.
Everything® Guide to Being a Paralegal
Everything® Guide to Being a Personal Trainer
Everything® Guide to Being a Real Estate Agent
Everything® Guide to Being a Sales Rep
Everything® Guide to Being an Event Planner
Everything® Guide to Careers in Health Care
Everything® Guide to Careers in Law Enforcement
Everything® Guide to Government Jobs
Everything® Guide to Starting and Running a Catering
   Business
Everything® Guide to Starting and Running a Restaurant
**Everything® Guide to Starting and Running
   a Retail Store**
Everything® Job Interview Book, 2nd Ed.
Everything® New Nurse Book
Everything® New Teacher Book
Everything® Paying for College Book
Everything® Practice Interview Book
Everything® Resume Book, 3rd Ed.
Everything® Study Book

SELF-HELP

Everything® Body Language Book
Everything® Dating Book, 2nd Ed.
Everything® Great Sex Book
**Everything® Guide to Caring for Aging Parents,
   $15.95**
Everything® Self-Esteem Book
Everything® Self-Hypnosis Book, $9.95
Everything® Tantric Sex Book

SPORTS & FITNESS

Everything® Easy Fitness Book
Everything® Fishing Book
Everything® Guide to Weight Training, $15.95
Everything® Krav Maga for Fitness Book
Everything® Running Book, 2nd Ed.
Everything® Triathlon Training Book, $15.95

TRAVEL

Everything® Family Guide to Coastal Florida
Everything® Family Guide to Cruise Vacations
Everything® Family Guide to Hawaii
Everything® Family Guide to Las Vegas, 2nd Ed.
Everything® Family Guide to Mexico
Everything® Family Guide to New England, 2nd Ed.

Everything® Family Guide to New York City, 3rd Ed.
**Everything® Family Guide to Northern California
   and Lake Tahoe**
Everything® Family Guide to RV Travel & Campgrounds
Everything® Family Guide to the Caribbean
Everything® Family Guide to the Disneyland® Resort, California
   Adventure®, Universal Studios®, and the Anaheim
   Area, 2nd Ed.
Everything® Family Guide to the Walt Disney World Resort®,
   Universal Studios®, and Greater Orlando, 5th Ed.
Everything® Family Guide to Timeshares
Everything® Family Guide to Washington D.C., 2nd Ed.

WEDDINGS

Everything® Bachelorette Party Book, $9.95
Everything® Bridesmaid Book, $9.95
Everything® Destination Wedding Book
Everything® Father of the Bride Book, $9.95
Everything® Green Wedding Book, $15.95
Everything® Groom Book, $9.95
Everything® Jewish Wedding Book, 2nd Ed., $15.95
Everything® Mother of the Bride Book, $9.95
Everything® Outdoor Wedding Book
Everything® Wedding Book, 3rd Ed.
Everything® Wedding Checklist, $9.95
Everything® Wedding Etiquette Book, $9.95
Everything® Wedding Organizer, 2nd Ed., $16.95
Everything® Wedding Shower Book, $9.95
Everything® Wedding Vows Book, 3rd Ed., $9.95
Everything® Wedding Workout Book
Everything® Weddings on a Budget Book, 2nd Ed., $9.95

WRITING

Everything® Creative Writing Book
Everything® Get Published Book, 2nd Ed.
Everything® Grammar and Style Book, 2nd Ed.
Everything® Guide to Magazine Writing
Everything® Guide to Writing a Book Proposal
Everything® Guide to Writing a Novel
Everything® Guide to Writing Children's Books
Everything® Guide to Writing Copy
Everything® Guide to Writing Graphic Novels
Everything® Guide to Writing Research Papers
Everything® Guide to Writing a Romance Novel, $15.95
Everything® Improve Your Writing Book, 2nd Ed.
Everything® Writing Poetry Book